Passage to Manhood

STUDIES OF THE WEATHERHEAD EAST ASIAN INSTITUTE,
COLUMBIA UNIVERSITY

The Weatherhead East Asian Institute is Columbia University's
center for research, publication, and teaching on the
modern and contemporary East Asia region. The Studies
of the Weatherhead East Asian Institute were inaugurated
in 1962 to bring to a wider public the results of significant
new research on modern and contemporary East Asia.

A complete list of titles in this series can be found online at
http://www.columbia.edu/cu/weai/weatherhead-studies.html.

Passage to Manhood

Youth Migration, Heroin, and AIDS in Southwest China

Shao-hua Liu

Stanford University Press
Stanford, California

Stanford University Press
Stanford, California

Printed in the United States of America on acid-free, archival-quality paper

Library of Congress Cataloging-in-Publication Data

Liu, Shao-hua, 1968–
  Passage to manhood : youth migration, heroin, and AIDS in Southwest China / Shao-hua Liu.
     p. cm. -- (Studies of the Weatherhead East Asian Institute, Columbia University)
  Includes bibliographical references and index.
  ISBN 978-0-8047-7024-8 (cloth : alk. paper) -- ISBN 978-0-8047-7025-5 (pbk. : alk. paper)
  1. Yi (Chinese people)--Drug use. 2. Yi (Chinese people)--Diseases. 3. Heroin abuse--Social aspects--China--Sichuan Sheng. 4. AIDS (Disease)--Transmission--China--Sichuan Sheng. 5. Young men--Drug use--China--Sichuan Sheng. 6. Young men--Diseases--China--Sichuan Sheng. 7. Migration, Internal--Health aspects--China. 8. Sichuan Sheng (China)--Social conditions. I. Title. II. Series: Studies of the Weatherhead East Asian Institute, Columbia University.
  DS731. Y5L63 2011
  362.196'9792008351095138--dc22
                    2010025604

Typeset by Bruce Lundquist in 10/14 Minion

For my parents,
Peng Mei and Liu Yi-huai

Contents

Illustrations

Maps

Figures

Preface

I REMEMBER VIVIDLY the sense of calm and comfort that settled over me as I made my way alone, cradling a hen in my left arm and a bag of rice in my right, along the mountain basin path in darkness. The hen was submissive; its low clucking consolingly answered my weeping. I had just returned from visiting a friend who had fallen seriously ill from AIDS. He had been bedridden for a week, and struggled to sit up when I arrived. Upon seeing him, I uttered the most common Nuosu greeting, "Is your body well?" He replied with the usual courteous response, "I am well." But he was not well at all. Knowing he would die soon, I had not brought a gift for this visit. I had learned to be pragmatic in this impoverished area. Instead I gave money to his family and asked them to buy whatever he liked to eat or use. Privately, I knew this was my condolence money for his funeral, my small effort to try and help the family prepare for his departure. I did not stay long because I felt bad for my friend, who insisted on sitting up while I was there. So I bid him a reluctant final farewell and left. Just as I was taking off my shoes to wade across the stream on the way back to my residence, my friend's young son caught up with me. He handed me the hen and the bag of rice and said these were from his grandmother, my friend's elderly mother. I politely declined them because I knew that even a hen was of great value to the poor seven-member household. But the boy insisted and repeatedly expressed his family's appreciation to me. I finally accepted the gifts and carried them home. The warm little hen was the only living being I could lean on just then, when I was wanting a comforting touch. This was not the first time, nor the last, that I would fall sad at seeing or hearing about a friend's surrender to AIDS or other drug-related illness. But the local people's courtesy, generosity, and resilience taught me not to become defeated or depressed in the face of life's hardships.

In one important sense, I consider this book to be a memorial to the endless suffering the Nuosu people have endured. I am deeply indebted to the local people of Limu who have helped, cared for, befriended, and taught me over the course of my sometimes emotionally challenging yet rewarding periods of research and writing, which stretched from 2002 through 2009. My heart belongs to all whose names cannot be listed here in consideration of their privacy. They are always on my mind. My fervent hope is to have recaptured and vividly portrayed their lives, suffering, and dreams in this ethnography.

Colleagues at Columbia University have been my most crucial mentors; they have advised and helped me in numberless ways. My deepest gratitude goes to Myron Cohen. Without his timely advice and guidance, I would not have been able to complete my research, writing, and publication. The enormous support and encouragement I received from Lesley Sharp, Carole Vance, and Kim Hopper have also been indispensable to my intellectual growth and professionalism, and I cannot thank them enough. I am also grateful to other faculty at Columbia University—Lambros Comitas, Ellen Marakowitz, and Mark Padilla—for their timely assistance with my research. Stevan Harrell, at the University of Washington, has always provided insightful advice and criticism concerning the Nuosu that I study. Several people have read different versions or parts of my earlier work and given me ideas for improvement: Svati Shah, Chiang Fei-chi, David Griffith, Andrea Sankar, Mark Luborsky, Ben Blount, Todd Nicewonger, Brian Harmon, Kerim Friedman, Hsieh Lili, and Sun Yanfei. I am grateful for their insightful comments. In New York City I have relied on the following people for friendship and intellectual inspiration: Ernesto Vasquez del Aguila, Wang Pin, Tung Chien-hung, Tan Ui-ti, Charles Ma, Chen Xixi, and Marcela Fuentes. They rescued me from my academic solitude over the course of what was long and sometimes lonely research.

For the professional assistance and information sharing I received during my research in China, I gratefully acknowledge the following scholars and friends in Beijing and Chengdu: professors Zhang Haiyang and Hou Yuangao at the Central University of Nationalities, who made my initial visit to Liangshan possible, and Wang Mingming, professor at Peking University, as well as Xu Xinjian, Xu Jun, and Shi Shuo, professors at Sichuan University, who helped me obtain permission for my year-long field research. The late professor Li Shaoming and professor Li Xingxing, at Sichuan Institute of Nationalities, taught me about

Liangshan and its history; Bai Shige, Baqie Rehuo, and Ma Erzi, all Nuosu scholars at the Liangshan Institute of Nationalities, generously shared their insights on the Nuosu and helped me settle in the field. I also thank Wan Yanhai, an AIDS activist who helped introduce me to Chinese scholars in the field of AIDS research. Weng Naiqun, anthropologist at the Chinese Academy of Social Sciences, Wang Jianmin and Pan Jiao, professors at the Central University of Nationalities, Zhuang Kongshao, professor at the Chinese People's University, and Ma Linying and Qin Heping, professors at the Southwest University of Nationalities, all were extremely generous in sharing their knowledge with me.

For their gracious help and warmhearted reception during my fieldwork in Liangshan, I cannot adequately express the depth of my appreciation to the following friends: Jimu Aluo, He Ying, Zhang Jianhua, Zhang Guifang, and Luo Qingguo.

Over the long process of writing and then working through the publication process, I am grateful to the following persons for sharing their experience and advice: Sara Friedman, Gardner Bovingdon, Lan Pei-chia, Huang Shu-min, Angela Ki Chi Leung, Anne Routon, Fred Chiu, Cheng Ling-fang, Ting Jen-chieh, and Anru Lee. I also thank Daniel Rivero and Madge Huntington at the Weatherhead East Asian Institute, Columbia University, for their help in making this book part of the WEAI publication series. My gratitude also goes to the three anonymous reviewers for their supportive and constructive comments for improving the book. Stacy Wagner, Jessica Walsh, and Carolyn Brown at Stanford University Press are extraordinary editors who provided exemplary professional assistance as it was needed throughout the publishing process. Without their help, this book would have taken much longer to see the light of day. I must also express many thanks to my assistant, Shannon Shen, whose help with proofreading and other tasks requiring painstaking attention to detail has been invaluable. Finally, there are almost certainly other people to whom I owe gratitude but who have not been mentioned here owing only to my own oversight.

The research and writing of this book were made possible by various grants and fellowships from the Weatherhead East Asian Institute, Columbia University. I also benefited from fellowships from the Chiang-Ching Kuo Foundation and the American Association of University Women. A two-year grant from Taiwan's National Science Council enabled me to write this book. Certainly the generous funding support, time allocation, and academic inspiration I received from Academia Sinica have been indispensable to my intellectual growth and the writing of the book.

Finally, this book is dedicated to my family. My mother, Peng Mei, has tolerated my incessant demands for freedom and independence, demands that were certainly unusual for a Taiwanese female of my generation. She has had to live with deep concern for my personal well-being as I have chosen to live and work in difficult areas and take on challenging tasks. My brother and sisters not only took care of my parents and grandmother while I was absent but have also been my most loyal supporters whenever I was frustrated and needed emotional encouragement. My adorable grandmother with bound feet, who left us at the age of 101 during the last phase of my long graduate work at Columbia University, had always encouraged me to see and experience the world beyond my familiar horizons. And my father, Liu Yi-huai, who left us nearly two decades ago, did not live to see his youngest daughter awarded a Doctorate of Philosophy. He would never have imagined that his Hunan accent, which I was accustomed to hearing from childhood, helped me pick up Sichuanese so quickly for this research. His reminiscences about his hometown in China and his compassion and caring for the mainlanders without families in Taiwan made a deep impression on me and taught me to always keep my eyes open to people's suffering while pursuing hope in life. This book is an embodiment of his legacy.

Passage to Manhood

Introduction

Bringing Peripheries to the Center

MODERNITY, the grand narrative of the twentieth century, has provided the backdrop for sweeping global social changes unforeseen in human history. China has been a particularly tumultuous arena of diverse modernization projects. This book examines the local ramifications of China's modernity drive in the lives of the minority Nuosu people in southwestern Sichuan Province (see Map 1). The Nuosu, classified as "Yi" in the state's ethnic identification project conducted in the 1950s, have been engulfed by the dual epidemics of heroin use and HIV/AIDS in the post-1978 reform era. Over the course of a half century, the Nuosu in Limu (see Map 2), one of the rural townships in Zhaojue County in mountainous Liangshan Yi Autonomous Prefecture, have taken part in various modernization projects imposed on them by the Chinese state. In what unfolds below, I show modernity to be a state-engineered political and economic force that is perceived, embraced, dissected, and challenged by the Nuosu in my ethnographic account of their transformations from tribalism to socialism to capitalism. The Nuosu's lived experiences and narratives will be recounted here in detail to show how they pit local actors against the chief agents of global modernity—the state governance and the capitalist market.

Notwithstanding the exploratory goals of my research, I never imagined I would be ushered into the Nuosu community and its modernity discourse by ghosts and bandits, both "deviant" entities that stand in direct contradiction to modern science and the Chinese brand of governmentality. Ghosts opened the door for me to the Nuosu peasants' living world, and a group of young "bandits," by sharing their perceptions of the world, helped me understand their sometimes tumultuous circumstances and motivations. These visible and invisible

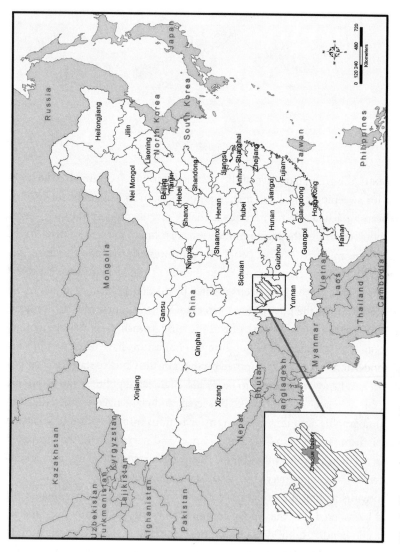

Map 1. Nuosu-dominant Zhaojue County, Liangshan Yi Autonomous Prefecture, Sichuan Province

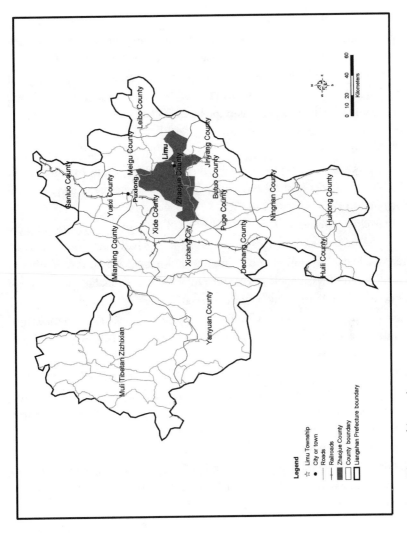

Map 2. Limu and its environs

players conveyed to me how overwhelming the influences of socialism and capitalism had become in local social life; they likewise broadened my understanding of how heroin use and HIV/AIDS have recently shaped Limu Township's marginalized Nuosu people. Let me begin with my "eventful" stories.

The Ghost Event

It was in early 2005 that I met my first key informant, the fifty-year-old Lati. A dapper man, Lati was a village cadre and a versatile Nuosu intellectual. Self-educated and frequently in contact with external officialdom, Lati has a good command of Mandarin Chinese. Lati's house sits by the main road in Limu, and he runs a small grocery store in the house. When I visited, I often found a few people sitting around chatting in front of Lati's flashing television screen. This drew me to Lati's place every day during the first few months of my fieldwork; I found it an ideal place to meet and get to know people. And best of all, with my regular visits, Lati cheerfully agreed to be my interpreter and assist me in my fieldwork in his spare time.

One chilly afternoon in early April I visited Lati as usual after lunch. Five men were present and discussing something in agitated tones as several children watched television. At that point, my Nuosu language skills were still rudimentary and I was unable to grasp the topic of discussion. So I just sat there acting as though I was enjoying the conversation. One of them suddenly stared at me and uttered the word *nyici* (ghost). "Nyici?" I repeated with both excitement and puzzlement, for I had finally been able to understand a word and enter their conversation. I had learned this word through readings on Nuosu etiology long before my arrival in Limu, but I had never expected to encounter, much less deal with, this term before I began inquiring into the relationship between illnesses and ghosts. "Yes, nyici, I know," I replied again in high spirits and, more important, in halting Nuosu. The men all turned and looked at me with interest when they realized that I *knew* what nyici was. Using their limited Mandarin, colored by strong Nuosu and Sichuanese, they began explaining to me the precise nature of the matter they were discussing. Fortunately, Lati had finished his routine grocery chores and rejoined us to be my interpreter.

Listening to their account was my first genuinely exciting experience in Limu. In neighboring Hagu Township there was a haunted house. A widow and her three children lived there, and they had been attacked by ghosts for about five consecutive days. Out of nowhere stones flew at the people and things in the house. It was a newly built house, but the stones had already broken a few tiles on the roof. People described the ghost attacks vividly. I was completely absorbed in the story and decided right away to pay a visit. When I expressed this desire, the people in the room looked at me earnestly and asked, "Aren't you afraid of ghosts?" I replied instantly, "It's a Nuosu nyici, and I am *Hxiemga* [ethnic Han]." All the men and children laughed at my pretentiously nonchalant response. Indeed, as a Hxiemga from Taiwan, local people thought me unusual because of my interest in Nuosu culture. Why would a seemingly well-educated and possibly well-off young woman be interested in the dirt-poor Nuosu? Furthermore, my interest in visiting the haunted house was beyond their, and especially beyond Lati's, imagination. Lati was a senior cadre who followed the official doctrine of the Communist Party, which for decades has called for China's modernization on the basis of scientific rationality and campaigns to combat superstition. Interest in ghosts certainly ran counter to the official line. But since Lati had agreed to serve as my interpreter, he could not help but accompany me on this visit.

When we set out, it was about three o'clock in the afternoon—a sunny day with few clouds in the sky. We had a long walk ahead, across the far-flung wet rice fields where people had begun channeling water from nearby streams to prepare for the transplanting of rice seedlings in the spring. We hopped over small streams at the boundaries between fields, and my shoes often sank into the sticky mud through which the farmers and their water buffalo had just ploughed. Lati looked at me sympathetically and helped me retrieve my shoes every time this happened. Finally, at about six o'clock, we arrived at the widow's house.

We saw three women and three children sitting out front. They stood up, greeted us, and told Lati that they were staying outside because they did not dare to go inside. I noticed that their pockets were filled with small pebbles and stone chips. The nervous women explained that they were hanging on to the pebbles and stones in preparation for a possible confrontation with the ghosts. Then they invited us in to take a look. It was a one-room house with a small yard. Inside was a small pen in which a horse and a few chickens were kept at night. The widow informed us that in the past they had also had a sheep and a pig but that the day before our visit she had killed the animals as a sacrifice in a ghost-expelling ritual.

On the night the ritual exorcism was conducted, the widow explained, a dozen primary school teachers and Hagu Township cadres came over to see for themselves about the rumored ghosts. Eventually flying stones hit everybody who attended the ritual, including the *bimo* (the priest or ritual specialist). The bimo claimed that there were four ghosts, one from the widow's (actually her husband's) lineage and a formidable *nuo* (traditional aristocrat) accompanied by his two slaves (the lowest social stratum in traditional Nuosu society). The widow and her seventy-two-year-old mother described for us how and whence the flying stones had come and struck them. The three children listened with horror and confusion in their eyes.

Suddenly, before Lati and I realized what was happening, everybody jumped up, yelled, and began throwing small stones in the direction of one corner of the house. We heard a noise above like something dropping on the roof. While cursing the ghosts, the widow's mother grabbed some ash from the hearth and tossed it into the air. I saw nothing besides the people's sudden commotion. I looked out the door and noticed that the sky had completely clouded over and a gusty wind had picked up. The atmosphere was creepy. About ten minutes later, everyone had finally calmed down. The sun had completely set and it was dark. The widow turned on the house's only 40-watt light. We picked up the conversation that had been disrupted by the recent commotion. I moved a little bit forward toward the hearth where a fire was lit. I wanted to feel warmth under such eerie circumstances. In doing so, I was facing the corner where, everyone alleged, a stone had just come from.

At around seven o'clock, I saw with my own eyes a stone shoot out horizontally from somewhere in that corner and drop in front of us. I was amazed at what I had just witnessed. Lati looked at me and inquired, "Did you see it?" I nodded without uttering a word. He picked up the stone and examined it, asking, "Do you think the stone has been burned?" He passed the stone to me; it was charred on the edges. "Yes, it has been burned," I said, turning it over in my hand. Then Lati said seriously, "There are many burned stones of this sort at cremation sites." Upon hearing that, I dropped the stone abruptly. It seemed ghastly.

Later on, I twice heard the sound of something dropping on the roof right above my head. I stood up and went to the troubled corner, where there was only a cupboard used for ancestor worship and for storage of household goods. I checked it and found no holes in its surface. It was too small to hide a person inside. I was wondering whether the stone had dropped from the roof, hit the cupboard, and bounced to the ground. This assumption, however, was unlikely because the stone had shot out horizontally, not in a curve. I went out and examined the roof from the outside and found no clue. I simply could not explain what had just happened and went back to sit on my little stool. We did not stay long because it was already late. Upon our departure, a few young men arrived. They were kinsmen and neighbors of the widow who, since the outset of these alleged paranormal events, had come to the house every evening after dinner to keep the family company through the fearful night.

The next day, the news of my witnessing a ghostly event spread quickly. After our visit, a couple of county and township officials paid a visit to the haunted house. From all accounts, everyone who visited the house had some sort of creepy experience. Around that time, a nationwide political campaign dubbed "Advance Education for Communist Party Members" (*gongchandangyuan xianjinxing jiaoyu*), promoting science as its key mission, had just been launched. Two days later, Limu's police chief ordered the local people to stop gossiping about the ghosts because, he claimed, the entire event was a fabrication.

After this order had been issued, three local policemen, including the chief, who was a Nuosu himself, called on me to hear my account of the incident. I told them what I had seen without any interpretation or using words like "ghost." They had plainly expected me to provide a clear repudiation of the ghost event because, they stressed, "any unscientific phenomenon is unlikely to have taken place." But I did not subscribe to this assertion and insisted that I had no idea what might have caused what I had observed on the night in question. They were unsatisfied with my response and left with the parting declaration: "They are all feudal and superstitious peasants!" Later, when I visited the widow again, she complained that the police officers had accused her of concocting the entire story and imposed a gag order against any further discussion of the event. It seemed to me that the widow and her companions had all exhibited genuine fear of the alleged ghosts, and yet the officials dismissed this emotional display as superstition and even a fabrication. This incident highlights government cadre and police condescension toward the presumably rustic and gullible Nuosu peasants.

After this incident, I quickly became known for my "witnessing" of ghosts, an incident reminding me of Geertz's (1973) experience at a Balinese cockfight, an event that involved illegal gambling. When the police raided the venue, the gamblers and onlookers fled. On the spur of the moment, Geertz fled with all the others and was hence recognized by them as part of the community. Similarly, the local people learned of my refusal to dismiss their belief in and fear of ghosts. Through this set of events, I found myself suddenly incorporated into the "we" group by the local community and in a position to establish good rapport there. My reputation as "a Taiwanese Hxiemga who is not afraid of ghosts" provided a credential with which I could call on people whom I had never met before. Afterward, strangers often greeted me saying, "I know you. Did you see the ghosts?" or something similar.

Discovering the "Bandits"

Another encounter that occurred soon after the ghost event further paved my entry into Limu's life world; it led me to understand young people's rising desire for a modern way of life. My initial research interests in the Nuosu and their struggles with heroin and AIDS stemmed from two previous research projects that had identified Nuosu lineage intervention as an effective drug-control strategy in Limu and another Nuosu community in Yunnan Province (Zhang et al. 2002; Zhuang, Yang, and Fu 2005). This finding attracted the attention of many anthropologists, who wished to discover the possible cultural implications of a syncretic merger between traditional and modern approaches to disease management. These interests were deeply impressed in my own mind before 2005. I eventually broadened my scope of analysis, however, to incorporate the role of individual actors within the relationships among the youth, Nuosu society, and the reach of political-economic reform. My frequent and close interactions with "delinquent" Nuosu young people helped me expand my horizon of understanding and opened my eyes to another dimension of the Nuosu's modernity trajectory, which includes state intervention, market expansion, youthful adventurism, and the commodification of goods and desires.

One day at the end of April 2005, I was strolling toward the hot-spring bathhouse located about two kilometers away from my residence at the township clinic. Taking a hot shower every few days, even in a filthy bathhouse rumored to be catering to the commercial sex trade, remained a most welcome activity during my extended stay in this cold and difficult mountain community. All of a sudden, a rattling farm tractor passed by and stopped a few meters ahead. "Are you going to the bathhouse?" a young man I knew asked loudly. "Yes," I replied. He gestured. "Come on! We'll give you a ride." Two men on the tractor helped me aboard, and I found myself sitting with a group of eight men in their twenties. Within a quarter of an hour, I learned that all of them had been in jail on charges ranging from heroin use and drug trafficking to burglaries in cities beyond Liangshan Prefecture. In excited tones, they recounted their mischievous conduct and criminal exploits. "So you are all *tufei* [bandits]!" I laughed heartily. And they shouted back cheerfully in unison, "Yes, we are!"

Qubi Muga, whose life course has run parallel to those "bandits," became my second key informant. I met the twenty-six-year-old Muga after I urged Lati to introduce me to more local people. Because Lati had become too busy to help me regularly after the ghost event, I was keenly on the lookout for another key informant. Early on Lati tried to find some educated girls to help me, but in vain. The young Nuosu women were too shy and too reluctant to talk around men, especially young men, because of the Nuosu's strong sexual taboos and strict gender segregation. In a later session, when Lati introduced me to a group of villagers, Muga greeted me, "They said you were not afraid of ghosts!" After this encounter, Muga agreed to replace Lati as my key informant.

Muga spoke the Han language with a very strong accent that mixed Nuosu grammar, Sichuanese, and Mandarin he had picked up on his urban journeys. He had never been to school. Very quickly, Muga became an indispensable friend and informant. We developed a relationship akin to siblings, so that his family, cousins, and friends became my quasi family and friends. Through Muga, I could interact more extensively with his brothers and other young men, and through them I learned that many Limu men between their late teens and forties had some prison experience. Many had even been behind bars more than once. Young Nuosu men often used their time of imprisonment as a marker for tracking what happened and when. For instance, one day when I was riding with Muga and another young man in his twenties in a minibus commuting between Limu Township and the Zhaojue county seat, I asked the driver, "When did this minibus first go into service?" "Maybe 1995?" the driver replied. Muga, sitting in the back, corrected the driver emphatically: "No, it was in 1997! There was no such minibus service when I was jailed in 1996. But I saw it running on the road when I was released in 1997." The other young man agreed, saying that he, too, had been imprisoned about the same time and had not seen the minibus before then.

The use of periods of imprisonment as markers in a timeline occurred in many of my conversations with young Nuosu men in 2005. And men in their thirties and forties also recounted similar experiences in which they, in their late teens or twenties, had participated in youthful misdeeds. Sometimes these stories carried a tinge of nostalgia, and at such moments I realized the compelling force of youthful adventure in impoverished Limu. These men simply wanted to experience a bigger world! This revelation provided a new analytical perspective for my examination of heroin use and AIDS in this rapidly changing community.

My Research in the Liangshan Mountains

Liangshan Prefecture covers approximately 60,000 square kilometers and is home to about 4 million people, with 44.4 percent (i.e., 1,813,683 people) of them Nuosu; Han Chinese make up 52 percent (2,121,231 people) of the prefecture's population; and the remaining population belongs to other ethnic minorities, such as Zang (or Tibetans) (Sichuan sheng 2002; see Figure 1). In general, the Han live in the better-off lowlands, in contrast to the Nuosu, who occupy the high hills. In certain poverty-stricken counties located in the high mountains, Nuosu make up over 95 percent of the local population.

In 2001 the Chinese state, in cooperation with international aid agencies, began investigating the spread of HIV infection in Liangshan. The government was alarmed at the high rates of HIV there: the Nuosu were less than 3 percent of Sichuan's provincial population, yet they constituted 59.6 percent of the province's HIV infections (China-UK 2001). Even by 2003, when HIV had begun to spread widely among majority Han people and other minority groups in Sichuan, the Nuosu still ranked at the top in terms of HIV prevalence (China-UK 2004). Unsafe heroin injection among young Nuosu men who had been migrating between rural Liangshan and big cities across the country since the mid-1980s played a major role in the local HIV/AIDS epidemic.

Initially, heroin use and HIV/AIDS were concentrated in Liangshan Prefecture's capital city, Xichang, and in two Nuosu-dominant rural counties, Zhaojue and Butuo (China-UK 2004). In recent years, however, both have spread to other Nuosu-dominant areas. By mid-2007, the number of reported HIV/AIDS cases in Liangshan had grown to 5,990 and occurred in all sixteen counties of the prefecture and the municipality of Xichang. Among them, Zhaojue County

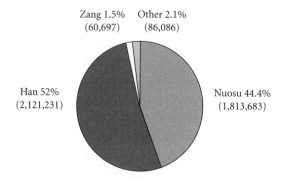

Zang 1.5%   Other 2.1%
(60,697)   (86,086)

Han 52%   Nuosu 44.4%
(2,121,231)   (1,813,683)

Figure 1. Population in Liangshan Prefecture. Data from Sichuan sheng (2002).

ranked at the top, accounting for 1,797 HIV/AIDS cases. The major pathway of transmission remained unsafe injection (46.34 percent). Nuosu (40.95 percent) and youths between the ages of twenty and thirty (78 percent) continued to be the most affected demographic groups. As HIV infections have continued to mount in Liangshan, they have alarmed disease control officials (Mose et al. 2008). The steady spread of HIV tells us that the effectiveness of intervention in Liangshan as a whole has been seriously compromised.

My main field research site was Limu Township, a Nuosu community located in a highland basin at an elevation of 1,900 meters (roughly 6,200 feet). Administered under Zhaojue County, Limu is the headquarters of both district and township government offices and is located approximately thirteen kilometers east of the county seat. The government identified Limu as one of the Liangshan communities hardest hit by heroin use and HIV (China-UK 2004). In 2005 HIV prevalence in targeted villages in the Limu basin was about 1.9 percent, or 78 infections out of approximately 4,000 residents. Local officials and health workers, however, believed that the real infection figure was much higher than the reported number.

Thus, my central question became: Why have the Nuosu, in Limu in particular, been so vulnerable to heroin use and HIV? Ancillary to that, how have they structured their lives around drugs? How have they responded to the twin epidemics of heroin and HIV/AIDS? And, finally, what types of cooperation or conflict did intervention practices introduce among state agencies, local society, and Nuosu individuals?

I trace these social problems back to the drastic changes the Nuosu went through in the twentieth century. The last century can be defined by modernity drives through which the world underwent rapid and comprehensive transformations toward "a post-traditional order" (Giddens 1991, 20). The Nuosu's entry into modernity has been for the most part externally induced and convoluted—beginning with their engagement in the opium economy in the early 1900s, followed by their reluctant surrender to socialism in mid-century, and, at the end of the century, their reckless embrace of capitalism. Their passage to modernity has brought them opportunities to obtain new wealth and improve their living standard, as well as the somber realities of an epidemic that mercilessly inflicts suffering in terms of lives lost and social dysfunction. Modernity is, as Giddens cogently observes, "a double-edged phenomenon" (1990, 7). In particular, late modernity, compared with the earlier modernity of industrialization, denotes an "age of flows" full of individual choices, precarious freedoms, and new inequalities (Lash 2002, vii). It is within this theoretical framework that I will examine heroin use and HIV/AIDS as by-products of the fast-changing political economy into which the Nuosu have been swept—voluntarily or involuntarily.

Modernity and Social Change:
A Political-Economic Perspective

The impact of modernity on the Nuosu began with the introduction of opium into the peripheral Liangshan region in the 1910s. It was at this historical juncture that a small group of the Nuosu elite was introduced to the production and trade of opium. This first wave of global influence linked the Nuosu to the outside world via one of the most profitable commodities of the early twentieth century. Using the lucrative profits from the drug trade, Nuosu noblemen obtained modern firearms, which allowed them to keep Liangshan a stronghold of tribalism and remain independent from the Chinese state.

After this first wave came the socialism that swept through many new nation-states in the mid-twentieth century. This second global drive for modernity compelled the Nuosu to be incorporated into the Chinese state and hence absorbed into the socialist modernization project. Premodern livelihoods enmeshed with traditional Nuosu systems of kinship and social hierarchy were quickly replaced by a modern political authority that dictated people's lives from birth to death in a rigid, territorially confined communal life.

After two decades of the turbulent experimentation that characterized socialist modernity in China, the Nuosu were again swirled en masse into the vortex of global neoliberal capitalism. In the wake of China's market reform in 1978, both traditional and socialist safety nets were removed, and new generations of Nuosu young people were exposed to the uncertainties of retreating state regulation of their livelihoods and to an emerging freedom of choice and mobility.

The dual epidemics of heroin and HIV/AIDS in Limu epitomize the most unfortunate outcomes of global modernity in a marginal locale. In a relatively short span of time, the drive to become modern has altered the position of the Nuosu in relation to the external world, reconstituted their internal social relationships, and given rise to greater consciousness of individuality among young people. These changes have in turn paved the way for the emergence of heroin use and AIDS, and generated conflicted local responses to these problems.

My analyses of the Nuosu's convoluted modernization process and its consequences to date are embedded in political-economic changes at the individual, social, and state levels. I examine the Nuosu's changing positionality from the top down—from the global and the state levels to the local—to contextualize them within China's nation-state building process and its development trajectories since 1956. I also analyze the problems from below, beginning with the local community, their rural markets, the emerging metropolis, and the state and international arenas, to see how local social responses to the dual epidemics also illuminate China's shifting political economy as well as cultural changes in Nuosu society. This two-way perspective provides a comprehensive picture of the intricate interfaces between the growing individualism of the Nuosu youth, the intermittent revival of indigenous social agency, and the continuous decline of state legitimacy. I hope to give full accounts of the complicated causal chain that has led to the emergence of both the heroin and HIV/AIDS epidemics and to focus on the failure of the state's neoliberal development blueprint in dealing with the local crisis.

In what follows, I lay out three facets of change—state, social, and individual—that the Nuosu have been subjected to over the course of the larger Chinese modernity drive in the past century. A simple causal link I wish to demonstrate is that changes emanating from the state have affected both society and individuals, and those changes in turn ricochet back onto the state itself. At the state level, two polarized modernity schemes—the central planning of socialist modernity and profit maximization in the markets of capitalist modernity—have thrown Nuosu society into disarray since the outset of their imposition. The drastic shift of state modernity discourses has put all actors in the postsocialist transition in a position of duplicity when confronting public issues. At the social level, modernization has meant the initial suppression— and later revival—of traditional Nuosu practices as the Chinese state floundered through a number of modernizing projects. The Nuosu have become a fixture in such programs; they can no longer remain aloof from the intrusions of state and global forces. Finally, at the individual level, modernity has altered individual aspirations and provided greater freedom of mobility and choice than ever before, all at a certain cost.

The Bipolar Drives of Chinese Modernity

Modernity has been the main political project of goal-oriented change, often initiated and orchestrated by nation-states, since the late nineteenth century. Nation-states, as Sassen specifies, are "the container of social process" (2007, 1). Scholars of all convictions have engaged in defining, delineating, or debating over the contours, trajectories, and impacts of modernity in transforming people's lives around the globe. Modernity theorist Anthony Giddens states that "the emergence of modernity is first of all the creation of a modern economic order, that is, a capitalistic economic order" (Giddens and Pierson 1998, 96). He depicts modernity as emerging from the capitalization of Europe and subsequently spreading worldwide (Giddens 1990). In light of this view, scholarly discourses on modernity tend to focus on how capitalism as a hegemonic ideology has schematically ordered and reordered people's activities, hierarchies, identities, and lives at large.

Nevertheless, modernity has never taken a single, monolithic form. Over the past few hundred years of human history, societies have experienced diverse forms of transformation that scholars have labeled in various ways—from early to late modernity, from modernity to postmodernity, and so on (Carleheden and Jacobsen 2001). Scholars have also used descriptors such as "alternative" or "other" to emphasize the global or non-Western characteristics of being modern and their multiple outcomes (e.g., Gaonkar 2001; Rofel 1999). To point to its diverse transformations is to notice that, despite its origin and orientation, modernity is not necessarily driven by capitalism. In some parts of the world, it has been engineered by other developmental ideologies—socialism, for example.

The shift of development paradigms demonstrates global competition among the multiple ideologies and models of modernity in the twentieth century. Competition between socialism and capitalism was most intense in the 1950s. In the capitalist world, from the 1950s to the 1960s, development was synonymous with modernization—defined, engineered, and directed by Western experts—in the newly decolonized third-world countries. This was the heyday of Weberian teleological social transformation, which suggests that industrialization, education, and technology acquisition can facilitate social or national movement from traditional types of social formation to a modern one (Leys 1996). By the 1970s, the focus of development had become economic growth (Edelman and Haugerud 2005).

At the same time, in another ideological zone, modernization projects pursued by socialist states did not emphasize economic growth alone but were characterized by a concentration of power and resources through centralized planning for purposes of modern nation-state building. Central planning, orchestrated by the state rather than by the invisible hand of the market, provided the fuel for a scheme of development that emphasized social equality over individual freedom of choice.

Despite the distinctions between these two competing ideologies, from the 1950s through the 1970s the idea of development was couched in terms of modernization around the world (Arnason 2002; Escobar 1995). The teleological transition from "backward" or "traditional" forms of social order to "modern" ones underpinned the various goals of development.

The period from the late 1970s through the 1980s, however, was a turning point for the global social and economic order; this was the period when neoliberalism gained growing influence in economies around the world, be they traditional, socialist, or capitalist. "Neoliberalism" can be defined as the "doctrines or policies that accord the market rather than the state the main role in resolving economic and other problems" (Edelman and Haugerud 2005, 7). The sway this doctrine gained worldwide yielded many unintended consequences, including the disintegration of the former Soviet Union and many of its Eastern European allies. This epochal shift has led to a categorical break from the modernization of the earlier era, namely, the advent of a late modernity and the emergence of a new phenomenon called "globalization." Since that time, "development" has become synonymous with globalization: it now means "participation in the world market" (17).

Although socialism had given way to neoliberal capitalism in China in 1978, socialist influences continue in people's everyday lives there, as they do in many so-called postsocialist states.[1] Postsocialism is not a teleological and unidirectional trajectory (Humphrey 2002). Social transformation in these countries is still in progress alongside the heritage of "actually existing socialism," which varies across diverse national contexts (Humphrey 1998; Verdery 1996). In China, recent social science literature has documented that late socialism or postsocialism is not a radical break from the past but instead a reconfiguration of socialist rationalities and practices that often creates new forms of inequality and problems, a consequence of the dramatic "plunge into modernity" (Beck and Beck-Gernsheim 2002, 2).

Globally, medical anthropological inquiries since the 1980s have underscored the importance of development as a key conceptual framework for understanding the spread, treatment, and consequences of diseases and maladies. In the field of illicit drugs and AIDS research, the political economy approach has tied the cause of such problems to externally imposed forces at different levels, from the institutional and national to the global (Baer, Singer, and Susser 1997; Bourgois 2003; Bourgois and Schonberg 2009; Farmer 1992; Parker 2001; Singer 1998). Paul Farmer (1992) spearheaded the ethnography of AIDS research with an explicit political economy perspective. By assessing a small village's contemporary epidemic and suffering, he convincingly shows how Haiti's history and complex development experiences have converged in a modernity trajectory that has left local people haplessly and hopelessly stranded. He pointedly asks, "Is AIDS caused by microbes or by poverty?" (Farmer 1992, 58).

The interplay between external forces—historical and global—and local crisis is also manifest in Bourgois's (2003) research on illicit drug use in East Harlem, New York City. In his analysis of why the young people there fell through the cracks, Bourgois criticizes the earlier behavioral approach to these social problems. He calls attention to racial and class inequality—not drugs—in the street. As he puts it, "Drugs are not the root of the problems . . . ; they are the epiphenomenonal [sic] expression of deeper, structural dilemmas" (Bourgois 2003, 319).

Hyde's (2007) investigation of the Chinese government's AIDS policies in Yunnan Province is also a case in point. The socialist government, following its teleological modernization scheme, labels "backward" ethnic minorities and sex workers, among other demographic groups, as AIDS "risk groups." This labeling converts the state's preexisting ideological prejudices against ethnic minorities into a representation of public health "fact."

By microscopically scrutinizing ethnographic details, these scholars situate social suffering in small or moderate-sized communities and juxtapose it with a larger political and economic context, be it the village, the city, the state, or the world. Their work makes an excellent case for how historical and economic development trajectories, under diverse modernity guises, have shaped local communities.

Inspired by these research insights, my study will emphasize two important areas that previous political-economic perspectives in medical anthropology have tended to downplay. First, I consider the development drives and trajectories, both socialist and capitalist, in the twentieth-century discourse of modernity. In doing so, I aim to emphasize that local people are not simply innocent "victims" but are also proactive agents who can be both losers and winners in the modernity drive. In other words, the articulation between the center and the periphery is not simply unidirectional, an imposition from the top; it is rather a dynamic interaction. The second emphasis of this study is related to the first, that is, individual agency is a crucial element in my analyses of changing modernity schemes. Individual voices are not treated merely as personal narratives of social suffering; they are also interpreted as expressions of young people's yearning and striving for a better way of life embedded in their desire to take part in the development going on all around them, in China's modernity. Capitalist modernity as a goal has introduced both bright and dark aspects to their new lives in the reform era. On the one hand, they are subjects of the state's modernity experiments, and their transitional vulnerability and suffering are particularly evident. On the other hand, capitalist modernity also offers them an expanded social horizon and life opportunities that they eagerly embrace.

The Changing Social Dimensions of Space and Time

Ever since Evans-Pritchard's *The Nuer* (1940), scholars have used space-time configurations as a perspective from which to understand the lived contexts of indigenous peoples. In a traditional society such as the Nuer, kinship principles dictate virtually every aspect of people's daily life, from physical residential units to conceptualizations of space (e.g., close kin live closer than distant kin) and time (e.g., the farther one travels away from one's personal residential unit, the more remote the lineal linkages through time). In contrast, in the post-traditional social order, organizing principles derived from other ideologies or referential frameworks crop up in people's everyday lives. This change has been the main transformation of modern society or modernity, and it is global in scale.

Recent multidisciplinary research has emphasized the space-time configurations as social constructs, particularly in relation to contemporary capitalistic modes of life. This line of research asks, for instance, how capitalism, as the hegemonic ideology, has schematically ordered and reordered the physical arrangements of activities (e.g., markets for trade, parks for leisure) and social ranking (e.g., rural versus urban). It has also inscribed new spatial and temporal patterns of social action and social imaginaries that affect people's day-to-day lives (e.g., Giddens 1990, 1991; Harvey 1989; Lefebvre 1991).

Nuosu people's experience of social transformation may deviate from the above-mentioned rule in that its key engagement with modernity did not come through capitalist penetration but through socialist governance. One conspicuous change after China forcibly incorporated the Nuosu into the Chinese state polity was the expanded horizons of space and time in the local Nuosu world. Giddens states that the modern nation-state is plainly "a type of social community which contrasts in a radical way with pre-modern states" (Giddens 1990, 13). The socialist Chinese state attempted to incorporate traditional Nuosu society into its grand, national collective entity, which aimed to synchronize different stages of development among its diverse nationalities according to the

Marxian-Morganian evolutionary paradigm: from primitive society to slavery to feudalistic, capitalist, and finally socialist society. To do this, the state first had to categorize and divide the entire population according to this hierarchical and teleological development scheme. Once the ethnic classification project was completed, the state then assigned these minority groups to an administrative hierarchy based on their size, distribution, and level of development. This hierarchy, which ascends from the individual Nuosu households to the village, from the village to the township, from the township to the county, then through Liangshan Prefecture to Chengdu (the capital of Sichuan Province), to Beijing (the capital of the Chinese nation-state), and ultimately beyond China,[2] expands the Nuosu's vistas via this new time-space dimensionality.

Despite the prelude of socialist modernity, however, the inward-looking collectives of the Maoist era kept the Nuosu largely unchanged in terms of their social and geographical mobility. In this sense, the socialist state shared a certain spatial commonality with traditional Nuosu lineages as it followed the blueprint of Maoist governance, which was based in confined and self-reliant "cellular" rural communes (Siu 1989). The Nuosu's spatial and temporal horizons began to change fundamentally only after the introduction of post-Mao market reforms, through which globalization has been able to penetrate to rural China.

With the collapse of the confined livelihood and command economy in the reform era, the Nuosu have been ushered into a late modernity that has created "emergent forms of life" characterized by cycles of social, political, and economic reconstructions across local and global horizons (Fischer 2003, 37). The constant flows of commodities, information, human labor, and capital both upward and downward, as well as increased personal opportunities and risks in the current globalizing era, have clearly led to the greatly broadened worldview that distinguishes today's Nuosu community from its previously centralized or mobility-restricted precursor under the collective system, whether tribal or socialist. Individuals can now move across spans of geography and socioeconomic status more freely than ever before. The markets "suck us (willingly) out of our cosy, dull, local niches and turn us into unencumbered actors, mobile in a world system, but setting us free they leave us exposed" (Douglas 1992, 15). The pursuit of a better life is now unequivocally driven by the criterion of capitalist success, namely, the amount of money one has and the scarce resources or privileges one can command with that accumulated money, rather than by the traditional or socialist moral economy.

The incorporation of the Nuosu into China's socialist polity in the 1950s and the global market in the 1980s has compelled them to see themselves as situated at the bottom of the territorial and economic hierarchy. So when the Nuosu people move, they are eager not only to move in geographical space but also in the sociocultural and political-economic space and time defined by the governing modernity scheme. The precarious position of Nuosu people in this modern nation-state is clearly manifested in their spatial and temporal marginalization on the state's development road map.

Changes in space and time perceptions may also change the dialectics of the local and the global. Global transformation often brings about unintended and uncertain outcomes, owing to the varied local particularities (Burawoy and Verdery 1999). For instance, under the conditions of top-down development, implementers may ignore local specifics and, not surprisingly, encounter unanticipated hurdles and failures. In the local governance of the Nuosu, the changing social space has had implications in line with what Giddens calls "disembedding" or "the 'lifting out' of social relations from local contexts of interaction and their restructuring across indefinite spans of time-space" (Giddens 1990, 21). Through this disembedding, to be discussed especially in Chapter 6, we see how globalization has indirectly set up the state agents' acceptance of global protocols for AIDS intervention. At the local front line of heroin and AIDS interventions, we also see how modern social institutions (e.g., administrative bureaucracy, police) and experts (e.g., public health workers) become the dominant authorities in deciding local affairs. The poor local footing of government agents becomes more pronounced the further removed the state's objectives and policies are from local particularities, an increasing trend within globalizing modernity.

Rising Individualism and Private Aspirations

In late modernity, opportunities and dangers are perceived and processed by individuals themselves rather than by predetermined aggregates such as families or communities. Individualization or individualism with regard to freedom and uncertainty has become a shared experience nowadays (Beck and Beck-Gernsheim 2002). The rise of individualism in the wake of China's market reform has been a focus in recent scholarship, especially in the arenas of consumerism, sexual desire, and private identities, which were largely stifled under socialist regimentation (see, e.g., Croll 2006; Farrer 2002; Rofel 2007; Yan 2003). Anthropological research, however, has pointed out that experiences of modernity are never homogenous or unidirectional. As Rofel (1999) argues, China's pursuit of modernity has accentuated generational and gender differences. Likewise, Litzinger (2002) argues that contemporary research on modernity in China tends to focus on Han-dominant urbanites and leave ethnic minorities at the margins. My research on the Nuosu can thus be considered a response to Litzinger's efforts, since it brings a peripheral minority back to the center stage of China's modernity discourses. Furthermore, I bring to the fore Nuosu young men who act on their individuality in line with market reform mandates.

Heroin is the focal point of my analysis of how modernity is desired and acquired by ordinary Nuosu young men. This leads to the question, why do they use drugs? One school of thought emphasizes "social exclusion" as the main reason youths take up drug use under peer pressure (MacDonald and Marsh 2002). This particular theory is not heuristic for the Nuosu because it does not explain why it is mainly Nuosu youth but not other neighboring groups who have this problem. Another approach proposes the concept of "consumer exoticism" as a key reason for drug use behavior when it is equated with fashion or a desired lifestyle (Jay 1999). Taking this perspective as my point of departure, I want to ask further: What circumstances contribute to drug consumption among the Nuosu youth, and what does it mean to them?

No one could have foreseen that modernity would make heroin available to young Nuosu and that drug use would become integral to their idea of a better life. The modern age is said to be epitomized by rapid, intense, and widespread flows of goods (Appadurai 1996). And few goods have as powerful an effect on society as drugs; its misuse indicates the crises around "modernity and human alienation" (Bourgois 1999, 2163). As I will lay out in Chapters 2 and 4, the life experiences of Nuosu youth under market reform have intertwined expanding individual liberty with the availability of novel commodities such as drugs and a yearning to claim a part in China's blossoming modernity.

There are two layers of individualism in my analysis of Nuosu youths' pursuit of modernity. The first reflects our common understanding of Western-style individualism. The decrease in family or community constraints on individuals has led to a growing craving on the part of young people for autonomy and freedom in making life choices. In the Nuosu case, the formation of a consumption-oriented individualism among the youth is combined intimately with their coming of age through migration to cities—a subplot to China's grand narrative of entry into the world of capitalist modernity. To a certain extent, this phenomenon underscores Yunxiang Yan's (2003) contention that China's market reform has been accompanied by the growth of young people's desire for individual autonomy and purchasable commodities.

The second layer of individualism relevant here—the other side of the coin, so to speak—is what Ulrich Beck calls "individualization" or "institutionalized individualism" in the context of late modernity (Beck and Beck-Gernsheim 2002). This type of individualism in the age of global flows focuses on "the fundamental incompleteness of the self" (xxi). In late modernity, individuals are not fancy-free monads but increasingly tied to other people, worldwide networks, and institutions. Under these circumstances their very freedom, in tandem with increasing individualization, is precarious, and risks encountered in the pursuit of opportunities are unavoidable because the individual cannot truly decide and shape life according to his or her own will. Individualization in this sense means "disembedding without reembedding" (xxii). In the Nuosu case, this means that as youths' individuality has increased and the previously constrained forms of livelihood have given way to individual choice, there has arisen an "institutionalized imbalance between the disembedded individual and global problems in a global risk society" (xxii).

The complexity of modernity is therefore clearly demonstrated in the dual meanings of individualism among Nuosu youth in the market reform era. It is a nearly universal phenomenon that youth stand at the forefront of dazzling social changes (Herdt and Leavitt 1998). They occupy the liminal stage in their life course and, therefore, can provide a key to understanding social change and its uncertainties at both the community and individual levels.

The transition from youth to manhood is often imbued with specific social meanings and embedded in particular practices. Anthropologists have noted that males in many societies, Trukese men in Marshall's (1979) research, for example, conform to idealized manliness by taking risks that may result in death or serious injury (Gilmore 1990). Likewise, Bumbita Arapesh youths of the East Sepik Province in Papua New Guinea engage in misconduct such as theft, vandalism, and sexual harassment as they attempt to become men (Leavitt 1998, 175).

Herzfeld's (1985) research on Glendiot shepherds' practice of goat theft as an informal initiation to manhood in Greece further locates manly selfhood in the tension between a marginal local community and the bureaucratic state. Within a contextualized understanding, Herzfeld shows Glendiot men's goat theft as beyond the stereotype of custom and criminality and unravels their performative focus as "being *good at* being a man" instead of "being a good man" (Herzfeld 1985, 16; italics in original unless otherwise noted). This research demonstrates an insightful analysis that situates men's conduct within macropolitical and -economic change.

Nuosu youths' expanded spatial and temporal possibilities, in the enticing guise of modernity, have led to their migration and pursuit of self-gratification in the cities. This uniform yet spontaneously adventurous behavior is an expression and demonstration of their masculine identity. In this sense, their outbound adventures are a case study in how noneconomic factors can determine human migration. Migration often has "*meanings* for a given society or for a sub-section of that society that cannot be reduced to clear-cut economic or social factors alone" (Boyle, Halfacree, and Robinson 1998, 72; emphasis added). In other words, economic determinism as a methodological paradigm in migration studies underestimates the complex motivations of human agency (Ellis, Conway, and Bailey 2000; Wright 2000). Nuosu youths' adventures toward manhood present us with an interesting view of how Limu's individuals enter China's new capitalist modernity in a relatively uniform manner.

A Medical Ethnography of Nuosu Postsocialist Transition

This book is at heart a medical ethnography of one corner of China's postsocialist transition. A medical ethnography, as defined by Arthur Kleinman, is "a description of a society through a medical lens, a systematic focus on the health-relevant aspects of social life" (Kleinman 1995, 205). In this study I look into life changes around the Nuosu's heroin use and the spread of HIV, both of which have come with China's postsocialist transition. In this light, this ethnography is also situated among the many other studies of postsocialist transitions globally, a growing area of anthropological interest in comparative research (Humphrey 2002; Kalb 2002).

Following anthropological tradition, I consider the ethnographic approach best suited to examining the multilayered meanings and practices of the institutions, policies, and actors in China's latest modernity discourse. It goes without saying that, by deploying this methodology, the researcher's personal background, social standing, professional experiences, and ways of living become closely intertwined with local contexts; the resulting encounters often give rise to unique challenges for the researcher and often rest in no small part on the researcher's luck as well. My encounters with ghosts and bandits mentioned in the opening sections have introduced my luck and personal perspective. If, as Michael Agar (1986) puts it, the ethnographic account mediates between the worlds of the readers and the subjects, I am eager to connect readers to the social world of Limu Township, where I conducted fieldwork for an accumulated twenty months, including the entire year of 2005 and sporadically between 2002 and 2009.

Even though my research was conducted in a community often regarded as peripheral, this ethnography is nonetheless compiled on the "multi-sited imaginary" (Marcus 1998). Ethnography dealing with multisited imaginaries may begin from a single locale to probe and expand into the encompassing external world. As Burawoy (2000) argues, the forces, connections, and imaginations that mediate the micro and macro worlds have become the three most important components of ethnographies in the globalizing world.

My reference to multisited imaginaries does not mean that I have actually conducted extensive fieldwork in the cities to which Nuosu youth migrated, although from time to time I did visit one city, Chengdu, which is on the receiving end of major Nuosu migration. During my long-term fieldwork, I spent most of my time in Limu and my principal field site remained this mountain township. My multisited representations are chiefly based on my informants' recollections of their lives in the cities, and I incorporate their stories into my analytical framework of Limu's social change.

Among the methods used, participant observation was the foundation of my fieldwork. My collection and understanding of the Nuosu verbal and nonverbal data were made possible through what Geertz (1983) terms an "experience-near" process. This is an ongoing process that hinges on close interactions with the local people. My Nuosu language capacity gradually improved as my fieldwork continued, and by the end of my year-long stay in 2005 I could carry on ordinary daily conversations. For more delicate matters, however, such as ritual chanting and legal dispute cases, I relied on my key informants, first Lati and later Muga, as my interpreters. They accompanied me when I conducted interviews or attended community events.

My understanding of Limu and its people also came from direct interviews with selected informants who were either knowledgeable about certain subjects I was exploring or trustworthy friends who gave me straight answers without concealment or pretension. I identified potential informants through the snowball sampling method, which is particularly well suited for the study of hard-to-reach people (Bernard 2002). This method enabled me to interview people such as drug users, dealers, and migrant workers. In total, I conducted in-depth interviews with fifty-six people, including high-level government officials, township and village cadres, ritual specialists (*bimo* and *sunyi*), traditional judges or mediators (*ndeggu*), lineage headmen (*suyy*), former and current drug users, people with HIV/AIDS, former and current health workers, migrant workers, drifters, and merchants.

My relatively long-term stay in Limu was nonetheless insufficient for me to experience comprehensively the complicated social processes and historical context that I aimed to unravel. To compensate for this shortfall, I considered the life-history method to be practical. According to Langness and Frank (1981): "Anthropologists who use the life-history method convey directly the *reality* that people other than themselves experience" (1). After numerous daily conversations and in-depth interviews, I constructed eight life histories, including those of an old granny (Qubi), a bimo (Jjike), and six former or current drug users. Their narratives will thread in and out of my account in the following chapters.

In June 2005 I conducted a door-to-door survey of all sixty-eight households in one *she* (the lowest administrative level, below a village) of Limu. I decided to conduct this small-scale survey mainly because I had had difficulties accessing the township government's statistical data about various aspects of local conditions. I used the household survey method to collect quantitative data and extrapolate the general conditions in this *she*—conditions that, I believe, can be applied to other communities in the Limu basin as well. My choice of the surveyed *she* was based on the consideration that it was near the township clinic where I resided during 2005, so villagers there knew me well and I knew them better than I did other Limu residents. My structured survey questions focused on the family tree of each household and the kinship relationships among them, as well as on the residents' drug-use history and the whereabouts of absent family members.

Throughout my field research in Liangshan, one of my greatest challenges was to secure official data for both heroin and HIV/AIDS, as well as other "unglamorous" data concerning, for example, the local poverty that officials did not wish to reveal. Occasionally I obtained scattered health data about Liangshan Prefecture, Zhaojue County, and Limu Township through unpublished reports, as well as from my consultation and conversation with health workers and officials. Data collection at the township and county levels was the most strenuous part of my fieldwork. In general, officials at these levels were reluctant to provide me with complete and unflattering data regarding the population, the farmland, the economy, and diseases. Officials often described these categories of data as "classified." They sometimes gave me partial figures, so I needed to use other means to construct as complete a picture as possible. I also realized that the data officials provided me should be treated with caution as to accuracy.

In China, gaps in the statistics gathered at different levels of government have been a long-standing problem (Cai 2000). My long-term stay in Limu enabled me to learn how officials at the village level and above collected and compiled data. Village cadres and lineage headmen established their own local databases concerning issues such as drug use. Data constructed at this level, before village cadres turned them over to the township government, tended to be the most reliable. Fortunately for me, several village cadres and lineage headmen were willing to share their data with me. But above the village level, numbers might be inflated or watered down, depending on the circumstances under which acquisition of the data had been commanded by higher-level offices.

Last but not least, this book deals with sensitive topics involving personal privacy: illicit drug use, HIV infection, burglary and theft, and conflicts of interest among state agents or between state agents and local peasants in a country that is still nominally following the socialist ideology. I have tried to protect the confidentiality of all parties involved by using pseudonyms for informants, lineages, and localities (*she*, village, and township). Using pseudonyms is our disciplinary convention, although it is not without problems. There remain practical difficulties when researchers try to protect the identities of their informants who live in small, easily identifiable communities (Hopkins 1993). Therefore, I have further disguised the identities of some people by changing their ranks in cadre status or in birth order without distorting the context of analysis.

Overview of the Book

Chapter 1 elaborates on Liangshan's development relative to two critical years in Limu's history, 1956 and 1978, to set the stage for the transformative effects of national and global development on the township. In Chapter 2, I describe Nuosu youth migration and how it has contributed greatly to the dual epidemics of heroin and HIV/AIDS. I argue that since the debut of China's market reform, out-migration has become a new rite of passage among young Nuosu men.

The epidemics of heroin use and HIV/AIDS have devastated Limu since the out-migrating youths brought these afflictions back to the township. In Chapters 3 and 4, I analyze how Limu's community leaders tried to cope with these emerging crises by calling for a reformulation of traditional kinship organizations and the reassertion of indigenous ritual authorities. I show how these traditional authorities have been weakened by the growing influence of the encroaching state, the ever-expanding market, and young people's rising sense of individuality and growing aspirations to seek pleasure beyond their stiflingly isolated mountain community.

Chapter 5 focuses on the state's efforts to intervene in the dual epidemics. I use Limu's leading AIDS intervention project, the China-UK HIV/AIDS Prevention and Care Project (hereafter the China-UK Project or simply the project), as a case in point to exemplify failed state intervention practices at the local level. Chapter 6 presents a case study that illustrates the emerging stigmatization of AIDS in Limu and identifies it as an unexpected consequence of state interventions, which brought the global antistigma agenda to Limu without adjusting it to local conditions.

In the Conclusion, along with an overview of my argument concerning modernity and social change, I raise two questions with regard to the influence of globalization. A revisiting of the state's changing role and the Nuosu's rising individualism may be essential for our understanding of Nuosu society in the future and others like it within and beyond China.

1 The Meandering Road to Modernity

IN AUGUST OF 2004, I sat discussing my interest in AIDS and contemporary Nuosu social change with several Nuosu friends who had gathered in Xichang, the capital city of Liangshan Prefecture. One of them, a high-ranking government official, half-jokingly remarked, "If you want to study how Communist governance has failed us Nuosu, go to Zhaojue County!" Then he added with a tinge of sarcasm, "And there, you will also see what effect the Han people have had on the Nuosu."

My eventual understanding of Zhaojue's recent history and the AIDS problem in the county confirmed this official's comments. During my intensive fieldwork in Zhaojue's Limu Township in 2005, I came to realize that all that remained in this county, after China launched its market reform in 1978, were the tatters of failed socialist modernity projects implemented over the previous two decades. The county had pointedly been bypassed in the capitalist development scheme; in 1978 the Liangshan prefectural government moved its capital from the county seat of Zhaojue County to Xichang City. Both the collective and the market reform eras have brought about controversial developments for the Nuosu in general and Zhaojue in particular. Problems of drug use and AIDS concomitant with the drastic social transformation of the Nuosu there have more recently been added to the long story of the county's hardships.

My examination of the historical twists and turns that have shaped Nuosu society must be understood within the sweep of China's modernization projects, which began in 1956. Once incorporated into the Chinese state, the Nuosu had little choice but to accept and try to adjust to its grand development plans. The shifting position of the Nuosu within the state has thus been a consequence of China's modernization efforts, which occurred in two distinct phases with uniquely different characteristics; these have produced diverse long- and short-term effects in Nuosu communities.

Watershed Events in Nuosu History

Within a mere fifty years, the Nuosu people experienced three distinct types of social life: kinship-based local autonomy (before 1956), socialist collectivism (1956–78), and market capitalism (post-1978). Beginning in the 1950s the Nuosu, a nonstate, pre-monetary, kinship-based society, was first forcibly incorporated into the Chinese socialist polity. It became one of the fifty-five officially recognized minority nationalities[1] and was subjected to radical transformation in order to acquire a "civilized" status. The top-down command governance established during the collective era firmly wrapped the Nuosu into the socialist state. Subsequently, Nuosu communities were relegated to the periphery of state-initiated modernization projects and marginalized during the market reform era, when capitalist-oriented development favored the coastal provinces and metropolitan regions over the poor, minority-dominant interior. In China's twentieth-century state-building process, the Nuosu suffered doubly, both as an "uncivilized" minority nationality and as rustic "backward" peasants (Cohen 1993; Litzinger 2000). The Nuosu's marginalization can be vividly seen in Zhaojue's recent history.

Zhaojue County is located in the so-called core area (*fuxin diqu*) of Liangshan, where the great majority of residents are Nuosu. Zhaojue County has perhaps the most concentrated Nuosu population in Liangshan: of the approximately 200,000 residents, nearly 97 percent are Nuosu, and the rest are mainly Han people, mostly government officials, teachers, and businesspeople residing in the county seat (Sichuan sheng 2002). This county encountered the Chinese Communists earlier than many other core areas, and in 1952 the new Communist government chose it to be the prefecture capital of Liangshan. Before then, no external state agency had successfully established a permanent presence in this remote Nuosu-dominant area enclosed by mountains.[2]

Old Liangshan as a Peripheral Power over Han Chinese

Prior to the 1950s, Liangshan had been an independent and sovereign territory, not ruled by either imperial China or theocratic Tibet. The Han referred to the Nuosu in Liangshan as *Lolo*, independent *Lolo*, or *Yi* (i.e., "barbarians").[3] Their relationship with the Han state had been both aloof and tense owing to their political autonomy and the practice of capturing and enslaving Han Chinese.

Traditionally, Nuosu society had four strata: *nzymo* ([Ch.] *tusi*, or ruler), *nuo* (black Yi, or aristocrat), *qunuo* (white Yi, or commoners), and *mgajie* and *gaxy* ([Ch.] *wazi*, or slaves).[4] Han state officials and individuals could not readily gain access to Nuosu-dominant areas without the protection of strong nzymo and nuo (Goullart 1959; Lin 1961; Winnington 1959).

Before Communist rule, Nuosu society had no consistent political organization or power structure above *cyvi* (Nuosu lineages and clans) (Lin 1961).[5] The Nuosu people recognize only a few dozen large clans, despite their sizable population in Liangshan (Ma 1999). Unlike the Han Chinese, who record their ancestry in written genealogies and usually commemorate only recently deceased immediate ancestors (Cohen 1990), the Nuosu memorize complete genealogies of lineages by rote (Hill and Diehl 2001). Teaching children to recite their genealogies, including both the father's and the mother's lines, has been an important part of Nuosu family education. Through the seniors' intensive instruction and the children's extensive drilling on lineage ancestors, most Nuosu children between the ages of four and six can recite family genealogies to thirty or forty generations and understand that they cannot survive without their paternal and maternal lineages (Ma 2003). Kinship principles traditionally dictated Nuosu people's social classifications, marital options, and residential distribution. Further, individual rights and obligations, as well as hereditary professions and public authorities, were couched in kinship terms. Social morality and cosmological beliefs were also embedded in their kinship universe.

Limu was a typical Nuosu community that had both strong lineage organizations and a strict social hierarchy. Limu was nominally a region that belonged to the nzymo lineage, the Lili,[6] while the de facto ruler in daily life was the resident nuo lineage, the Ma. Under the nuo, there were two sizable qunuo lineages, the Lewu and Anyu, and several small- to medium-sized qunuo lineages. Before the 1950s, slaves were said to be either Han Chinese who had been captured by nuo and qunuo, or their offspring.[7]

The traditional Nuosu way of life was subsistence agriculture, with sheep and goat pasturing in the mountains. Their main crops were buckwheat, corn, and potatoes (Lin 1961). In the pre-state era (circa pre-1956), the Nuosu in the core area did not have a currency-driven market economy or fixed marketplaces; barter was the main way of obtaining the goods and services that people did not produce by themselves. The few Nuosu people who had experience of market mechanisms at that time traded primarily on the ethnic borderlands of Liangshan, and that trade had everything to do with opium.

The Introduction of Opium to Liangshan

China was overwhelmed by opium consumption in the late nineteenth century. By 1906 about 16.2 million people, or 3.6 percent of the total population, were daily opium smokers (Courtwright 2001, 33; Newman 1995, 787). The ever-growing demand for opium, as well as the promised profits from this cash crop, bolstered mass poppy production in southwest China, especially in Sichuan Province, beginning in the second half of the nineteenth century (Bello 2005; Trocki 1999).

Around 1910, Han people introduced poppy cultivation into Nuosu areas, with the assistance of certain nzymo and nuo, and grew it in remote and isolated mountains as a way of evading the anti-opium campaigns launched by the Qing court (Zhou 1999). In subsequent decades, opium planting became widespread in Liangshan because Nuosu landowners, mostly nzymo and nuo, realized that they could use it to trade with Han people for silver ingots or dollars (*tuotuo yin* or *bai yin*[8]), cloth, salt, and other everyday commodities. Opium soon changed the Nuosu landscape. As historian Doak Barnett commented after a trip to the borders of Tibetan and Nuosu areas in Sichuan in 1948, "Most Yi [Nuosu] were farmers, and one of their principal crops was opium" (Barnett 1993, 415). The Chinese government's surveys of Liangshan in the early 1950s, including Nuosu core areas as well as ethnically mixed areas, also indicated that between 50 and 80 percent of the households, both Han and Nuosu, engaged in poppy farming and that 50 to 60 percent of the local populations smoked opium regularly (Sun, Shi, and Zhu 1993, cited in Zhou 1999).

Opium altered the closed economy of Nuosuland most significantly by involving the Nuosu in a monetary trade that tipped the balance of the Nuosu-Han relationship. The influx of sudden wealth through the opium trade also brought with it deadly new weapons—guns, rifles, and bullets—that replaced the Nuosu's old weapons, such as bows and arrows, poles and sticks, leather shields, and long knives. New armaments enabled the locally powerful Nuosu to protect their clans and dependents, to feud with their Nuosu enemies and other ethnic groups, and to capture more Han slaves for opium production and other labor (Lin 1961; Sichuan sheng 1999; Zhou 1999).[9] Opium trade usually took place in the periodic markets held on the borders of Nuosu-Han habitations, not within Nuosu-dominant areas (Leng and Ma 1992; Liu 2007). Occasionally opium was also bartered between the Nuosu themselves in exchange for slaves or other needs. For example, a qunuo who wanted to smoke opium had to exchange food with the opium-growing nuo.

The introduction of opium to Nuosu society presented a novel and luxurious commodity whose consumption occurred along the lines of preexisting social strata: mainly only wealthy and powerful people could enjoy it. The embodiment of social hierarchy and wealth status in the consumption of opium is part and parcel of contemporary Nuosu reminiscences concerning this substance. An old *bimo* (ritual healer), who is classified as a qunuo, rehearsed a Nuosu saying: "'Opium is the food and candy of nzymo and nuo.' Only nzymo, nuo, and well-off qunuo could afford to smoke opium." For this reason, he himself took up opium smoking in the 1940s, for the sake of "gaining face."

Limu, like other Nuosu areas in old Liangshan, underwent changes brought about by the introduction of opium and new weapons. Before 1950 only a small number of Han people traveled to Limu as merchants. They paid protection fees to the powerful nuo for permission to enter Nuosu territories and for escorts composed of armed nuo and their slaves. The eighty-two-year-old granny Qubi, who had spent her whole life in Limu, recalled in 2005:

> I first saw Han people when I was around six or seven years old. They didn't have a "horse's head" [i.e., look monstrous] as we imagined. [*Chuckle.*] . . . Han merchants came to us to exchange cloth and salt for sheepskin and pig bristles. Nuo might exchange opium for silver ingots, and we qunuo women exchanged eggs for thread, which we used to make clothes. Han merchants had to ask nuo for permission and protection beforehand, lest they become slaves.

Opium brought great fortunes and power to the Nuosu. Nevertheless, the enormous power they wielded over various ethnic groups, including the Han in this border area of the Southwest, evaporated after the establishment of the People's Republic of China in 1949. When the new Chinese state launched the Democratic Reform in minority-dominated peripheral areas in 1956, the imposition of state authority rapidly and drastically transformed Nuosu society in terms of its social structure and its relationship with the Han.

1956 as the Beginning of Socialist Modernity

The establishment of the Chinese Communist polity in Liangshan in the midtwentieth century marked the beginning of the Nuosu's modernization experience and eventually ushered them into a socialist version of the "Brave New World." Socialist China attempted to transform the Nuosu in line with its goal of achieving a unified, modern nation-state. All previous Chinese polities—whether imperial or nationalist—had attempted to define just who are properly Chinese and determine how to "civilize" the peripheral "barbarians," but as Harrell (1995, 1996) points out, socialist China instituted the most sweeping and systematic measures to achieve these goals. Socialist China adopted the Marxian-Morganian evolutionary theory to justify the transformation of "backward" cultures and societies into "advanced" ones. The state agents for modernization projects, such as ethnologists who studied and categorized the minorities, described the Nuosu according to the state's established typologies. The state relegated the Nuosu to a low rung on the human societal development ladder, classifying them as the only remaining "slave society" extant in China in the 1950s.[10] Fixing their identity as members of a uniquely backward "slave society" was only the first act of the state's official stigmatizing of Nuosu people and communities. As Giddens has noted, "The practical impact of social science and sociological theories is enormous, and sociological concepts and findings are constitutively involved in what modernity *is*" (Giddens 1990, 16). In other words, this official label would be integrated into the contemporary Nuosu's construction of the self (Hill 2001), and it has continued to negatively inform the Nuosu about their own culture, society, and people.

From the 1950s to the late 1970s, China experimented with socialist modernity through centrally planned governance in order to realize the utopian Marxist goal of equality. As William H. Sewell argues, however, totalitarian states' practices have never been successful in achieving cultural uniformity. The typical cultural strategy of such powers is "not so much to establish uniformity as it is to organize difference. They are constantly engaged in efforts not only to normalize or homogenize but also to hierarchize, encapsulate, exclude, criminalize, hegemonize, or marginalize practices and populations that diverge from the sanctioned ideal" (Sewell 2005, 172). Under the Chinese state, the Nuosu have experienced these transformations within only one or two generations.

The Democratic Reform

The socialist state's enormous army "liberated" Liangshan in 1950. Two years later, the Communist government chose the county seat of Zhaojue County to be the capital of Liangshan Prefecture in its efforts to firmly establish itself in the Nuosu core area. Its initial governance simultaneously upset the Nuosu social hierarchy and incorporated that hierarchy into the party-state. Slaves were released from the control of the nuo. Some of the slaves, dubbed "progressive proletarians," became core cadres in the party. At the same time, cadres in the Liberation Army in Zhaojue County were ordered to assign members of the traditional Nuosu aristocracy to new governmental positions in 1951 because "their functions were crucial" to mediation between the ruling newcomers and the local Nuosu populace (Luo 1999). The incorporation of local elites into a new governmental apparatus where they acted as state-community intermediaries was a common practice in the early days of socialist China (Harrell 2007).[11]

The new socialist state did not immediately introduce the sweeping changes to Nuosu areas that it instituted in Han-dominant areas. The state moved ahead gingerly with its socialist projects, largely owing to its dread of long-standing Nuosu power and its sensitivity toward minority-Han relations. The government waited four years before it initiated any large-scale project in Liangshan; but in 1956 it finally undertook a major program called the Democratic Reform, which ran until 1958. Resistance, especially from the nuo, to the state's imposition of power over Nuosuland sparked violent protests, military confrontations, and killings in many parts of Liangshan, Limu included.

The Communist government tagged local nuo who resisted the state projects with the label *tufei* (bandits). Granny Qubi remembered the fighting between the Communist army and the nuo in 1956:

> Tufei [i.e., nuo] didn't welcome Han people in Limu. They attacked government offices. Soldiers fought back and killed nuo and their slaves. Later that day, I saw soldiers carrying away dead bodies, countless men and boys. That sleepless night, I thought there would be no more men left in Riha [Village], because so many of them had died in the fight. The non-stop bark of the guns—*da-da-da-da!*—tore through the skies. . . . I was thirty-three years old then. It was the Year of the Monkey.

A bimo from the Qubi lineage recalled his father's death in an accident during the Democratic Reform:

> I did not learn to be a bimo with my father because he died during the *da tufei* [antibandit] campaign in 1956, when I was only eleven years old. My father, carrying a sheepskin on his back, was returning from a ritual service in another village; he arrived at our village in the midst of the gun battles. He was accidentally hit by a stray bullet. We didn't know if it was tufei or the Liberation Army that shot him. We are a bimo family and ritual practices have to be handed down within the family. So my mother sent me to an old bimo in Wupo Township to study Nuosu ritual texts and practices with him. I didn't learn during the daytime or at night. I learned around the time when roosters crowed. I stayed in Wupo for only two years because the government prohibited "superstition" after the tufei rebellion.

During the Democratic Reform, the Communists also began an antifeudal-ism campaign. To this end, they abolished the traditional social hierarchy and prohibited kinship organizations and related cultural practices. Traditional authorities faced vehement attacks in the name of egalitarianism. In Limu the majority of nuo, save a handful of "progressives" who had been placed as tokens in high positions in the local government, had been classified as "enemies of the people" and were barred from their role as traditional leaders. The Communists declared that nuo were exploitative "slaveholders" and "landlords" (*dizhu*). Even now, older people in Limu who lived through those political campaigns use the Han Chinese terms *dizhu* or *tufei* to refer to nuo.

After the Democratic Reform, the state's legitimacy and bureaucratic administration were securely established. The old Nuosu social landscape assumed a new configuration through the measuring and codifying of land units and the formal recording of their inhabitants. The goal of such modernist statecraft was "to make a society legible" (Scott 1998, 2). It simplified or standardized—or in Weber's terms, "rationalized"—the objects that fell within the state's purview. This was followed by the hierarchical ranking of the objects and the regions in which they lived to achieve the centralization of power. Under a uniform territorial classification with a clear hierarchical system of administration, the state can gradually eliminate diversity. The Chinese state's legibility project turned the Nuosu landscape from one primarily based on complex bonds such as social hierarchy and kinship into one defined by administrative boundaries (counties, townships, and villages). One of the first locales in the core areas to undergo socialist reform, Limu was divided into eight villages. Four of them, Luja, Muha, Riha, and Tange, are located in the basin area, while the other four sit in the adjacent high hills.

The socialist Chinese state saw Nuosu religion and lineages as a threat to the creation of a unified state and authority, a type of governmentality seen in many Asian countries during the nation-state building process of the twentieth century (Keyes, Hardacre, and Kendall 1994). During the Democratic Reform, lineage headmen became targets of political campaigns because of their authority over ordinary people. Individual loyalty to lineages was shifted to the party-state. The government ordered that *ndeggu* (traditional mediators or judges) stop performing their mediation roles and that people abide by the state's legal systems and institutions. The government alleged that bimo and *sunyi* (shamans or traditional healers) practiced superstitious tricks and preyed on the "ignorant and backward" peasants. All these campaigns aimed at creating a sturdy base for the socialist modernity the state would impose on the Nuosu in the following decades.

The Minority Project

It was around the time of the Democratic Reform that the state initiated the ethnic identification project—a key approach to making the population "legible." Many ethnologists and local officials, both ethnic Han and minorities, began ethnological investigations into minority areas under the banner of socialist nation building (Guldin 1994; Mullaney 2006). Owing to the political need to simplify diverse populations, the state reduced the number of ethnic groups from the over 400 self-reported groups to 56 nationalities (Gladney 1998).[12] As such, this classification project lumped Nuosu of the Liangshan region together with several other groups elsewhere, such as the Lipuo, Nasu, and Yala, under the broad and state-coined ethnic category "Yi."[13]

The state's teleological ideology characterized "unsinicized" minorities as the most "backward." In the 1950s, Chinese Communist Party Chairman Mao Zedong called on cadres and intellectuals to do "minority work"—that is, to go to ethnic minority areas and "rescue the backward." This call came in tandem with the socialist development ideologies that considered unsinicized minorities to be like children who needed to become cultured (Harrell 1995, 1999).

The introduction of biomedicine and science-based rationality was part of the minority work; this was essentially an attempt to root out traditional beliefs and ritual healings. Limu was one of the first core areas to be equipped with a medical team in the 1950s (Meigu xian 1992; Sichuan sheng 1999). The current Limu Township Clinic was officially established in August 1957, soon after the launch of the Democratic Reform (Sichuan sheng 1999). This clinic was designated to serve the entire district and was thus more important than ordinary township clinics that provided health care mainly for the township residents. Many Han health workers, responding to Mao's call, became the "sent-down youth" and came to work in Limu. These Han workers selected a few local Nuosu youths and trained them to become barefoot doctors, whose chief function was to promote biomedicine and public health. I will discuss the introduction of biomedicine to the Nuosu and its influence on Limu in more detail in Chapter 5.

Rural Collectivization

Socialist campaigns and minority work grew in intensity and scale in the late 1950s. To control both the public and private arenas, the state implemented a collective way of life—the people's communes—to replace the traditional family and community. Each village became a production brigade. Under the brigade were production teams (now called *she*). People belonging to the same team received rationed meals at the collective kitchen and ate in their own homes. The collective dining system was established in 1960 in Limu but lasted for only about two years. The limited portions of allocated food, based on the workpoints each person earned, amidst the agricultural chaos translated into widespread hunger between the late 1950s and the early 1960s. Nationwide, nearly thirty million Chinese died during the massive starvation (Kleinman and Kleinman 1997, 16). Mueggler (2001) also describes extensive famine in another Yi (Lòlop'ò) community in Yunnan Province. As my informant Granny Qubi bitterly recounted the misery of their hunger, the memory rekindled sadness in her deeply wrinkled face:

> One of my daughters was so famished she ate rice bran and grass. She couldn't stand the misery any longer so she hanged herself at the age of eighteen. And we couldn't hold a funeral for her as we had done for others before. Even if it were allowed, there was no food we could have saved to hold a funeral. Besides, no one would have had enough energy to walk to the ceremony. We were all too hungry and weary.

The deprivations caused by collectivization were intensified in 1966 when the Cultural Revolution was formally launched. This campaign attacked all established customs and practices, as well as the intellectuals in the country. As Mueggler describes, the socialist state used an array of "ritualized methods" during its political campaigns, including the Cultural Revolution; these practices were intended to both mobilize the masses and enmesh them through engagement in public performances. In this way, the masses exhibited their loyalty to the party-state. These rituals were designed to transform the state "from personified external Other to abstract internal Other" (Mueggler 2001, 288).

It was through these rituals that traditional authorities such as lineage headmen and ritual specialists repeatedly suffered the humiliation of public criticism and beatings, or underwent numerous thought-reform sessions. The state aimed to eradicate their influence from the very consciousness of the Nuosu and so to solidify its own power over the people. The nuo, as slaveholders and landlords, once again faced the most stringent political attacks. "Many nuo men were jailed or killed. Their women and girls were punished, ordered to stand on small rocks as people spat on them and threw pig dung on them," recounted Granny Qubi.

"There are not many nuo in Limu now. Most of them perished at the time." As the state's grip on Nuosu society grew tighter, social activities related to kinship organizations and traditional rituals were banned almost completely.

Culture, however, can hardly be uprooted overnight, as we have learned from the experiences of former colonies and brutally governed areas worldwide. Certain significant aspects of Nuosu culture, such as the traditional Nuosu concepts of kinship, persisted even under the harsh circumstances of socialist reform. The continued importance of lineage and the way Nuosu adults insisted on teaching their children about their genealogies during the collective era contributed to the survival of a distinct Nuosu ethnicity. In addition to the Nuosu's persistence in teaching their children kinship, other traditions such as funeral rituals sometimes escaped the socialist government's critical gaze. A Nuosu scholar, Ma Erzi, tells how his father risked practicing a "feudalistic" custom—sacrificing a goat at his grandfather's funeral. Similar accounts clearly show that many local people resisted giving up Nuosu customs (Ma 2003).

Among the people who had gone through socialist reform, bimo generally remembered the Cultural Revolution as particularly painful. Because their priesthood status was inherited, any interruption in one generation could cause this heritage to be lost. Only in the isolated high mountains or under special circumstances, such as with the tacit support of village cadres who were themselves Nuosu, did traditional practices continue. One sixty-year-old bimo of the Jjike lineage, famous in both Zhaojue and Limu, admitted that he had dealt with outbreaks of infectious diseases like measles and diarrhea on four occasions between 1966 and 1972:

> I practiced during the Cultural Revolution. The government did not know about that. Once, a team head asked me to perform rituals to cope with an outbreak of cholera. I chanted the ritual texts in the ceremony, and every villager held a wooden knife to expel the ghosts of disease.

A seventy-four-year-old Jjike bimo who lived in the high hills around the Limu basin told me how bimo up in the mountains continued their practices during hard times:

> My father and I kept practicing intermittently because people wanted us to do it for them. You know, as bimo, we had to perform rituals whenever people called on us. But it was difficult at that time. Mao Zedong ordered us not to believe in spirits and ghosts. We tried to perform the rituals at night secretly and hid the

texts in the woods during the day. But there were a few years when we didn't dare to do anything at all.

An old sunyi told me that she did not play the drum, as ritually required, when she performed services secretly at night during those years: "There was no *dong-dong-dong.*"

These ritual specialists took great risks in continuing their traditional practices. The more respect or fame an indigenous authority commanded, the worse he or she suffered during the numerous political campaigns. The seventy-four-year-old Jjike bimo told me about one of his experiences: "They said I was one of the *qi da pianzi* [seven major deceivers]." He could still accurately pronounce the accusation in Mandarin Chinese though he barely spoke the language. He remembered this Mandarin charge because the "progressive" Nuosu cadres who carried out the political campaigns viewed speaking Chinese as a means of becoming genuine members of the new China.

> [Nuosu] peasants didn't scold me. Only cadres hit me. Peasants still wanted me to perform rituals after the political campaigns. But I dared not do it. . . . Later on, after the Cultural Revolution had ended, a village cadre said to me, "We can practice superstition now [*xianzai keyi gan mixin le*]!" Opening up [*kaifang*] . . . do it [*ganle*]!

A Great Leap to Capitalist Modernity in 1978

With the death of Chairman Mao in 1976, which brought an abrupt end to the ten-year purge of the Cultural Revolution, the nearly three-decade-old dream of socialist modernity seemed to have died. Deng Xiaoping emerged as the post-Mao leader, and his epochal Reform and Opening policies and refocus on modernization in 1978 were to bring the economy "very quickly to where it would have been had the Maoist experiments not intervened" (Skinner 1985, 412). Ever since, China has embraced capitalism with socialist undertones; it has made an incremental shift from a planned economy to a market economy under the guiding hand of the Communist Party. With the government's vertical bureaucracy still intact, the state could implement the new policies using the top-down approach it had depended on during the collective era; in other words, local initiatives had to reflect the policies and interests of higher-level agencies and institutions.

Even today, the Chinese Communist Party still exerts extensive domestic control, a fact that contrasts sharply with the situation of other postsocialist states. In view of this, we can identify two unique characteristics of China's transformation from socialism to capitalism. First, China's entrance into the market economy has not been accompanied by the turbulent takeover of party power in domestic politics.[14] Verdery (1996) describes the postsocialist market transition in former Soviet Union states as a process in which the state's visible guiding hand is replaced by the invisible hand of the market. In today's China, these two hands *simultaneously* govern the lives of the people, especially those who live in remote rural areas.

Second, the Chinese state's public discourse retains much of the official rhetoric inherited from the collective era—still speaking, for example, of equality, selflessness, and service to the people. However, from the outset of market reform the state has gradually retreated from its commitment to egalitarianism in practice. To address uneven development in the reform era, the central government has announced many policies concerned with poverty alleviation. But in practice most of these assistance programs quickly fade, both in funding and spirit, as they flow down the chain of command from the national government to the local level. The bureaucratic hierarchy filters out most of their promised benefits and turns these policies into empty rhetoric.

Rural Development Bypassed

Liangshan has been marginal to the Chinese state's modernization projects, regardless of the state's ideological inclinations. The socialist development that took place between the 1950s and 1970s brought limited progress to most Nuosu areas. In comparison to other minority regions and to China as a whole, Liangshan Prefecture ranked at the very bottom of the economic development scale at the end of the 1970s (Heberer 2001). Similarly, in the reform era, China's capitalist development scheme has also largely bypassed Nuosuland.

Market reform shifted the official emphasis from rural areas to urban ones when the government began prioritizing economic development over ideological commitment. In 1978, when the government moved the prefecture capital, with its many financial resources and government offices, to Han-dominant Xichang City, Zhaojue County and Limu Township suffered dramatically. Subsequently, many sent-down youths—mostly skilled and well-educated Han people coming to the Nuosu region in response to Mao's call for "minority work"—left rural Liangshan. Zhaojue County alone lost 995 sent-down workers between 1979 and 1992; of those, 235 were college graduates and 760 were high school or vocational school graduates (Heberer 2001).[15] The success in rural public health had previously relied in considerable part on these youths as medical trainers, barefoot doctors, school teachers, and office workers. Rural public health faced serious challenges when the flow of sent-down workers reversed in the early 1980s.

The transition from socialism to capitalism quickly translated into social disparities. The gap in living standards between the core regions and the peripheries of development has rapidly widened. In poor peripheral regions, chronic problems have included waves of infectious diseases and new epidemics, low-quality school facilities, and understaffed public services (Bloom and Gu 1997; Feng et al. 1995). These problems have only been aggravated since the 1990s as economic development elsewhere accelerated.

Levels of education demonstrate the extent of underdevelopment and marginalization of the Nuosu periphery. According to the 2000 population census, in Zhaojue County as a whole, 37 percent of the population above the age of six had had no schooling at all. The illiteracy rate among residents fifteen years of age or older corresponded to nearly 40 percent of the cohort (Sichuan sheng 2002).[16] Limu, with a total population of 8,726 people in 2005, is not the poorest township in Zhaojue County, owing to the relatively moderate climate of the Limu basin and its relative convenience for transportation; yet Limu's low schooling rate contributes to the county's unimpressive literacy rate. In Luja Village, for example, according to the village steering committee in 2005, only 39 people out of approximately 1,800 had officially completed schooling above the primary school level.

Even with the market reforms of the 1980s and 1990s and China's ambitious Great Western Regional Development Program, launched in 2000, 130,000 people in Zhaojue County lived under the state-designated poverty line of 1,000 yuan (or about $125 per year) in 2004.[17] In the same year, 43,168 people (or almost 21 percent) out of a population of 207,712 lived below the local poverty line of 625 yuan ($78) per capita per year (Liangshan 2005) (see Figure 2).

A baseline survey of households carried out in Limu in 2005 not only reveals the severity of local poverty but also spotlights the bureaucratic way of dealing with this problem. This household survey, conducted by the Limu Township government, included inventories of cash income, crops, livestock, and domestic fowl; and it concluded that 260 (or 11.7 percent) of the total of 2,210 households in Limu fell under the local poverty line of 625 yuan in 2005. Information from village cadres, however, suggested that the actual number of poor households in Limu was likely to be double or triple the number re-

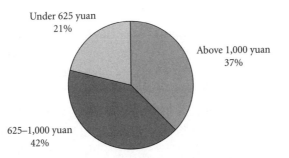

Figure 2. Percentage of population above the poverty line of 1,000 yuan, under the poverty line of 1,000 yuan, and under the poverty line of 625 yuan in Zhaojue County in 2005. Data from Liangshan (2005) and personal interviews at the Antipoverty Office in Zhaojue County.

ported in the township's statistics. When this survey was first conducted in June 2005, the results showed over 900 households living under the poverty line. The township government considered this startling figure to be unacceptable and asked village cadres to reduce the number. I witnessed the meetings in which village cadres gathered to discuss which households could be taken off the poverty list. For example, one village had about 348 households, 81 of which were assessed by village cadres as living below the poverty line. In the end, only 33 of these 81 poor households made it onto the final list, and all of these families had net per capita incomes of less than 300 yuan ($37.50 in 2005) (see Figure 3).

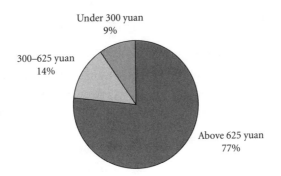

Figure 3. Estimated percentage of household income by category in Luja Village, June 2005. Original data obtained from the Luja Village Steering Committee.

Agricultural Labor Surplus

Collectivism ended in Limu in April 1981 with the local government's implementation of the farmland-redistribution-to-household policy (*baochan daohu*), in which the government allocated to each adult (over the age of eighteen and of either sex) 0.8 mu of paddy fields and 1.0 mu of nonirrigated farmland.[18] Each household also received 1.0 mu of woodland, because people need wood for construction and for fuel.[19] Peasants greeted this policy with enthusiasm and worked harder than before to increase agricultural production to enrich their own lives. No longer did they have to hand everything over to the communes.

The benefits of farmland redistribution did not last long in Limu because of continuous population growth caused by both natural increase and immigration. For example, in 1981 Luja Village had 340 households that shared all the allocated farmland. By May of 2005 the number of households had grown to 406. When young men marry, they must establish their own households while continuing to work on the limited farmland they share with parents and brothers.

The birth-control policy instituted in 1979 adopted various criteria that reflect not only rural-versus-urban discrepancies but also those between ethnic minorities and the Han majority. In Han-dominant rural areas, some provincial governments permit a second child if the first child is a girl, or the husband marries uxorilocally, or a family has produced only one son for two generations in a row (Greenhalgh 1986; Honig and Hershatter 1988). In minority-dominant areas, the state allows minorities to have more children than Han people (Whyte and Gu 1987). Such leniency is due mainly to the state's wish to avoid conflict between Chinese authorities and minority groups. The combination of rural residency and minority status allows each Nuosu woman to have up to three children in Limu and other rural areas in Liangshan.[20] In spite of the birth quota, many Nuosu families have more than three children, especially in out-of-the-way localities.[21]

In addition to natural population growth, the Limu basin's long-established reputation as the "rice barn" of Liangshan has prompted many immigrants from the surrounding high hills to relocate there, often with the assistance of their resident kin. Although impoverished, Limu still outshines other Nuosu locales in the mountains, where severe climate and inferior infrastructure make living difficult. The relatively fertile land and agreeable weather make this basin area arable for several staple crops, including rice, buckwheat, corn, and potatoes. Rice, a coveted crop in the eyes of Nuosu farmers, is grown only in the lowlands or basins of Liangshan. Limu residents make rice cakes instead of buckwheat cakes during funerals to better treat their relatives or friends who travel from the high mountains to attend these events. Traditionally, Nuosu people did not like to live at low elevations, where hot summer weather makes it difficult to herd sheep and goats, which supply important sustenance in Nuosu daily life and are needed for ritual practices. Therefore, Limu's relatively fertile basin environment, with its appropriately cool temperature, attracts people who reside in the high mountains but wish to improve their living conditions. To live in Limu, in the eyes of high-mountain dwellers, signifies a modern way of life, although the term "modern" is defined relatively. In comparison with most Han areas, Limu remains an impoverished locality.

Land has become scarcer in Limu owing to the steady growth of the total population and the unchanged supply of farmland. The total agricultural production remains stagnant, while people's living costs increase. Faced with this, the local government is eager to improve the local economy through whatever means available.

The Local Mode of Economic Development

Postreform China's halfhearted political enthusiasm for socialist utopia has given way en masse to profit making. Since the 1980s, the state has encouraged small start-up enterprises at the township and village levels to increase local revenues (Huang 1998). Two types of entrepreneurship developed in Limu characterize local people's embrace of capitalist modernity. The first is the periodic market, which has facilitated the circulation of goods and services and heightened the importance of money in sustaining an emerging commodity-based livelihood. The other is the cement factory, which both exemplifies the commodification of cheap local labor and resources and constitutes an unscrupulous economic development project that overlooks environmental concerns and equal access to employment. I will now consider these two cases of entrepreneurship to highlight the local conditions resulting from market reform.

Establishment of the Periodic Market

The Nuosu peasants' initiation into a capitalist way of life has been, ironically, accomplished through an anachronistic Han peasant commercial institution, the periodic market. G. William Skinner, who spearheaded the study of periodic markets in rural China in the late 1940s, saw peasant marketing as an evolutionary departure from subsistence-oriented societies, signaling "the onset of the transformation of a traditional agrarian society into a modern industrial society" (Skinner 1964–65, 3). The Nuosu periodic market, however, distinguishes itself from the Han peasant market in several significant ways. Unlike Han Chinese, who have been used to market mechanisms for a long time (Gates 1996), the Nuosu, especially in the core area of Liangshan, have experienced market forces in their own society only recently. Moreover, the Limu periodic market was created not by the Nuosu themselves but by the state commerce offices as a move to enhance rural trade. Once again, the Nuosu were forced to learn to live with a new institution. In subsequent years, the periodic market has broadened the Nuosu's economic involvements and worldview. More strikingly, the changing economic factors have affected local morality, rationality, and sense of identity (Liu 2007).

The Limu periodic market was first established in the mid-1980s, when the Zhaojue County government instituted *ziyou shichang* (free markets) to facilitate rural trade after farmland redistribution. The market meets, according to the Gregorian calendar, on the ninth day of a ten-day cycle, in an open area about the size of a basketball court. In the month of February, when it is not a leap year and there is no twenty-ninth day, local people automatically change the market day to the first of March. Though the scale of the periodic market in Limu is modest, the marketplace has become a magnet in the local landscape, and market days have become something akin to weekends in most modern societies. Hundreds of local people converge in Limu's market every ten days. The market enables people from neighboring communities to meet their needs and provides them an opportunity to trade their domestic products for money. Other periodic markets in neighboring Nuosu areas are on different schedules, held one day between the first to the tenth of every cycle, so the markets do not compete for customers.

In Limu, as elsewhere in the region, a market day follows a predictable pattern. Beginning at about nine o'clock in the morning, itinerant merchants arrive at the trading grounds, where they arrange their goods for display. Around one and a half hours later, once peasants from the surrounding hills have arrived, the market buzzes with activity. Men and women, children and adults, arrive on foot and on horseback and hitch their animals along nearby thoroughfares. The market ends at three o'clock, giving people enough time to walk back to their homes in the high hills before dusk.

It was through the periodic market that the majority of the Nuosu in core areas were first introduced to money. As I noted previously, before 1956 only a small number of the Nuosu people, mostly nuo and nzymo, exchanged opium with Han merchants for silver dollars and certain goods at the old markets located in the ethnic borderlands of Liangshan. Between 1956 and 1981, state-run collective stores (*yingye bu*) instituted the use of money, but the practice remained very limited in scale. Most consumable goods were allocated or acquired according to a collective workpoint system. Only in the reform era did the official currency (yuan) begin to be widely circulated.

The Limu market is divided into several broad sections for various trade activities, with some small sellers carrying their goods around the marketplace to find customers. Goods sold vary from agricultural produce, to hand-made products, to mass-produced commodities imported from large cities or even foreign countries. On sale are new and used clothes, shoes, videotapes, pirated compact discs, household goods, seeds, pesticides, and popsicles. The market also draws barbers, cobblers, and tinkers. Entertainment is provided in the form of video-viewing stalls.

The current popularity of the periodic market was not achieved overnight. It took more than a decade, beginning roughly in the mid-1990s, for local Nuosu people to become fully accustomed to the market's rhythms, its amenities, and the calculation of profit margins in trade. Now the market has tremendous influence over at least three major aspects of the lives of local Nuosu. First, it has introduced new mediums of exchange (i.e., the market-place for trade and the use of money), as well as the circulation of goods and services above and beyond traditional subsistence-oriented ways of life. This has further encouraged new economic rationalities (e.g., the maximization of personal gain and profit margins in terms of cash), with interesting effects on the local moral economy. For instance, the presence of the market has led to the demise of the traditional taboo against intra-Nuosu trade, particularly with regard to foodstuffs. In premodern times, Nuosu home-grown produce was used exclusively either for domestic consumption or for cementing kinship and community ties. The market, however, has brought the moral economy based on reciprocal kinship principles into a complementary relationship with impersonal trade rationality. Recent research on Nuosu entrepreneurs in Liangshan cities also indicates the destabilization of the traditional moral economy and a weakening of kinship-based identities under the current market drive (Heberer 2005).

Second, the periodic market has shaped or reshaped the identity of the local people. The presence of the periodic market has made the Limu basin more like a quasi-urban town in the mountains. One meets friends, greets strangers, shops at a variety of stalls, and explores novelties on market days. As a variety of people from different localities gather in the marketplace, identities take shape along new vectors. Residents of the Limu basin view themselves as "more modern" than people from the surrounding high hills. This identity shift has everything to do with living near the marketplace, more actively participating in trade, and enjoying better material living standards. Basin residents now look at the mountain people as "dirty" and "backward"—an ironic twist, since the Han Chinese used these same terms to describe the Nuosu of Liangshan as a whole. One often sees basin residents gather to gossip with amused expressions about mountain dwellers on their way to the market, although many of these visitors may actually be their yet unrecognized kinsmen.

Third, the periodic market, despite its traditional modus operandi, has become indispensable to how Nuosu peasants fashion a modern way of life. Marketization and commodification have expanded the desires of local people, especially the young. Young people's pursuit of companionship, pleasure, and novelties through the market has become part and parcel of Limu's modernization. The market provides Limu people a glimpse of what lies beyond their village, beyond the Nuosu world, even beyond China, owing to the diverse walks of life and commodities gathered in the local marketplace (Liu 2007).

Privileged Local Enterprises

Just as local people began to learn about the capitalist way of life by familiarizing themselves with the periodic market, they also began to learn about capitalism's conversion of human labor to a commodity through the operation of local enterprises in Limu. The basin is now home to a power plant, a cement factory, and four hot-spring restaurants that can be counted as enterprises. These provide only limited work opportunities and income to the local people, yet they have a considerable effect on Limu. All these enterprises involve government officials from the village to the county level who have invested in them.

The hydroelectric power plant was constructed in Limu just recently. But instead of providing Limu residents with much-appreciated service, the plant has drawn the ire of locals because it sporadically discharges huge volumes of water into the river. This prevents peasants from wading across the river to their farmland and has occasionally drowned careless people and livestock. Because the local population lacks the education and skills necessary to operate the plant, nearly all its employees hail from outside Limu and even beyond Liangshan. Even worse, the locally produced power has not reduced the cost of electricity or enhanced the reliability of the power supply in Limu. Since the plant has gone into operation, most Limu residents have continued to rely on firewood for cooking or warmth. Because of their low income levels, most local people who can afford to install power meters use only one small light bulb (40 watts) to light an approximately 6 × 4 meter single-room house.

Recently the local government has cautioned that in a few years villagers will no longer be allowed to use forest timber for house construction or firewood for cooking or keeping warm. The government formulated this prohibition as part of an environmental protection plan, and similar concerns have recently been incorporated into China's national economic development projects. However, many peasants continue to use firewood because they simply cannot afford to buy electric cookers. And while the state gradually imposes restrictions on the use of forest wood for house construction and fuel, officials and powerful businesspeople nevertheless legally tap local natural resources in the name of economic development. Local enterprises seem to be exempt from environmental protection regulation. The cement factory in Limu constitutes a glaring example.

The cement factory has left ugly scars in Limu's landscape. The factory acquires lime by blasting limestone from a mountain that rims the Limu basin and then processes the lime into cement, which is bagged daily to be transported to other localities. The cement factory had originally been constructed by the prefectural government in a different locality in 1966. After the launch of market reform, the prefecture transferred the factory to the Zhaojue County government, which later sold it to private Han entrepreneurs. The factory began operations at its current site in 1997. Since then, two stripped and scarred hills, devoured by the previous and the current production operations, have become the predominant visual irritant in Limu.

The cement factory is said to be the most profitable industry in Zhaojue County. In 1996 it netted the county government over 2.2 million yuan in profits (Shi et al. 1999, 71). The township officials told me in 2005 that its annual profits had reached nearly 3 million yuan in recent years. Muha Village, where the factory is located, is said to be the only entity in Limu that gains some benefits from this enterprise.

An Enriched Village in Trouble

There are always two sides to every coin. Muha Village has suffered enormously from both the heavy airborne dust and the blasting that occur in the course of cement production. On the factory grounds, one can neither see the sky clearly nor breathe easily. Village laborers commonly have respiratory problems although they are given two masks per month; few of them, however, complain about it. During my one-hour stay in the tiny, shabby workers' lounge, my notebook accumulated a thick layer of dust on its pages. The wet rice fields adjacent to the factory were also covered with dust, and the farmers complained about the low output of these fields. The explosions in the mountain, which occur two to three times daily, cause thunderous noise and quakelike effects that I felt in my residence two or three kilometers away. Nearby residents, of course, suffer even more.

Even given its role in creating all these potential and real hazards to people's health and the environment, the factory is still the main source of income for Muha Village. The village steering committee and the cement factory signed an agreement that gives village cadres the authority to recruit workers. In 2005, sixty-two male villagers, mostly from Muha Village, were employed in the cement factory. Many of them belonged to the same lineage as Lewu Munyo, the party secretary of the village. Limited in number, the factory's paid positions were highly sought after. Villagers had to bribe village cadres to be recruited as workers. Once a villager was employed, one of his sons would be entitled to succeed him in the future. The workers in the factory were divided into two shifts, and each worker earned approximately 450 to 600 yuan each month; their income was contingent on the output of cement each day.

When I visited the workers' lounge, a few laborers were having a late lunch. Their bodies were covered, from head to toe, with ashen dust. Some were sitting or sleeping on the ground, with their lunch of rice stored in heavily smudged kettles they brought from home. I could calculate the number of laborers on duty that day by counting the chalky bags hanging on the wall. These bags contained clean clothes, which the workers put on after finishing work. They told me that they had to pay about 5 percent of their monthly salary to the village steering committee, 2 percent to the two foremen, and 6 percent to the county tax office. Although nearly all workers complained about the payments they made to the steering committee and the tax office, they treasured their jobs because they received a steady income greater than what they could earn in seasonal agricultural production.

Other Muha villagers also worked for this factory, using their privately owned tractors to deliver cement. The village committee estimated that in 2005 a total of 140 Muha villagers out of approximately 300 households were employed there; most of these workers were men.

Muha villagers had other work opportunities as well, such as working at its four hot-spring restaurants. The area's natural hot spring used to benefit all Limu residents, but now most local people can no longer enjoy it for free because the water is channeled to these restaurants. The hot-spring restaurants were established, one by one, in the late 1990s, in cooperation with various government offices or individual officials. In addition to dining services, some restaurants also provide hot-spring bathhouses, karaoke, and—clandestinely—sex services. The waitresses and workers were hired mainly from Muha Village and occasionally from other villages in Limu or even beyond. These restaurants employed a small number of Han sex workers, who were virtually invisible during the day. Few local people could afford the pricy food at the luxurious restaurants and had to settle for occasional use of the bathhouse. Most of the restaurants' customers were cadres and officials from Limu, from the county seat of Zhaojue County, or from other cities including Xichang.

The local peasants gave many reasons for their aversion to these restaurants. One concerned the peasants' belief that work in these restaurants consisted chiefly of sex-related jobs for women. "We Nuosu don't serve people that way," my informant Lati declared. Another was the equally strong belief that cadres and officials were embezzling money from their workplace so that they could afford the entertainment there. Every day at about sunset, especially from Friday through Sunday, the usually empty lots in front of the restaurants were packed with cars and vans that belonged to various government offices. "They are all state cadres eating state money. How can they afford an expense of over 1,000 yuan per night at these restaurants when their monthly salary is just about that amount?" one villager sneered. Whenever I asked about the restaurants' customers, local people generally responded with similar remarks. Several people who lived close to one restaurant told me that they had witnessed a farce involving several county officials. As the men loitered in the restaurant around midnight, they were confronted by one official's enraged wife, who made a real scene both inside the restaurant and in the woods nearby.

Anthropologists conducting fieldwork in many societies, but especially postsocialist ones, often encounter conversations about official corruption. People's talk about such endemic corruption constitutes one perspective of local society on both the state's imagined governance and its agents (Haller and Shore 2005). In Limu nearly all peasants have heard of or witnessed corruption, so few of them trust officials to have a fair policy, much less to enforce one. A retired health worker commenting on the local government's STD (sexually transmitted diseases) prevention project sarcastically noted, "Those cadres in government offices are the real 'high-risk' group."

In spite of these controversies, Muha Village is generally better off than other villages in the Limu basin because of its local enterprises. Yet Muha villagers have to pay dearly for those benefits. In the market reform era, as money and material consumption have become imperatives in daily life, the economic development of Muha Village has been accompanied by a transformation of values and desires that has motivated many young people to seek levels of personal gratification, mostly in a material sense, that they had never enjoyed before. Muha's young men have taken the lead, followed by other young men in the Limu basin, to migrate to cities once they became familiar with market mechanisms and the use of money. Young Nuosu men's adventures in the larger capitalist markets of the cities have, since the 1980s, ushered them into heroin problems.

2 Manhood, Migration, and Heroin

There is nothing to do here, no money or fun. We want to see a big city and make money there. It's fun in the city if you have money. I come home very often but stay only for a few days, and then I take off to the city again. My friends are all out there. I am quite good at stealing and have been caught only once.

ONE SPRING DAY in Limu in 2005, as a thirty-five-year-old Nuosu man related to me his experiences as a migrant making a living in the city, I was struck by his vocal inflections and facial expressions, which conveyed an almost youthful excitement. Later on I would observe similar expressions in other Nuosu men, whose ages ranged from the mid-teens to the late thirties. In each case, the speaker was clearly re-experiencing past emotions as he explained why he had taken off to the city and what his livelihood had been while he was away from home. Migration to cities often coincided with drug use, drug dealing, theft, burglary, imprisonment, and, occasionally, illness or untimely death. I eventually came to realize that, as a unique stage in the life-course transition, such experiences constituted the shared practice and memory of most young men in Limu. This oblique path into manhood among Limu's Nuosu youth can be regarded as a local repercussion of the changing reality of the Chinese nation-state—in effect the life-course change of the entire society, when even remote regions yield to forces of the globalizing market economy. Metaphorically speaking, the Nuosu youths' venturing out for fun, drug use, or opportunities has become a new "rite of passage."

The concept of a new rite of passage among Limu's young men registers their experimental forays into manhood and autonomy in the context of market reform. It is through this lens that I see both the positive and negative consequences of their life-course transition. On the one hand, their marginal socioeconomic status makes them easy victims of China's globalizing market. Their lives in the reform era have been full of seemingly insurmountable difficulties: unemployment, poverty, bewilderment, danger, and suffering. On the other hand, they have embraced their newly gained freedom of choice and experimented with both the Nuosu concept of masculine identity and novel ways of life. Despite the disadvantages that Limu youth face, their yearning for—and initial steps toward—capitalist modernity are simultaneously reckless and self-fulfilling.

The New Rite of Passage to Manhood

The seminal concept of rites of passage can help us unpack the significance of the youthful transition that Limu witnessed in the 1990s. Arnold van Gennep (1960) first came up with this concept to understand the interlocking relationships between society and its individual members' life stages. He shows that all rites of passage are marked by three distinct phases: separation, transition, and incorporation. For example, when making the transition from childhood to adulthood, young people are first removed from their normal structural positions and, consequently, separated from the conventional values, norms, sentiments, and practices of daily living associated with those positions. This concept was further elaborated by Victor Turner (1967, 1969) to analyze the processual changes of the individual's status—a condition that he calls "liminality." It is during the liminal state that people are both forced and encouraged to reflexively examine themselves and their own society and culture. In other words, liminality is "a stage of reflection" (Turner 1967, 105). Turner (1969) further uses the concept of "communitas" to describe the rise of a new esprit de corps among people who, having shared the trials of liminality, develop a newly invigorated homogeneity and comradeship when they successfully transfer from their previous position to the new one.

Anthropologists usually employ these concepts to describe formal or institutionalized transitional rituals in traditional, preindustrial societies; however, Turner (1969) argued that, because the formation of communitas and its changing relations to a society's power structure are universal, rites of passage can be found in all types of societies. Researchers since then have applied these concepts, directly or indirectly, to the examination of life-course transitions in contemporary capitalist societies (e.g., Herzfeld 1985; Hopper 2003; Modell 1989).

These concepts provide real utility for the analysis of why Nuosu youths who were born or grew up in the market reform era have navigated through their life-course transition with such a high degree of uniformity. This new rite of passage has never been consciously acknowledged by the Nuosu; it represents a kind of spontaneous and individual adaptability among these young men. Their attraction to the allure of the city, their readiness for risk taking, their development of a work ethic and the ability to cope with loneliness, and finally their willingness to terminate this transitory period—all pertain to testing their masculine identity. This initiation into manhood manifests both their maturing to adulthood and their successful performance of manliness.

The Youthful Transition

For this analysis, I define Nuosu "youth" as men between their late teens and thirties, a period when their adulthood and manhood are settled. This broad definition of youthfulness is based on the argument that the category "youth" is a sociocultural construction and individualized psychological life phase rather than a universal, fixed biological life stage (Amit-Talai and Wulff 1995; Sharp 2002; Wallace and Cross 1990). The term "youth," rather than "adolescence," best conveys the flexible nature of this identity, which is framed by individual experiences and talents (Sharp 2002, 15).

Strictly speaking, Nuosu society does not specify a fixed age for the commencement or termination of the liminal transition for males. In Nuosu cultures, the transition from childhood to adulthood can occur anytime from thirteen to thirty years of age. In general, when boys reach the ages of thirteen, fifteen, or seventeen[1] and are ready to hone their individual maturity and social skills, society encourages them to take part in lineage meetings, inasmuch as the boys are already aware of public affairs. After thirty, the young adults are considered "seniors" (Ma 2006, 373–74).

Anthropological research points out that, in general, boys' initiation rituals are more elaborate than those of girls (Herdt and Leavitt 1998). The Nuosu practices, however, are contradictory to this norm. There are no institutionalized initiation rituals, such as puberty rites, for Nuosu men. In contrast, Nuosu women's life transitions are clearly marked. Tradition dictates that when a girl reaches thirteen, fifteen, or seventeen, she will change her skirt from a child's style to that of an adult during an initiation ritual. She also goes through a mock marriage ritual to signal her entrance into adulthood. She may either marry a designated husband, preferably her cross-cousin, or symbolically marry a tree, a hearth, or something else that signifies her fertility-ready status or household responsibilities. After these rituals, she becomes an "outsider" to her natal family and no longer participates in domestic rituals as a family member.

Whether a person is formally initiated into adulthood or not, local Nuosu believe that he or she must have a child to reach full social maturity. Childless couples, regardless of their age or whether they have established a financially independent household, will not be seen as a genuine family or a complete social unit.[2] In contrast, a person—even if quite young—will acquire the status of respected adult once he or she has a child. This changed status is embodied in a woman's attire: she wears a different style of hat once she becomes a mother. For men, however, there is no such status-shifting marker, although having children is a widely recognized prerequisite for manhood.[3]

According to Nuosu cultural perceptions of manhood, a youth who is ready to become an adult and to establish a stable family must have acquired the following personal qualifications: he must participate in public affairs; he must have mastered the work capacities and skills to become financially independent; he must be recognized by his natal family and lineages as having achieved the status of a responsible member; and finally, he must possess a stable state of mind. Men who beget children or reach their thirties often become disenchanted with drifting in the cities or using drugs and decide to settle down. Substance use in this context is part of the experimentation that many have passed through at this stage, as Gutmann (1996) observed in regard to heavy drinking among men in Mexico. Nuosu youths who have experienced the outside world, whether happily or miserably, are likely to be more willing to become responsible husbands, fathers, and breadwinners. Before going through this process, however, they find that the omnipresent market forces trigger their desire to be modern and lure them away from their mountain community in search of new life experiences.

A New Way of Life, a New Masculine Identity

The Nuosu male's desire for adventure also registers in the ideal practices of modern masculinity, which conflate erstwhile social dramas of male mobility and new meanings of manliness. In the old days, the best way to demonstrate one's masculinity was to engage in wars with other ethnic groups or feuds with other lineages. Hunting and martial skills played an important role in boys' and men's daily lives (Ma 2006). A man who was able to demonstrate his fighting prowess and physical stamina across Liangshan or even beyond Nuosuland through defending the reputation of his lineage and kin and capturing slaves or acquiring goods from Han areas by whatever means would achieve high social status and fame (Y. Liu 2001). As with the Han Chinese, mobility is essential to masculinity and bravery (Kohrman 2005). In the postreform 1990s, the most courageous youths were allegedly those who dared to explore the world beyond their confined hometowns. Market-style criteria for measuring success in a capitalist economy have become acceptable standards by which to evaluate the capability and masculinity of Limu youth. Ironically, the youths replay the old dramas with a new outlook that inspires them to become idealized men by undertaking audacious adventures.

Some Nuosu migrants who have made money by whatever means, legal or illegal, have bought cellular phones for themselves and their family members and have become role models for younger people who have yet to venture out. Young men have brought novelties from the cities back to Limu and showed off fashionable styles and a new affluence that other peasants have seen only on television programs and karaoke-VCD shows. This material success may help explain why other people in Limu do not disdain those who have been released from prison and why young boys follow them with adoring gazes. Even those who remain behind share a fascination with the outside world.

These adventurous youths, who typically behave as though they are more modern, more sophisticated, and better informed than those who stay home, tend to hang out with other recent returnees from cities. Usually people who have spent time in criminal-detention facilities or drug-rehabilitation centers can speak better Han Chinese than their fellow peasants. During incarceration, they may even have learned new skills, such as guitar playing, with which they can entertain their families and neighbors once they return home. Indeed, where else can young people meet so many people from different parts of China and hear stories foreign to the Nuosu peasants? The peculiar moral neutrality in this peripheral community toward misdeeds done in the city is embedded in the complexity of traditional Nuosu masculinity mixed with the currently pervasive yearning for capitalist modernity, a complexity that has driven Limu youth to migrate cohort by cohort.

Migrant youths, after returning home, recast their ways of living in terms of diet, physical hygiene, housing styles, concepts of fashion, commitment to traditional cultures and practices, and ideas of social relationships. Some of these changes are revealed in their newly acquired appreciation of Han foodways. As one twenty-eight-year-old young man commented in 2006, "Those of us who have been out for a while will not be satisfied with Nuosu food any more: it is not hygienic, and it is too dull. It's too difficult to stay home and eat such food day after day." Another young man declared, "Han people have smarter brains than ours because they know how to eat diverse and nourishing food." Likewise, since the 1980s, young men have stopped wearing the traditional forehead braids and earrings that used to signify Nuosu manhood. Most young men have begun wearing dark, Western-style sport coats, shirts, and polo-style T-shirts that have become the most popular male clothing sold in the periodic market. Young men now consider Nuosu clothes embarrassing to wear and alienating in urban life. From time to time, in wintry months, one might even encounter returning youths wearing exotic hats or costumes they acquired in Xinjiang, Tibet, the northeastern regions, or cities elsewhere in China. These returnees stand out as they stroll among the Nuosu peasants, who generally dress in the uniformlike dark *vala* (cloak). Exotica in Nuosuland as elsewhere signal the expanded world of the globalizing markets.

In the following section, I examine the social process of Nuosu youth migration and its consequences in Limu. It is necessary, however, to bear in mind that, given the variation and diversity seen in manly behaviors in a society, *men as men* have never been homogenous (Connell 1995; Cornwall and Lindisfarne 1994; Gutmann 1996). There are doubtless exceptions to my general portrayal—for instance, a few young men never migrated at all. But even if they eventually spent the entire course of their lives in the traditionally defined Nuosu way within the confines of Nuosuland, they nevertheless dreamed about the outside world, like the others, and they often expressed their envy of men who acted on their thirst for adventure.

Adventurous Youths on the Move

Beginning in the 1980s, young men from Limu joined China's "floating population" in search of fun and adventure. At that time, public transportation connecting Limu to the outside world was limited.[4] Puxiong, in the neighboring county, has been the key staging point for most Limu people and other Nuosu who, using the train, leave for cities beyond Liangshan. The main road connecting Limu and Puxiong was not well constructed; even now it takes three to four hours traveling by bus between these two points on a winding, cement-paved road that stretches only 140 kilometers. Yet despite the difficulties of transportation, Limu youths have journeyed to big towns and cities such as Xichang, Chengdu, and Kunming and even as far away as Beijing and Urumqi in Xinjiang. They have traveled mainly by way of the major railways from Liangshan, heading southward, eastward, northeastward, and northwestward. Han people have jokingly dubbed the low-fare trains packed with Nuosu youths "barbarian trains."

Early Exploratory Journeys

The movement to the cities began in the face of persistent, crushing poverty in Limu as China's market reform took off. "The first time when I went out [in

1983], the grain in our field was not enough to feed us," said Hielie Yyrre, who was thirty-eight years old in 2005 and one of the first young men to venture out to Chengdu. Limu's allocations of scarce farmland to individual households in 1981 had been insufficient to feed the local population that continued to grow. Moreover, the agricultural season in Limu lasts only from mid-March through October, with work concentrated mostly in April, May, June, and October and with no more than ten days of intensive work in each of these months. A young woman explained to me why her male peers migrated: "There's nothing to do here beyond agricultural seasonal labor." Short intervals of agricultural labor on the limited amount of arable land often left young men idle, and idleness fueled their desire to explore the outside world. In addition, China's gradual relaxation of restrictions on mobility since the 1980s had made it possible for Nuosu youths to pursue their footloose fantasies.

In the 1980s most floating youths had only vague ideas of what to do in the city. Hielie Yyrre's first migration experience exemplifies the shared memories of his cohort. Yyrre recalled his first journey to a city north of Liangshan in 1983. He and a kinsman walked an entire day through a shortcut on the mountain trails from Limu to the railway station at Puxiong. At Puxiong they waited for freight trains coming from Dukou City (renamed Panzhihua City in 1987), a dusty, polluted town famous for metal products and heavy industry that lies on the border between Liangshan Prefecture and Yunnan Province. When they saw the freight train coming, there were already many young Nuosu men sitting on top, so they jumped aboard and were headed to Chengdu.

"Why did you go out then?" I asked Yyrre. "No idea," he replied. "Seeking a job?" I insisted. "No. No idea," he stammered a bit shyly. "I just know we wanted to see a very, very big city." "Then what did you see later?" I prodded him further. "Not much. We were frightened by the others when we got to the city at night. So we climbed back on the same train as it turned back from Chengdu to Dukou. We didn't see anything in the city because [everything] happened so quickly and it was at night."

On encountering strangers who questioned their reasons for going to the city, Yyrre and his kinsman were intimidated and immediately fled. Having returned to the station at Puxiong the next day, they lodged and ate in the home of a lineage member they had never met before.[5] They spent the entire third day walking the mountain trails back to Limu. Yyrre's and his kinsman's ignorance about the outside world did not diminish their desire to venture out again. He was clearly embarrassed at his failed first journey and tried to save face by recounting his later trips to Chengdu, where he succeeded in mediating conflicts between troubled Nuosu "brothers," an event that I will relate shortly.

Eating Up and Robbing the Han

Many youths in Yyrre's age cohort (i.e., in their thirties in 2005) had similarly rocky first journeys outside Limu. For those who eventually reached and spent time in the cities, the social and economic challenges quickly became acute. After wiping out their meager cash reserves, some migrants managed to pay for transportation back home; others resorted to theft and burglary to survive. These illicit means not only were strategies for getting by in the new environment but also reflected on the implicitly contested Nuosu-Han relationship in a way that bolstered the youth's masculine identity.

In rural Nuosu society, stealing is seen as extremely shameful conduct. The youths, however, justified this behavior in the cities because "it's a place of the Han people," a circumstance that exempted them from the moral strictures of their own society. An old Nuosu saying—"Looting and devouring the Han is as enjoyable as eating a sweet radish!"—justifies the youths' misconduct in the cities. Yyrre further viewed their urban misdeeds through the lens of entrenched ethnic conflict: "It is said that we [Nuosu] often fought with Han people in old times. In the past, before liberation, we only stole from you when we had enmity against you. During our grandfathers' generation and before, we felt great animosity against Han people. This hatred seems to have passed down to the current generations." Yyrre's comment is reminiscent of the Nuosu maxim that someone who successfully steals valuables such as slaves or livestock from rivals will become the protagonist of laudatory tales (Y. Liu 2001, 112). To distinguish their conduct from that of other "troubled" ethnic groups (in the eyes of the state), another Nuosu man added, "We only steal. We never kill people. Unlike the Tibetans, we don't carry knives."

The quick and easy money to be had in the cities excited many migrant youths, and thereafter theft and burglary became commonly accepted behavior among them. Peers followed peers in learning and practicing this "trade." They often worked in small groups of two or three and broke into people's houses in the middle of the night. The less audacious or unskilled would usually take the role of lookouts. The loot was divided according to the thieves' skills, audacity, and role in the job. This method of obtaining easy money soon became widely known in Limu; many youths who had yet to migrate were already fully aware of it. Sometimes the sheer appeal of these daring activities drew more youths to cities. They called their perilous pursuits *haoshua* (seeking fun). The oft-recited statement in Mandarin, "*You qian jiu haoshua, mei qian bu haoshua*" (you can have fun if you have money, but no money means no fun), has become a pet phrase used to justify both migration and theft among the opportunistic youths of Limu.

Nuosu Brotherhood in the City

Since the 1980s, the wandering Nuosu youths in China's rapidly expanding cities have developed a kind of fraternity based on their shared places of origin or kinship ties. Conflicts might erupt among regionally based Nuosu groups who occupied different "turfs" in a city. Yyrre explained the situation in Chengdu: "People from the county seat of Zhaojue County clustered in the North [Railway] Station of Chengdu City, while the South [Railway] Station was the turf of the Limu people. People from Butuo County usually went to Kunming."[6]

Most drifters stayed outdoors at night or in shabby and cramped flop-houses, which charged 10 to 20 yuan per person per night. Sometimes a few young migrants would rent a suburban house or an apartment from Han people. In general, the drifters' living conditions were wretched unless they could make regular money through theft. With such crowds of unstable youths living together, away from their elders' supervision and in an alien environment, fights often broke out over the division of stolen money and property or over women or simply out of bad temper. Before the mid-1990s, the police were not particularly concerned about violence among the wandering youth. Nuosu youth migrants might occasionally rely on traditional ways of mediation to solve their problems. Yyrre was one of the *ndeggu* (traditional mediators) recognized among the Nuosu youths in Chengdu. He told me about the first time he mediated a fight between two groups whose conflict centered on the South and North Railway Stations in Chengdu:

> My words carried weight among our peer brothers when I was eighteen years old. Many young people couldn't understand advanced Nuosu language, but I could because I'd liked to listen to ndeggu and *kenre* (traditional debaters) since childhood. I first mediated a conflict in 1985 between the two groups in Chengdu. Limu people from the South Railway Station went to the North Station and were attacked there. Then Zhaojue people from the North Railway Station came to the South Station and were attacked in return. So the fights

went back and forth. Everybody was entangled. I joined in too. We fought at the edge of the city, and the police did not care about it. We fought violently with clubs and stones for a day and a night. The fight escalated in severity. Some Limu brothers asked me to negotiate because the two parties knew about me. So . . . another man—of the Asu lineage from Zhaojue County—and I served as ndeggu. At the periphery of Chengdu, hundreds of Nuosu brothers gathered for the negotiations. We bought liquor and agreed to let bygones be bygones. Then the conflict was settled because many of us were relatives.

Disadvantages in the Urban Economy

Since the early 1990s, more and more young men have migrated to cities for various periods of time because transportation has become more convenient and reliable; furthermore, the Nuosu youth have become more experienced at moving about and surviving through their kinship and community networks. According to 1992 statistics compiled by the police department in Zhaojue County, 2,000 to 3,000 migrants had left the county for cities (Zhang 2002). The population of Zhaojue County was 201,292 in 1990 and 207,712 in 2000 (Sichuan sheng 1999, 2002). Few drifters or migrant workers have secured identification cards, nor can they change their *hukou* (household registration) from rural Liangshan to the city. The great majority of Nuosu migrants have moved to cities only temporarily or in a circular manner.

Limu basin has been one of the major sources of out-migration in Zhaojue County because of its relatively convenient location. A few Limu elders told me that over 70 percent of the local young men had headed off at least once by 2005 and that the outflow was ongoing. Limu had no systematic migration statistics that I could access for verification. My knowledge of the situation in the community developed as I analyzed the scattered information I gathered from village cadres, township officials, and my youth informants. By my estimate, over 600 young people (mostly men) from the three villages of Riha, Luja, and Muha in the Limu basin, with a total population of approximately 4,000, had migration experience. My own household survey in one *she*, Riha Village, in June 2005 revealed that only eleven of its fifty-three male residents between fifteen and forty years of age had never migrated. Among those who had yet to venture out, nine were in their late teens and expressed dreams of venturing out some day.

The best lawful employment opportunities awaiting Limu youths were construction jobs. Since the late 1980s, a housing boom and growth in factory construction have become a testimony to China's rapid urbanization in former suburban or rural areas adjacent to large cities, mainly in Han-dominant regions beyond Liangshan. Many small-scale hydroelectric power plants have also been under construction in the mountains of southwest China. Before the 1990s, few Nuosu people had the contacts or opportunities to land temporary work at these construction sites. After some time, however, a few Nuosu who had worked for Han employers on construction jobs returned home to recruit other Nuosu men for new projects. This networking resulted in small-scale, semiorganized migration. Each work crew of this sort typically has one man from Limu as the foreman, plus a dozen or so Nuosu workers. One such foreman, who had led other young men to work on power plant projects, told me: "Han employers like Nuosu men for constructing power plants because we are used to the mountain climate and can work very well at high elevations." Village cadres, elders, and young men welcomed this kind of organized migration for work. These networks, however, provided only limited opportunities because the projects required only a small number of temporary laborers.

Not all laborers could make money by working at this type of job. On average, the pay for construction work was between 15 and 30 yuan (US$2–3.75 in 2005) per day, depending on whether employers provided food or not. Sometimes laborers had to wait without any pay if the work was suspended or delayed. For example, a man told me about his experience in Urumqi, Xinjiang, where he worked in April 2005 on a project that paid 30 yuan per day, but because of heavy snow he worked for only fifteen days that month. Although he was on the construction site ready to work every day, his pay for April was calculated on the basis of the number of actual workdays, so for that month he earned a total of 450 yuan. Sometimes workers were not paid at all after toiling for a period of time because the employer would not agree to the payment the foreman had promised. In other cases, workers received no pay because the foreman had absconded with the money. On one occasion, Limu's court magistrate called on me to take minutes—because I was the only person who could write and was available at that time—for a dispute of this sort between workers and a foreman. As far as I know, most workers faced with this problem simply gave up any hope of recovering their lost income because they had little social recourse for seeking assistance.

Protections the extended family network may provide to disadvantaged individual migrants may be ineffective if the political and economic environment remains very hostile (Kwong 2001). Most young Nuosu migrants—at least until recently—have not flourished in the cities. Their situation differs considerably from what Gates (1996) describes regarding Han Chinese who used their small sums of capital and extended kinship ties to sustain family-based businesses—what Gates calls "petty capitalism." Nor are Limu migrants' experiences comparable to those of the successful migratory entrepreneurs who hailed from Wenzhou City and formed influential business enclaves in Beijing (Zhang 2001). Other than their kinship and community networks, which have grown in strength since the 1990s, Nuosu youth have not had the capital, either monetary or social, or the skills to establish their own niche in China's expanding urban economy.

Nuosu youths carved out their enclave as more and more migrants from rural areas and of diverse minority ethnicities were competing for limited job opportunities in the cities. Each Nuosu group claimed a specific neighborhood as its own territory, where the youths loitered, stole, and socialized. It is not surprising that most Han urbanites found these activities intimidating and were uncomfortable with such congregations. Also disturbing to many city residents was the Nuosu youths' poor command of Han languages. And since the early 1990s, when heroin was introduced into the floating Nuosu community, their situation in the city has worsened markedly.

The Liminal Transition Toward Chaos

Market reform has inadvertently engendered the resurgence of illicit drug use in Liangshan (Zhou 1999). The combination of China's open policy toward international trade and its proximity to the Golden Triangle has contributed to an increase in the trafficking and consumption of heroin (Reid and Costigan 2002). In the 1990s, it was estimated that 90 percent of the heroin trafficked to China originated in Burma (AHRN 1997). Four possible trafficking routes starting in Burma spread heroin to different areas in East and South Asia (Beyrer et al. 2000). Liangshan, located on the border of Yunnan and Sichuan, sits on one such route, linking Burma to China's hinterland through Yunnan Province, along which heroin is transported and shipped nationwide.

Jonathan Spence's (1975) analysis of opium smoking in the Qing Dynasty can help us grasp the ramifications of heroin use in Limu and Liangshan at large. In brief, heroin use and trade, like opium production and addiction in the past, have both moral and economic implications. The general impression concerning opium in China, among both academics and ordinary people, is that it was negative and devastating; but this may be too simplistic. Some scholars have shown that opium as a commodity has gone through a moral transformation over time and that its social and cultural meanings, such as its use in leisure and fashion, have been excluded from previous research (Dikötter, Laamann, and Xun 2004; Lin 2004; Zheng 2005). In Chinese history, the use of opium was not necessarily evil in the view of many ordinary people. For example, Zheng (2005) relates opium use to the cultures of consumption of other substances such as tobacco and tea and demonstrates how, at one time, the smoking of opium as a luxury item was a sought-after lifestyle and led to the creation of paraphernalia of artistic value.

The moral and economic issues surrounding heroin use in Limu also stand in sharp contrast to our general impressions of opium smoking in the past. Thus my discussion of heroin use and its social repercussions in Limu must take into account the cross-cultural backstory—the Nuosu's reminiscences about opium, their newly gained freedom and expanding desires, China's transition toward a global market economy, and the persistent attempts by state authorities to exert control over stigmatized minorities. The convergence of modernity, masculinity, lifestyle, and substance consumption we find in the drug is the matrix in which we examine the problem of heroin use among Nuosu youth.

Déjà Vu of Yeyi Among the Nuosu

When young Nuosu men first encountered heroin, they called it *yeyi*. In the Nuosu language, *yeyi* originally signified opium, but now there is no semantic distinction between the two substances, save the difference in the temporal sequence of their appearance in Nuosu society and their physical quality, opium being in the form of black, gummy dough and heroin a white powder.

In the eyes of many Nuosu elders, opium is an illicit but harmless substance. A few of my elderly informants believed that they had been leading healthier and more vigorous lives because of their opium-smoking habits. A bimo in his seventies told me, as I observed how he prepared opium for smoking, "I smoke opium so that I can stay in shape, avoid illness, and work well. I've smoked opium since the age of eighteen. Now, you see, I can still perform rituals and do farm work in the field."

In the early 1990s, when yeyi (heroin) made a dramatic entrance into Nuosu lives, the innocuous connotations of yeyi (opium) likely encouraged Nuosu youths to accept it and overlook its devastating effects. "This 'medicine'[7] is as good as yeyi [i.e., opium] in making you feel good and happy," a former heroin user confided to me. Many other users also told me that people who had introduced heroin to them had described this new drug as a good medicine or substance. Heroin's effect of providing temporary relief from stress and pain led many Nuosu youths to appreciate the drug when they could not find sustainable economic opportunities abroad. Some said that using drugs helped them sleep because many of the unemployed youths had to live outdoors or in flophouses.

Obviously, their ready acceptance of heroin was connected with their search for pleasure and the historical associations of opium, a luxury item enjoyed, as mentioned in Chapter 1, by aristocrats and well-off commoners. The old saying, "Opium is the food and candy of *nzymo*," is often recited with a hint of amusement among young heroin users. Like opium in old times, heroin quickly became a marker of fashionableness, social status, and economic success.

Indeed, the most common experiences users worldwide associate with heroin are relaxation and an enhanced sense of well-being (Pearson 1987; Pilkington 2006).[8] Nuosu youths also saw it as a commodity that only capable and affluent men could obtain by means of cash, a token of value most Limu farmers were short of. This drug-use mentality echoes the concept of "consumer exoticism" that Jay (1999) proposes in order to explain why people use drugs. A mentality similar to that of Nuosu youths is traceable to Akha highlanders in the Golden Triangle, where drug use is a "pleasure-based" consumption activity that epitomizes the pursuit of capitalist modernity (Lyttleton 2004).

Heroin's positive effects made it a welcome form of entertainment among Nuosu youths. The role of heroin in Nuosu male sociality was at this point comparable to that of the currently pervasive cigarette sharing and smoking among Chinese men (Kohrman 2007). Well-off young migrants treated their friends and helpers in the cities to the new drug. Yyrre, the ndeggu who mediated among disputing brothers in Chengdu, enjoyed such treats in exchange for his services.

> When yeyi became available and after we had successfully mediated a conflict in Chengdu, the culprits had to buy drugs as a form of indemnity to make up to the complainants, in the same manner as people in Limu do when they buy liquor as a form of apology after the completion of mediation.

Yyrre himself began using heroin in 1995, and after that people bought heroin instead of liquor for him as a token of appreciation for his mediation. Yyrre remembered these furnishers' comments: "They said, 'He [Yyrre] doesn't drink now. Buy him drugs!'" Heroin has strong potency as a psychoactive drug and, in short order, its use became prevalent among the migrant youths. "Now, nobody will fight in the city. Heroin has paralyzed them; they have no more energy to fight!" Yyrre pointed out the connection between the cessation of turf wars and the rise of heroin use in Chengdu.

Once heroin gained popularity among Nuosu youths, their hometowns also witnessed a surge in its availability. By 1993 yeyi in its heroin version had become so widespread in some Nuosu communities that elders were compelled to appeal to the government for intervention.[9] Soon after its introduction in Limu, yeyi swept through the community. In the Limu basin, only a handful of households remained untouched; according to the head of Luja Village, Limu's drug use grew rapidly in 1995, a year when his 1,200-resident village had over 200 drug users. In 1995, cadres of Muha Village estimated that only three households out of a total of seventy-eight in one of its *she* had no family members involved with heroin. My own 2005 household survey, in retrospect, illustrates the severity of the Limu basin's drug problems: thirty-eight out of fifty-three men between the ages of fifteen and forty had once used or were still using drugs.

By the mid-1990s heroin—in Limu as in the cities—had become a popular and fashionable source of entertainment, a treat for guests and ritual specialists. One bimo who was a former user told me that his first taste of heroin occurred when his ritual clients treated him to the drug. Heroin's popularity seduced young men into trying it even before they embarked on migration. Others picked up the habit although they never migrated. Those who did not flourish in the cities or enjoy drugs there might eventually fall into heroin use after returning to their own communities. Agga Shyzzi, who was thirty years old in 2005, relates the miserable conditions in Chengdu and his rash surrender to heroin after coming home:

> At the age of seventeen, I followed the others and went to Chengdu for fun. I didn't work, and I didn't steal. I was a young boy and knew nothing. Once there, my heart beat so fast that it was almost skipping beats. Heartbroken! This is not our hometown. Others tempted me to steal and play there. But I was unable to steal anything. I was not experienced. I was starving for lack of money to buy food. My heart ached and my tummy groaned. I was thinking I'd never leave home again if only I could get back there. Eventually someone who made money through burglary gave me some, so I could come back. I never went away again.

Shyzzi did not use heroin while he was in Chengdu because he lacked money. The ironic and sad development was that, upon returning home, he had ready access to money, and that made this coveted drug affordable in Limu. Shyzzi began using it in 1995, two years after his fizzled adventure in the city.

The recollections of another former user may sum up the prevalence of drug use in Limu at the time:

> Nearly all young men at that time used yeyi. Anyone who didn't use got no respect from his friends. When you treated friends to meat, they would not be pleased. When you treated them to liquor, they would not be pleased. But when you treated them to yeyi, they were pleased.

Transient in the Drug Trade

As the increased supply of heroin fostered the demand for it, the growing demand helped further increase the supply. On average it took about two to four months for Nuosu youths to complete their circular migration. Unless they lacked money to pay for the return trip, most of them voluntarily returned because they were unaccustomed to long stretches away from home. "Coming home to see the family," "coming back to help out during the busy agricultural seasons," or "coming back for seasonal ritual practices"[10] are the most common reasons young men offered when explaining their decision to end a migration. Once home, they might stay for a few days up to a few months. For the drug addicts, their willingness to stay home also depended on whether they could sustain their habit at home. With both returning migrants and some residents in need of drugs, supplying heroin became a profitable enterprise.

In the 1990s selling heroin in Limu quickly generated handsome profits on initial investments. Local cadres and wealthy villagers, especially elders who had more savings in hand, engaged in this business. The former party secretary of Riha Village was eventually incarcerated owing to his involvement in the drug trade. It was said in Limu that many well-constructed houses belonged to people who, at one time or another, had dealt in drugs. For many local residents the heroin trade provided a shortcut to becoming well off.

My household survey provides a glimpse into the arc of Limu's drug trade: 11 out of the 252 residents had traded or were trading drugs, and 7 of these 11 had been incarcerated because of their illegal activities. I believe the actual number of people involved must have been higher, but it was difficult to get accurate numbers because, by the period of my fieldwork, selling heroin had become a mark of shame, an activity to which traffickers would not readily admit.

Limu's drug trade has been gradually declining since the mid-1990s, when local people began to condemn the negative effects of drug use on the youth and the government began to tighten its drug-control enforcement. The arrest and punishment of drug users and traffickers has become strict. According to China's criminal law, conviction for trafficking or trading 50 grams or more of heroin can carry the death sentence.[11] I remember one occasion in January 2005, when I hired a taxi from Xichang to Limu. As we entered the township territory, the taxi driver, who was Han, suddenly pointed to a gorge by the road-side and said:

> In December of last year [2004], six drug dealers who had been sentenced to death were executed by shooting there, and two of the criminals were from Limu. Altogether, two were men and four were women. All were Yizu [Nuosu]. A big crowd of people gathered by the roadside to watch.

After hearing that story, I felt uneasy every time I passed the gorge because I opposed the death penalty and, even more, was appalled by the idea of a public execution. The government's intense law-enforcement policy against drug trafficking significantly reduced Limu's drug trade. Still, some people continued to engage in small-time drug dealing, and most of these were women.

Gendered Relationships with Drugs

By viewing the Nuosu youths' venturing out and using heroin as part of their initiation into manhood, we can also get a sense of how these new activities were shaped by and have reshaped gender relations. West and Zimmerman (1987) coined the expression "doing gender" to account for everyday conduct and interactions seen appropriate to their sex by the actors. "The 'doing' of gender is undertaken by women and men whose competence as members of society is hostage to its production" (126). Heroin use among male Nuosu youth has meanings intertwined with purchasing power, social status, male dominance, and leisure pursuits that, at some point, could be only attained in the cities. Young Nuosu have projected their somewhat essentialized gendered expectations onto the activities of drug use and trade.

Generally speaking, Nuosu women are subordinated to men even in the contexts of migration and drugs. Women usually follow their husbands or sexual partners back and forth between Limu and the cities. Very often Nuosu women first encounter heroin by engaging in small-scale drug dealing rather than by using the drug. Their customers are all Nuosu, most of them acquaintances. Nuosu rarely use or trade heroin with people outside their own ethnic group. The reason, as one young female drug dealer told me, concerns the Nuosu's "fear that Han people may turn them in to the police."

Women's association with male drug users has often been instrumental not only in their sale of drugs but also in their involvement in drug use (Rosenbaum 1981; Taylor 1993). Limu male youths usually begin using drugs for reasons such as fashion, conspicuous displays of wealth and social status, peer pressure, and stress relief. But Nuosu women take up heroin not so much for their own pleasure or in response to same-sex peer pressure but because of their relationships with men who are drug users themselves. Oftentimes women engage in drug trade to earn a profit and support the drug habits of their male partners. Sometimes women begin using drugs or move from small to increased dosages because they have failed to persuade their men to abstain or simply want to keep up with their men by joining them.

Men's and women's patterns of drug use are also manifested in their different attitudes toward profit making and work responsibility. In general, only men engage in major drug trades, whereas women participate in retail person-to-person dealing under the aegis of men. A Nuosu woman succinctly summarized this gender difference: "Boys would steal to make big money. Girls are not capable of theft, so they earn small sums through drug dealing." She added, "There are not enough drugs for boys to use; how can they sell them?" Young men often expressed their reluctance to earn petty cash through minor deals. During everyday conversations I had with people in Limu, I often heard them say something like, "Men work for big money; small money is for women."

In Limu, as in any other Nuosu village, women generally perform work that includes farming, collecting firewood, carrying water, feeding animals, cooking nonmeat foods, and caring for families; none of these activities generate real income, let alone quick profits. In my observation, young men often abstain from farm work (except for plowing and harvesting) and household chores even when they have nothing else to do. When I asked why men did not help their women, they responded with comments akin to the following: "Those [tasks] are minor. They [women] can handle them. Men should do big things and earn large sums of money." My observations suggest that, in normal cases, young men who stayed at home did not engage in major endeavors. They simply pretended they were busy engaging in something important.

Women's particular styles of selling drugs capitalize on their roles as mothers. In recent years, pregnant women have become more active in organized heroin trafficking than men. Despite their traditional subordination to men, women are also going through changes, which I will relate in Chapter 4. It is a common practice for young women to take their own children or "borrow" children from poor families to accompany them during drug deals. Usually the police are more lenient with pregnant women or women with young children and less likely to incarcerate them, or such women can post bail more easily (Ma Linying 2001). I remember a telling episode in late 2005: Based on charges of drug dealing, police officers in Yunnan Province arrested two young women from Limu and sent them back to Liangshan's detention center. The women's families petitioned the village's Communist Party secretary to grant them a year's release, until their infants no longer needed to nurse. The children were only four and five months old at that time. The village party secretary, who was also a lineage headman, acted as guarantor that the women would return to jail in one year, whereupon the police agreed and released them. One year later, however, they did not return to jail. Instead, they migrated to Chengdu, where they again engaged in drug dealing.

City Segregation

Drug prices vary according to policing conditions, and drug use methods hinge on personal financial circumstances. The cost of heroin varies depending on the location in which a sale occurs: in general, the price increases as the distance between its place of origin, Burma, and the location of the final sale expands. I compiled a list of heroin prices in different localities in 2005, on the basis of drug users' estimations. On average, heroin cost between 100 and 200 yuan per gram in Kunming, 400 yuan in Liangshan, 500 yuan in Chengdu, 800 yuan in Beijing and Xi'an (Shaanxi Province), and 1,000 yuan in Inner Mongolia. Furthermore, the prices fluctuated in relation to whether or not law enforcement had increased its efforts to crack down on illicit drugs. In Chengdu in August 2005, for example, 1 gram of heroin cost 500 yuan, but in November of the same year it cost 900 yuan because the police had tightened their enforcement. Usually drug users spent between 10 and 20 yuan to buy a small packet of heroin, the size of one mung bean. The frequency of drug use and the quantity hinge upon the user's habit and financial circumstances. Better-off users may take heroin three times a day; poorer users could only afford to satisfy their craving once every few days.

Poor heroin users commonly take the drug intravenously. According to a survey of 1,649 arrested users in six rehabilitation centers in Sichuan Province, 48.8 percent of them injected, and the majority of these were peasants, illiterates, and young people (China-UK 2001, 12). To satisfy the craving through injection takes only one-fourth to one-fifth of the heroin needed for smoking.

According to the testimony of one of my informants, "You needed 100 yuan [to pay for heroin] by smoking, but only 20 yuan by injection [to have the same effect]." Therefore, to save money, many poor users change their method of administration from smoking to injection.

Injecting heroin may more cheaply satisfy one's addiction, but it also increases the chances of spreading blood-borne diseases through needle sharing. Research has established that the first injection of drugs may be riskier than subsequent injections because the novice drug user may fail to properly plan that first injection. Proper planning stems from experience, but new users often lack experience or their own injection equipment (Sherman et al. 2002). This careless behavior may have paved the way for the spread of the AIDS virus among injectors.

In the mid-1990s, using heroin by injection had become prevalent among Limu youths stranded in the cities. The misery of these users and small-time drug dealers had become visible in the city landscape. Drifting young Nuosu often injected drugs outdoors and rarely bathed. At Chengdu's South Railway Station, as recently as March 2009, one could still easily spot the Nuosu drug users and dealers hanging around in groups outside the station. In wintertime these young men squatted for warmth on the cement-paved sidewalk in a circle around a pile of burning firewood. Young women brought along their own or others' children, who played on the sidewalk or in the roadside plant beds. These people all looked shabby and listless. Their used syringes and needles, as well as discarded trash and dirt, lay scattered around the plant beds.

The congregation of Nuosu drifters in Chengdu, many of them involved in theft, burglary, heroin use, and the heroin trade, quickly attracted the attention of city authorities and residents. Since the mid-1990s the city police have stepped up their enforcement against drug-related crimes, and the Nuosu population has, in response, shrunk considerably. I have no systematic data as to how many youths drifted around the cities in the 1990s. A few young people told me that the number at that time was much higher than it has been more recently. In 2005, I estimated the numbers of city-based Nuosu migrants to be from 300 to 400 in Chengdu, 500 to 600 in Xi'an, 300 to 400 in Inner Mongolia, and 300 to 400 in Beijing.

By the mid-1990s, Chengdu urbanites had developed strong negative stereotypes of the Nuosu drifters. Many residents came to believe that all Nuosu youths must be drug users or dealers, as well as thieves. A Han friend of mine who was a news reporter in Chengdu once asked me, before my departure to Liangshan in December of 2004, "How do you dare to go to the Liangshan Yi

[Nuosu] area? In truth, Chengdu residents are very fearful of the Yi people. The newspapers here either totally ignore them or report on them as criminals." It was neither the first nor the last time I heard Han people invoke this stereotype of the Nuosu. Because of this stigma throughout the city, Chengdu had become an even less viable place for migrating Nuosu youths.

To rid the city of this menace and regulate the floating population, the Chengdu authorities set up a police task force in the mid-1990s that targeted mainly the Nuosu and another minority group, the Tibetans. In recent years, a residential community around Chengdu's South Railway Station, with the approval of the city police, organized a group of guards who, armed with night-sticks, cordoned off the entrance of a nearby market to prevent any Nuosu without identification cards from entering. City authorities and residents both attempted to stop Nuosu people from drifting in and making their living environment a dangerous one.

The Closure of a Contorted Rite of Passage

The Nuosu migrants' accounts of detention after being arrested for drug use or other crimes are quite similar and represent a particularly sad chapter in their story. I first listened to such an account during the second month of my residence in Limu in 2005, sooner than I had expected. Lewu Shuomo, twenty-seven years old and from Riha Village, along with his cousin, knocked on my door one evening. He introduced himself upon seeing my surprise: "I have met so many different people while traveling outside, so I'd like to get to know you." Usually, only those Nuosu who have had many migration experiences and have interacted with outsiders before could possibly have found the courage to approach a stranger like me. Owing to his initiative, I invited them into my house and listened to his story, the first of many like it that I would hear later.

Shuomo began by commenting on the helplessness and hopelessness of Nuosu youths locked away in the mountains and his frustration at being unable to find a stable job at home despite his better-than-average education as a high school graduate. Suddenly, and without prompting from me, he confided to me his drug use and detention experiences:

> I went out just for fun in 1996. . . . To be frank with you, I felt stressed and homesick so I used drugs. Then, I was caught by the police and was sent to the rehabilitation center in Chengdu. It was awful there! Twice a day for a few days, the wardens fed us a kind of red liquid, claiming it was medication that would

reduce our craving for drugs. They also had my blood tested. Old inmates beat up new inmates. I had no clue as to why they beat us. There were only two Nuosu, and the rest were all Han people. One of my ribs was broken. I was weaker than the others and deserved to be hit: no one had forced me to use drugs! And it cost my family dearly to get me out of there after three months. Had I not paid the fee, which was itemized and charged to my family as the cost of my stay at the center, I would have been sent to another detention center in Ebian, which had a notorious reputation for mistreating inmates. But, alas, even after ten years, I tell you, I have found no way to kick the drug habit for good. . . . I still, once in a while, smoke a bit when I get drunk.

Today those Nuosu youths who migrated for fun and adventure in the 1980s and 1990s and were imprisoned on charges of drug use, drug dealing, or burglary are no longer young adults. Many people of this cohort have expressed their reluctance to live miserably again in the cities. As research has pointed out, drug use may "age out," and the so-called street culture of the drug users may be more of an age-grade phenomenon (Glick Schiller 1992). This youthful experience is akin to that of Mexican men as described by Matthew Gutmann: "Heavy drinking . . . has been . . . largely a *male* stage through which many have passed. . . . Although some youth do not ever leave this stage, most of them do get out in one way or another" (Gutmann 1996, 189). Limu elders told me that, because of penal punishment and Limu community control (which I will discuss in the next chapter), over 40 percent of Limu's drug users had successfully kicked their habits by the early 2000s. These successful youths survived their "rite of passage" and began a new phase of life in various ways. Some of them took jobs as construction workers, more street-smart youths made money by hustling, and still others simply returned home for a settled life there.

Nevertheless, a small number of this cohort were unsuccessful in this transition. Their failed experimentation fits a pattern in which "certain forms of liminality are riskier, more easily derailed" (Hopper 2003, 21–22). As I will show shortly, some died of drug overdoses or during imprisonment. Drug injectors had a harder time kicking the habit than those who smoked. Some of them failed to be assimilated into the city's Han-dominant capitalist way of life, nor could they return to Limu to settle down. As their transitional situation became routinized and their sense of betwixt and between extended, their liminality became a "social and cultural *limbo*" in the cities (Hopper and Baumohl 2004, 355). They could not have strayed further from their dream of a glorified manhood.

When China's economic development brought little change to the Liang-shan region in the 1990s and early 2000s, conditions in the mountain com-munity of Limu remained stale. Limu youth in the early 2000s shared dreams similar to their predecessors a decade earlier—the yearning to venture out. In comparison with the drifters in the 1990s, the cohort of young men in the 2000s were clearly aware of the potential problems of heroin because they had wit-nessed its devastating effects on the older cohort of Nuosu migrants. With so many of their older brothers, sisters, fathers, uncles, and neighbors returned home safely after early adventures involving drugs and burglary, the younger generation seemed eager and ready to undertake those legendary urban ex-ploits themselves. Unfortunately, this newest cohort did not learn from the experiences of their predecessors; they simply repeated that life course and its mistakes, and the cities have become increasingly hostile to their visits. The institutionalized inequity and risks such disembedded individuals encounter in capitalist modernity, as Beck and Beck-Gernsheim (2002) point out, loom ahead of the younger cohorts of Nuosu drifters. Stigmatized, undereducated, and inexperienced, the recent cohorts of Nuosu youths have predictably been unable to share in the fortunes of the new, market-oriented China.

A Damaged Hometown

Local history testifies to how drugs have transformed Nuosu society since the nonstate era, first through the introduction of opium cultivation and trade and now heroin addiction. Unlike opium, which at one time brought awe-some power and fortune to the Nuosu elites in relation to Han people, heroin has further strained this already socioeconomically marginalized community. Contemporary young Nuosu have lost money and lives in the purchase and consumption of heroin trafficked from afar. Theft rose in Limu after heroin use there became prevalent. Drug addicts stole from their own homes and their neighbors to buy heroin. In the past, Nuosu people despised theft in their own communities; it was one of the most shameful types of misconduct. Today it has become a common social ill in Limu.

Many young men, to sustain their drug habits, have depleted their family savings. Some even sold their own houses or land to immigrants who moved from the high hills to settle in Limu.[12] Jjike Lassyr, at the age of forty, a widely known former drug user and dealer, successfully abstained from his heroin habit and was elected the head of Luja Village in 2003. Lassyr admitted to me that, between 1993 and 1995, he spent nearly 180,000 yuan (approximately US$22,500) on heroin. He was just one of the many drug addicts who used up all their money reserves, earned partly through drug trade, and family property on heroin.

In recent years, village cadres in the Limu basin began to prohibit the sale of houses and land to outsiders. They said that Limu would become dominated by immigrants if such sales continued. In 2005, during the biannual meeting of Luja Village, Lassyr admonished the attendees, most of whom were elders because so many young men were away from home. At the heart of his lecture was the warning: "In the future, when our children grow up, they will no longer have farmland. Luja Village used to be the territory of Jjike and Jjiebba lineages. If you continue selling our land to outsiders, Luja Village will become the land of people from the [surrounding] mountains!"

The precipitous decline in the health of Limu youths has been even more alarming. In the 1990s many young men appeared dazed and listless because of drug addiction. A restaurant owner in Limu who contrasted the before-and-after conditions of the heroin epidemic noted that before the mid-1990s, fistfights among young males were commonplace at the periodic market. Once heroin use became prevalent, the youths were paralyzed in a drug-induced heedlessness.

What also distinguishes heroin from opium is that the former can be injected, and this has wrecked lives mercilessly. No systematic public health statistics have been gathered on the consequences of drug addiction in Limu. Tuberculosis has been a common infectious disease in Liangshan. A Zhaojue County doctor who sometimes came to Limu to treat patients reported that after drug use became prevalent, it was difficult to treat tuberculosis patients because so many of them used drugs, which exacerbated existing health problems. At the Limu Township Clinic, where young stay-at-home drug injectors and drug-injecting migrant returnees came for treatment, health workers often found it difficult to inject medication. The patients' legs and arms were just too damaged from their frequent heroin injections. Sometimes health workers could inject only through the jugular vein in the neck. Parents of drug users often commented sarcastically about their children's adroitness at drug taking: "Their injection skills are much better than those of the [health clinic] doctors."

An Unrehearsed Ritual for Life and Death

Sadly but predictably, death and social affliction followed the heroin-addicted migrants back to Limu. With so many young people constantly venturing out for easy money and drugs, it was not a total surprise that in Limu and neighboring Hagu Township, 275 known drug users had died by 2001. In 2005, local elders and village cadres estimated that there remained 216 known drug users in Limu out of a population of 8,726. In one *she* of about 500 residents in Luja Village, 13 young men had died from heroin overdoses alone between 1998 and 2005. In addition to drug use, diseases (e.g., AIDS) and injuries—from lashings by policemen or city residents to accidents that occurred during migration—contributed further to the loss of young lives in Limu. Given these conditions, orphans have become a social problem. Grandparents are often compelled to care for their sick children or orphaned grandchildren.

Yyrre belongs to the first generation of Limu's youth migrants. One day I asked him whether he knew how many young people had died while sojourning. After replying that two-thirds of his friends who first ventured out in the 1980s had died, he began to recite their names, one by one. I felt uneasy and sad listening to this ritual-like recitation. A man from the Jjike lineage counted ninety-nine deaths among his kinsmen in Limu and neighboring areas between 1995 and the middle of 2005. "All these dead kinsmen were the most talented people. Only the best young men had the ability to leave home and make money for their drug habits." This comment ironically reminds me of the Nuosu's traditional belief in military prowess and exploratory masculinity, which has been part and parcel of the motivation behind Limu's youth migration.

Funerals have constituted the final rite of passage for these youths, whether they perished at home or far away in big cities. To the Nuosu, funeral ceremonies held at home are indispensable occasions for kin to mourn their dead. On the opposite side of the globe, Smith (2004) shows that, in Nigerian culture, at-home ritual burials for migrants who died away from home can be indicative of ties between the deceased and their place of birth. Although Limu's funerals are not as extravagant as those of the Nigerians, they are similarly important social events that demonstrate close social relationships, personal fortunes, and familial duties. Elders who organize these events have tacitly accepted this painful reality and help to complete the life cycle of their dead young men, in accordance with traditional Nuosu funeral practices (see Figure 4).

The Nuosu belief in three souls after death also governs the significance of at-home funerals. Nuosu peasants have been practicing outdoor cremation since time immemorial. They believe that one soul remains at the cremation site.[13] The second soul is attached to *madu*, a spirit tube, kept by the deceased's family. The last soul goes to their ancestors' place, where the Nuosu originated, said to be in today's Yunnan Province. Following this Nuosu worldview, when the deceased's family provides proper rituals officiated by bimo at home, the

Figure 4. Kinsmen distributing meat (pork and beef) and rice-and-buckwheat cakes to funeral participants

last two souls reach their rightful places, and in turn the afflicted family can resume its peaceful existence. Therefore, all Nuosu consider it a natural responsibility that they carry the bodies or at least the bone ashes of their dead kinsmen home, regardless of whether the kinsmen were drifters, burglars, drug users, or AIDS patients.

Most of the dead migrant youths were cremated legally in the cities and then brought back to Limu by kinsmen or friends. Sometimes, however, there were exceptions. The practice of either bringing the dead body home or cremating the deceased outdoors according to Nuosu tradition is contested because it differs drastically from the state-approved "modern" cremation carried out in funeral homes. Indeed, even though the state promotes cremation in state-run funeral homes, not all Nuosu peasants could afford its cost—about 2,000 yuan—given the annual net income per capita in rural Zhaojue County of only about 730 yuan in 2004. Therefore, it became a significant financial burden for Nuosu kinsmen or friends to legally cremate their dead peers in distant cities. My informant Muga told me a story that vividly portrays this predicament and the conflicts between the Nuosu way of cremation and the mortuary rules of the modern state:

> Numerous young people died outside. They didn't have the money to get cremated at funeral homes. It cost 2,000 yuan! So the only way is to cremate them secretly outdoors. As far as I know, forty to fifty people from Limu and the neighboring townships were cremated outdoors in the cities. I personally cremated eight people in the cities of Chengdu, Xi'an, and Nanjing. Six of them were my Qubi kinsmen, and the other two were members of the Lewu lineage from Limu. Their families asked me to help burn them out there and bring their bones and ashes home.
>
> One time, in the middle of a cremation on the fringes of Xi'an City, policemen suddenly arrived and accused me of being a murderer. I told them, "I didn't kill him. He was my own brother! We Yizu[14] do this to the dead all the time." I showed the policemen the dead man's hukou. I thought it might be needed, so I had brought it with me from Limu. I also gave the policemen the telephone number of the Zhaojue County Police Station. They made a call to Zhaojue and realized that we Yizu do cremate the dead this way. So they didn't arrest me but warned me not to burn bodies this way any more. I've been to Xi'an for this purpose several times. The policemen over there are already acquainted with me. Upon seeing me, they reminded me that I can't burn bodies outdoors again and suggested that I do it at funeral homes. I asked the policemen, "They don't have money to be cremated at the funeral homes, so can the Bureau of Civil Affairs help out with the cremation costs?" They replied that only the dead without families could get such assistance. I don't know what we can do in the future. But I don't dare to cremate my kinsmen and friends again in Xi'an. I would be arrested on murder charges!
>
> People often asked for my help in this matter because they didn't speak Han languages and knew no one in the cities. And I always did them this favor and didn't have time to make money for myself! . . . Ah, the bones of drug users are black, different from people who die naturally.

The Bureau of Civil Affairs cremated people who died on the city's skid row or in jails and had no one to claim their bodies. Family members of the dead had to pay a sum of money, generally between 500 and 1,000 yuan, to retrieve the ashes and bones from the Bureau. I remember a funeral that was held in Limu, right after the Nuosu New Year in 2005. On this occasion, attendees mourned the deceased without his ashes and bones being present. This young man had died in the Emei Labor and Education Camp while under incarceration. The camp sent the body to the funeral home for cremation right away. His family and immediate kinsmen did not have enough money to pay for the cremation and could only see the picture of his ashes and bones provided by the camp at the funeral home.

Muga recalled another incident involving the cremation of a kinsman in Nanjing. The incident shows simultaneously both the sorrowful and the hilarious aspects of following their traditional Nuosu way of "dealing with the dead" in Han-dominant society.

> We hired a cab to move the dead body to the fringes of Nanjing. We wrapped the body with a sleeping bag and placed it in the trunk of the cab. We Yizu working on construction sites often carry sleeping accommodations from one place to another. So it's not unusual for us to put bundles and bags in car trunks. But just as we were about to begin burning the body in the middle of nowhere in the suburbs—I had just started pouring gasoline along with ten kilograms of beans on the body so that it would be completely burned in half an hour—the cab driver returned and shouted at us. Someone had told him that he had just delivered a body. He said that his family relied on this cab to earn a living but that he wouldn't dare to drive it any longer because it had carried a body. He wanted us to keep his cab and give him money in return. We told him that we didn't have money for his car. After a long argument, he left with our 500 yuan.

Similar stories are familiar and widespread among Nuosu migrant youths. One of them tells how several Nuosu youths secretly carried a dead body by train, car, and bus all the way from a big city to their mountain home, although I have never interviewed anyone who actually witnessed or participated in the event.

The Emerging HIV/AIDS Epidemic

Failing to secure for themselves a share of China's newfound wealth, many Nuosu youths have emerged from their life transition disillusioned. Others left behind afflicted widows and small children when they perished. And still others have returned home and placed new burdens on their kin and communities. The heroin epidemic peaked in Limu around 1995 and remained acute until 1999. Limu residents have since then experienced a new, plaguelike loss of young people. In 1995 the Chinese government imposed compulsory HIV testing on arrested drug users and dealers at detention and rehabilitation centers.

That same year the first case of HIV infection in Liangshan was reported among Nuosu drug injectors (China-UK 2004). Blood testing among drug users eventually indicated that the AIDS virus had spread among Nuosu youths through contaminated needles and syringes they shared and that infected youths who returned to Limu had brought the virus with them. Limu Township reported its first case of HIV infection in 1997.

The heroin-induced HIV/AIDS epidemic in Limu reached an alarming stage in the late 1990s, when various international organizations, in collaboration with the Liangshan prefectural government, began working in this Nuosu community. In 2001 the China-UK Project, which was sponsored by the British government, launched broad-based blood tests in Limu's three basin villages to signal the start of its official operations. Responding to official orders from above, village cadres mobilized villagers between the ages of fourteen and sixty to submit to a blood test for HIV in Riha Village (China-UK 2004, 27). My neighbor Mahxi Ggurre described the scene: "Cadres ordered everybody between fourteen and sixty to go to the waterfront pasture for blood tests. The doctors drew our blood according to the household registration list. So everybody had to go. I went too. And I tested HIV positive during that blood test."

The initial tests in these three villages showed an alarming rate of HIV infection: 96 of the approximately 1,000 participating peasants tested HIV positive; that is, the prevalence of HIV cases was 9.6 percent of the sampled population, or 2.4 percent of the three villages' population (approximately 4,000). Among the 96 reported HIV infections, 61 of them were tracked by the township government and health workers in 2002. In Zhaojue County as a whole, 96.52 percent of the HIV-infected people were between the ages of fifteen and forty; most were males who had injected heroin (China-UK 2004, 27). When the results were made public, Limu quickly became known as one of the worst-hit areas of Liangshan in connection with the heroin-engendered HIV/AIDS epidemic.[15]

Although drug use has declined since the late 1990s, the outbreak of HIV/AIDS had just begun to ravage Limu at that point. Having come through their chaotic initiation from youth to manhood, how do the young men reflect upon its unexpected and sorrowful consequences? Comments by thirty-one-year-old Anyu Shiyi reveal the extent to which Limu youths' attitudes toward manliness and adventure have led many astray:

> I was sent to the Labor and Education Camp in Ebian because I had three burglary convictions: in 1995, 1998, and 2001. [*Shiyi gives a beaming smile.*] Last

year [i.e., 2004], after I returned home, a doctor in the clinic visited me, saying I was HIV positive and asking me to attend the AIDS education session once a month in the township clinic. . . . Am I afraid of AIDS? Nothing to fear! Dying at home should satisfy my father: it's better than dying away from home!

The failure of many Limu youths to negotiate their rite of passage in the market reform era has further tarnished Nuosu people's ethnic pride. Along with their previous classification as a "backward slave society" under the rubric of socialist modernity, the Nuosu must now deal with yet another stigmatizing label: they are a "plague" society. All the while, the Nuosu have had to cope with the long-standing obstacles of chronic poverty and marginalization. In the face of the ongoing miseries in Limu, young Nuosu in their late teens and early twenties are more than ever ready to venture out. They share the feeling of their predecessors that there is neither hope nor fun at home.

3 Multivocal Drug Control

AROUND 1994, when heroin use in Limu was on the rise among the youth, a small group of lineage headmen began to mobilize their kinfolk and deploy kinship institutions to try to contain the emerging problem before the state intervened. But heroin's popularity continued to run rampant between 1995 and 1999 and wreaked devastation across the whole community. It was in this context that the image of heroin use underwent a complicated process of change from being "fashionable" to being "delinquent."

Like earlier drugs such as opium, heroin experienced a similar historical change worldwide: once a popular substance, it has come to be considered a social evil. This transformation points to the complexity of medico-pharmaceutical, political-economic, and sociocultural factors surrounding the production, acceptance, circulation, and control of such substances (Courtwright 2001; Dikötter, Laamann, and Xun 2004; Trocki 1999; Zheng 2005). Once the discourse that defines a substance negatively grows dominant, drug control then comes to represent a long and hard-fought social mission, one that gives rise to many conflicts of interest among groups and individuals with a stake in the controversy. The national pain and social unrest brought about in the wake of opium control campaigns instituted by the Qing court, the Republican nationalists, and the Chinese Communists provide poignant examples of this from the pages of modern Chinese history (Bello 2005; Lin 2004; Qin 2001; Zhou 1999).

Historical archives preserve accounts showing how drug control campaigns are implemented and resisted at the levels of the nation, the provinces, and sometimes the counties. The everyday and subaltern situations and laypeople's acts and responses therein are only marginally noted, if not dismissed altogether, in the stories that are readily accessible.[1] In contrast, this chapter will examine the fine grain of contemporary China's drug control efforts through the grassroots and everyday antiheroin campaigns that took place in Limu. These actions are embedded in the broader contexts of China's and global antidrug crusades. More important, they illustrate how drug control has been made possible or impossible by folk institutions in a reforming socialist state.

Inquiring into Community Campaigns

Drug control has been a key concern of poverty-stricken Limu Township for over a decade. Community campaigns were self-initiated at first and then, later on, mandated by the state. As one village cadre stressed, "The township government wanted lineages to shoulder the drug control responsibility." The key question thus becomes, are kinship institutions as a form of social control anachronistic in the market reform era? More to the point here, under what circumstances can kinship groups play a role in an effective grassroots alliance for drug control? As I will show shortly, the complexity of Limu's drug control activities points to changing social relationships under the influence of capitalist modernity.

The local community's measures to combat the emerging epidemic of heroin use present us with an ironic yet intriguing development. The Chinese government had labeled Nuosu kinship institutions "feudalistic" and banned their activities during the collective era. But in the subsequent shift toward market reform, the state has assumed an increasingly liberal approach to many aspects of social life. One striking example of this has been the state's tacit permission for local communities to resuscitate indigenous institutions. Limu peasants revived their kinship organizations in the early 1980s. At the outset, the themes of the gatherings were primarily lineage solidarity and how to cope with the capriciousness of market reform. Kinsmen pledged to avoid fighting kinsmen, to help each other with conflict resolution, and to cooperate generally for the sake of cohesion. By the early 1990s, as heroin use was spreading among young people, the main theme of lineage gatherings shifted from solidarity to the drug problem. It is in this context that the revived lineage organizations mobilized for drug control in the mid-1990s.

Shortly afterward, local police also stepped up drug control enforcement in the mid-1990s. By that time, it was not unusual to see youths openly taking heroin along the main roads; only later, when lineage pressure and local law enforcement worked simultaneously on the problem did this behavior begin to move out of public view. Two of my young male neighbors recalled the government's initial arrests in 1996:

> Many of us young people sat around the square in front of the primary school watching a video program. Most of us did not have TV sets at home at that time, so we gathered there to watch paid videos. All of a sudden, four policemen came out of nowhere and asked us to put our hands at the back of our necks. At that time, we were all taking drugs and had heroin in our pockets or bags. No one listened to the police. Everybody ran and hastily threw the drugs behind the TV set. The police arrested a five-year-old boy who happened to pick up a small packet of drugs! His lineage headmen complained to the police about their arrest of an innocent kid and finally were able to take him back home. Since then, no one has dared to carry drugs openly. . . . The government's law enforcement tightened in 1998, when drug use here reached its peak.

Since that time, local law enforcement efforts have paralleled grassroots antidrug campaigns, which put the police and lineage authorities in constant competition with each other. This sort of conflict is embedded in the chronic, simultaneously collaborative and antagonistic state-society relationship in the Nuosu community. Unlike other state policies, drug control was initiated and led by the local community owing to the urgency of the problem for grassroots survival. Initially, some of the local responses seemed to be effective. But their efficacy quickly diminished as time went on, and each subsequent wave of the community campaigns had a shorter and shorter life span.

Additionally, the limitations of grassroots efforts would become salient as local health problems developed. When Nuosu peasants began their drug control campaigns in the mid-1990s, AIDS had yet to become a crisis. As the HIV/AIDS epidemic grew in the late 1990s, the lineage drug control campaigns continued, but local people admitted they could only deal with heroin—not with AIDS, too. The grassroots campaigners had neither clear ideas about prevention nor adequate medical resources to tackle HIV/AIDS. When state health care support finally arrived after 2001, it remained limited in scale. (Chapter 5 will examine the state's AIDS intervention.) The lineages' method of responding to the AIDS threat was principally to help the victims and their families with farm work or provide care to orphaned children. Community meetings rarely presented comprehensive information about preventing HIV transmission through noninjection pathways, such as sexual and mother-to-child transmission. When local cadres and headmen addressed the problem of AIDS, it was treated as a thorny issue linked exclusively to heroin injection—as if AIDS would disappear once heroin was removed from the local landscape. The remarks of Lewu Munyo, the party secretary of Muha Village and the leading figure in Limu's drug control campaigns, showcase the local strategy:

> AIDS is actually more damaging than drug use, but local lineages are not ready to handle it. Lineages haven't found practical ways of understanding and dealing with AIDS. We can only control drug use and the drug trade, as well as prevent young people from floating out, and hope that AIDS will diminish accordingly.

Community participation in local health-related campaigns is by nature political, and whether such campaigns are effective depends on the prior history of citizen participation (Midgley 1986; Morgan 1993). In this regard, the role of the state in shaping community activism is in fact crucial, especially in a country where state-society relations are antipathetic. China's compulsory Democratic Reform of 1956 and subsequent governance did not cultivate a sound partnership with Nuosu society. State control over the people is a recurrent theme. In Limu's drug control campaigns, the state demanded that local communities remain "self-reliant," a message that drew on the rhetoric of civilian participation in state-initiated or -sanctioned campaigns—a common practice of the collective era. As a consequence, local campaigns waxed and waned over time as peasants realized that their own real constraints and the state agents' erratic efforts and underfunded intervention programs presented insurmountable obstacles. Predicated on an ill-conceived policy of self-sufficiency for solving local crises, such measures simply "aimed at minimizing the need for costly public health infrastructure" (Sherraden 1991, 261).

The result of collective drug control endeavors from 1994 to 2006 is debatable. Both the peasants and the state agents involved were ambivalent toward them. This ambivalence was rooted in the conflation of and tensions among traditional symbolic power, personal economic interests, and state authority—three domains that concurrently shaped Limu's drug control mechanisms. These practices illustrate the resilience and constraints of Nuosu tradition when faced with a watchful state and the seductions of capitalist modernity. In the following reconstruction of Limu's decade-long drug control efforts, we will see how its grassroots campaigns became problematic and controversial.

The Convoluted Trajectory of Local Drug Control

A Model Cadre and His Village

The first wave of drug control campaigns was launched in a *she* of Muha Village in 1994 where most of the households belong to the Lewu lineage. The campaign there was headed by Lewu Munyo, a *she* cadre. Lewu Munyo was thirty-two at the time and had boldly undertaken many pursuits with impressive success. In this campaign, he resorted to the simplest, toughest, yet most effective approach to drug control: he, along with his followers, had drug users and dealers tied up and beaten. In addition, Munyo and the lineage headmen organized all families of the *she* into self-monitoring watchdog units (*lianzu*), each comprising five households. The rule was that the entire unit would be punished should any of its members violate antidrug rules.

One year later, thirty-one of the *she*'s seventy-eight households were already free from involvement with heroin. This was an impressive turnaround since at the outset only three households had not been engaged in drug use or trade. Munyo's strong-arm approach and its initial effectiveness earned him the approval of lineage headmen and the parents of young addicts alike. To expand drug control in Muha Village, Munyo called on fifty-one elders of all of its lineages, and they agreed to expand the campaign from the *she* to the entire village. Accordingly, village cadres and lineage headmen signed pledges to monitor their own young members' behavior and organized a group of patrolmen to catch drug users and dealers. They believed that young villagers who drifted to cities without clear purpose were at greater risk of taking drugs, so they also signed a protocol aimed at preventing young people from heading off to urban areas. Every month they gathered to review each household's situation. All households in each watchdog unit were fined from 500 to 1,000 yuan if any member of the unit violated the protocols, either for drug use or drifting.

Lewu Munyo and the patrolmen commonly used confinement and sometimes corporal punishment to deal with arrested drug users or dealers. Patrolmen might handcuff and beat delinquents in their office, but they also provided food as well as painkillers to alleviate drug users' withdrawal symptoms. It typically takes about two weeks for the craving for heroin to abate, but some people needed as much as a month of such treatment before the cravings tapered off significantly. This deterrent approach effectively intimidated drug users and dealers in the village. Many ended their involvement in heroin, while others left Muha Village to continue their drug habit or business elsewhere.

The government supported such lineage-based efforts as the primary method of intervention and engaged in various forms of collaboration with the local community. As the leader of Limu's antidrug campaign, Lewu Munyo was quickly promoted to deputy head of Muha Village in 1996. A year later the township government promoted him to the position of the village's Communist Party secretary, and the central government declared him "the nation's premier exponent of drug cessation medical science" (*quanguo jiedu yixue xianjin geren*). In 1999 Lewu Munyo received another promotion, this time to become deputy head of the Limu Township government in charge of drug control, while he also retained his position as the Muha Village party secretary. In that same year, the Sichuan Provincial Communist Party Office celebrated Lewu Munyo as one of "The Best 100 Village Party Secretaries" (*baijiacun dangbu shuji*). Drug control in Muha Village enjoyed its highest profile in the late 1990s when Lewu Munyo's expanding political power reached its peak, with state officials lauding him as the genuine answer to drug control.

Imitating the Model Village

Having witnessed the initial success of Lewu Munyo's drug control program in Muha Village, the lineage headmen and cadres in other villages followed suit and established their own. Individual lineages and whole communities held meetings and rituals to publicly declare their antidrug agendas. One such meeting held in a *she* of Luja Village exemplifies grassroots creativity and effort in reformulating and mobilizing their traditional social institutions. I paraphrase below what the presiding cadre, Anyu Aja, recounted.

It was a sunny day in October 1998 when an early winter chill descended upon the Limu basin. Lineages of one *she* in Luja Village held their first joint antidrug meeting. Cadres had sold a share of the *she*'s remaining collective woodlands for 3,000 yuan and used the funds to buy an ox, a goat, a pig, and a chicken for the ceremony, which would take place by the flat waterfront pasture of the *she*. This *she* had about 500 residents, over 200 of whom happened to be home at the time, and all attended the event. People sacrificed the animals and cooked them on the spot. Women and children sat together at the periphery of the gathering ground. Headmen and lineage members who also served as cadres spoke one by one, underscoring the importance of community accord and people's compliance with both state rules and Nuosu norms. Young men and older boys distributed meat and liquor to each participant (children also drink at these occasions). People enjoyed the treats as the headmen and cadres continued their lecturing.

This antidrug assembly was an expansion of ordinary lineage meetings. The *she* had twelve lineages, three of them large and the other nine small. The nine small lineages grouped together to form a quasi lineage that provided support among its members and took part in public activities as if it were a single lineage. Headmen of these four lineage groups (three actual and the fourth fictive) promised to control their kin members' behavior. They asked young drug users to forswear their addiction in a conditional curse ritual: if the drug users violated the ban, they would face spiritual punishment.

During such meetings, local people at times invited bimo to officiate in drug-resistance rituals, which included killing a dog or chicken as a warning to lineage members that, should they use drugs, their misconduct would result in grievous punishments akin to the fate of the animals. To intensify the power of the rituals and their compacts, some lineages asked drug users to drink a concoction of chicken blood and liquor (Figure 5). This meant that the vows of drug users to abstain were sealed with blood, so they would suffer the gravest consequences if they relapsed.

Figure 5. Ritual for drug control: a *bimo* (priest in turban) kills a chicken, then a mixture of liquor and chicken blood is poured into the bowls

State agencies encouraged local drug control to be modeled after that of Muha Village and many of the other villages in Limu followed suit, but none of them had comparable success. The flows of heroin and its users and dealers extended well beyond the confines of individual villages. Peasants soon discovered that many Muha Village users simply sneaked off to other villages to continue their use or trade. Cadres in other villages did not necessarily possess the power or personal charisma of Lewu Munyo. Moreover, the other villages were not as uniform in terms of lineage composition as was Muha's population. Among the three villages in the Limu basin, Muha is the only "lineage village," that is, the majority of its residents belong to the same lineage. The other two villages, Luja and Riha, with their more diverse composition of several medium to small lineages, were unable to match Muha's drug control success and additionally suffered a great deal of internal strain.

Individual Aspects of Drug Control

As lineage-run drug control programs placed enormous social pressure on users, individual abstainers underwent their own painful and protracted struggles. Many of the successful abstainers had to leave Limu, sometimes with family members or relatives by their side, in order to avoid the ready availability of heroin there and escape the peer pressure to use. The legendary story of Jjike Lassyr, the forty-year-old head of Luja Village in 2005, provides an example. In the preceding chapter I mentioned that Lassyr estimates that he spent nearly 180,000 yuan (approximately $22,500) between 1993 and 1995 on his heroin addiction. His determination to kick his habit earned him the respect and acclaim of his kin and fellow villagers. Here is Lassyr's poignant account of his experience:

> In November of 1995, after the Nuosu New Year, I went to Meigu County to get away from heroin. Heroin was everywhere in Zhaojue County but unavailable in Meigu at the time. My brother-in-law, for the sake of his sister and nephew [i.e., Lassyr's wife and son], accompanied me over to Meigu. My wife sold a pig for 700 yuan and bought two grams of heroin for me to use in a fashion that would enable me to gradually reduce the amount I was using. My heroin addiction was too strong and could not be stopped abruptly. Early on, I divided one gram into ten portions, and later, the second gram into twenty portions. Two months later, I had finished the two grams and bought five boxes of sleeping tablets instead. . . .
>
> I don't remember how I did it. I was going insane. I didn't wear shoes while strolling on the street. My brother-in-law bought me a pair of shoes and cried. I

cried when I saw him crying. I walked to a relative's house in Meigu. A lineage granny killed a pig for me and cried. She said, "Your ancestors were all fine and well. How did you become like this? You are as paralyzed as a wandering dog!" I felt sorry for these relatives. I stayed in her home for two days and nights. On the third day, my brother-in-law helped me get up; I felt like dying. I puked and puked until I threw up blood. I told my brother-in-law, "I am going to die." He said, "If you live, your family lives; if you die, your family dies." I passed out again. . . .

Six months after I went to Meigu, I finally succeeded. I came back to Limu. My mother said joyfully upon seeing me, "You have returned from hell." All my family and kin members cried for me, happily. I swore to my lineage headmen and kin, "I'll kill myself if I use drugs again." At that time, many people claimed to have been successful in stopping their drug use, but they later relapsed. My wife didn't believe me [to be completely clean] and told me privately not to kill the pig for a futile celebration. But I convinced her to kill the pig for our kin. She finally believed me, and tears welled in her eyes.

It is true that many heroin users in Limu were unsuccessful in their attempts at abstinence. Some of them circumvented lineage controls by moving in and out of their communities to avoid punishment. They purposely avoided lineage meetings. This directly challenged the reach and efficacy of lineage control in each village.

Drug problems remained chronic in Limu, and the lineage watchdog system, which seemed to work well early on, eventually fizzled out as internal dissension crept in. Even people who had ended their involvement with heroin found their households still asked to pay fines to the watchdog unit for another member's violations—a situation that gave rise to loud complaints about the unfairness of group punishment and the trouble that a few violators caused entire units.

As more and more lineages and villages tried to control their members only to encounter similar difficulties, Lewu Munyo, who had by this time secured the township government position as the top drug control official, began discussing another grand plan with Limu's headmen.

Joint Township Campaigns

In 2001 Limu peasants began to carry out multivillage and multilineage drug control campaigns, and the local Limu-Hagu Antidrug Association was founded. This coalition of all the lineages and villages in Limu and neighboring Hagu Township was acknowledged by newspersons and Liangshan officials to be the first known grassroots antidrug association in China. Lewu Munyo served as the honorary deputy chair of the association because, as he said, "Although I founded this association, I am a [township] government official and cannot work in a civilian association. Only peasants are eligible."

The support and participation of lineage headmen were the cornerstones of this grand social experiment. Although its drug control efforts crossed the boundaries of lineages, villages, and even townships, its basic control mechanisms and compliance enforcement measures were still essentially kinship based. Most residents in these two townships are related—affinally or consanguineously—so they were not hesitant about cooperating. In March 2001 each household in the two townships contributed 1 yuan to a fund that paid for holding the association's inaugural ceremony. I was told that nearly 1,000 people took part in this event. Local and county government officials also came to lend their support to this regional grassroots antidrug activism.

At the outset association organizers adopted drug-control measures similar to those that had formed the basis of previous single-lineage or single-village efforts, only on a larger scale. For example, Luja Village, with 299 households, was divided into twelve watchdog units, including eleven lineages and one multilineage unit consisting of several fragmented lineages. Each watchdog unit comprised one to two dozen households. The association also recruited groups of eight to ten male villagers, recommended by lineage headmen, as volunteers to patrol public areas and arrest drug users and dealers. Some of these patrolmen were former heroin users themselves and had firsthand experience with the common behavior of delinquents. Upon arresting a user or dealer, the patrolmen could confine the offender in the association's office and charge a fine of 500 to 1,000 yuan. Most of these fines were used to fund the transportation and meals of the patrolmen on duty.

The township government sanctioned the association's instituting its own rules for drug enforcement. The distinction between the state and society in this context is simultaneously clear-cut and fuzzy. In the interests of efficient governance, state agents may encourage local communities to do things beyond the state's judiciary capacity and even beyond the state's legal boundaries. Lewu Munyo, as the official in charge of drug control, distinguished the state's role from the peasants' this way:

> We, as officials, have to abide by state law: we cannot beat the offenders, nor tie them up with ropes. But the state allows peasants in civilian associations (*nongmin*

minjian) to beat and tie up offenders, as long as no deaths occur. Peasants set their own rules, and we in the township government tacitly support them.

Still, the formation of such a large civil association was not without political implications in a state that still embraced socialism, if only rhetorically. Lineage headmen and village cadres had not forgotten how the Chinese government branded Nuosu kinship organizations "feudal" during the Democratic Reform (1956–58) and the Cultural Revolution (1966–76). They moved gingerly and with self-restraint as they mobilized their kinship networks to take a hand in public affairs. This caution was manifest in local leaders' carefully chosen words in their negotiations with state agents. During lineage meetings, headmen and attending cadres would first announce existing state policies related to Limu. In documents the association submitted to government offices, the Nuosu term *cyvi* was translated as the Mandarin Chinese *jiazu*. In academic use, *cyvi* is usually translated as *jiazhi* (literally, *jia* "home" and *zhi* "branch"), not *jiazu*, which denotes Han concepts of lineage. The academic use of *jiazhi* probably reflects scholars' attempts to highlight the particularities of Nuosu kinship organizations and thus to distinguish Nuosu lineages from those of Han society.[2] The headmen's strategic preference for the Han-generic *jiazu* over the Nuosu-specific *jiazhi* was clearly based on their sense of being politically correct:

> *Jiazhi* does not sound good. It brings to the surface bad memories of cyvi being suppressed and headmen being beaten during the Cultural Revolution. At that time, jiazhi was criticized as a feudal remnant whose main function was to engage in local feuds. It also sounds like an organization that is in competition with the village Communist Party branches (*gongdang cun zhibu*). In contrast, jiazu is a friendly, unproblematic term, and thus safer.

To promote its antidrug campaigns, the association adopted a practice Chinese Communists commonly used during the collective era—organizing a performing troupe—which transformed policy pronouncements into public performances. The troupe organizer adapted Nuosu folk songs and dances to antidrug-themed performances that attracted local audiences at Limu's periodic market. Peasants watched the performances for both entertainment and information.

In the beginning the association infused Limu residents and government officials with new hope that the entire community would participate in drug control. Patrolmen worked hard and believed that they were doing a significant job.

According to association statistics, patrolmen arrested seventy-three drug users and seventy-one dealers, as well as confiscating 22 grams of heroin, between 2001 and April 2005. The association also gave classes for arrested drug users. It was said that patrolmen arrested only dealers who were involved in minor drug dealing. People believed, and some association members also confirmed, that "patrolmen did not dare to arrest big-time drug dealers for fear of retaliation." Patrolmen would not respond to this statement but admitted they were unable to deal with desperate drug injectors.

Despite their limitations, the association's achievements received widespread recognition and set an example for grassroots drug control elsewhere in Liangshan and beyond. Many government bureaucracies above the township level paid visits to the association and viewed its antidrug performances. Laudatory remarks from the national government (e.g., praise from Luo Gan, the secretary-general of the Central Commission of Political Science and Law) and the national news media (e.g., China Central Television) elevated the association from a local phenomenon to a model for China's nationwide war on drugs.

State agencies at the township and county levels saw this publicity-attracting association as one of their political achievements; to better impress visitors (most from high-level government offices or major media agencies), the Zhaojue County government helped renovate the association's shabby offices and asked its hard-core members to continue drug control in conjunction with the county government. The association carried out its efforts, driven by both its original motivation and its desire to meet the expectations of higher-level state officials. Besides the superficial office makeover, however, the association received only limited financial support from the government and worked on a meager budget that relied heavily on fines levied against arrested users and dealers. Eventually the association faced controversies arising from its disposal of these funds. Worse yet, it stepped on a political landmine when it exercised authority in direct competition with that of local police working in drug enforcement.

Sandwiched Between the State and Society

By 2004 the endeavors of Limu's antidrug association had begun to lose momentum. There were two main reasons for this. First, the association's enormous financial burdens triggered something near collapse. Even though the practice of fining delinquents and related household units was stipulated in the association's original charter and had been accepted by all lineage headmen as well as the township government, people complained—as before—about the steep fines imposed on innocent households and the elderly. Before long, the association suspended fines for watchdog units, which meant that it virtually abandoned enforcement by means of close-knit kinship and community ties. After pulling the watchdog system from its program, the association continued its efforts by dealing directly with individual users and dealers. Patrolmen still had the power to arrest and fine delinquents, because lawbreakers were afraid that if they did not cooperate, the patrolmen would turn them over to the police.

Despite the revocation of group punishment, villagers continued to question the disposal of the individual fines and expressed their growing distrust of both the cadres and the patrolmen who imposed penalties. Patrolmen had often been seen eating at local restaurants or drinking beer in the association office. People believed they were using fines to fund consumption of what counted locally as luxuries—not for legitimate on-duty purposes. After a while, suspicion of patrolmen ran through Limu peasant society. Local state agents, including the police, officials, and health workers, also criticized the association for its "swindling." On one occasion I listened to a peasant who complained about fines levied by patrolmen and by the police; his comment demonstrates the negative image of state agents and the patrolmen in the eyes of poor peasants:

> The police are corrupt. They fine drug users and dealers and put the money in their own pockets. But they are *guojia* [the state]; they can do whatever they want, and we peasants have no say in their behavior. But patrolmen are not government; they don't have the power to fine people or to use the fines for their own entertainment.

The patrolmen had their own complaints against such widespread criticism. Hielie Yyrre, head of the patrol and also the aforementioned ndeggu among drifting Nuosu youths in Chengdu (see Chapter 2), explained the association's dilemma:

> We [the antidrug association] once asked the county and township governments for money to help sustain our work. But they [the government officials] said, "You belong to *minjian* [the civilian sector] and should serve the people. You have to resolve the funding problems by yourselves." They have state salaries and we have nothing. If they had done their jobs, we wouldn't have had to get involved [in drug control].
>
> . . . I think I am doing a great service for our community, but it turns out drug users and dealers and their families, as well as the military and police

force, all dislike me. . . . There has been a lot of turnover among us patrolmen. Some brothers [patrolmen] became worn out; others left because there were no benefits; still others departed in search of better pay. . . . Many of our wives and children have complained, "Why bother doing it? Do something else to make money!" But lineage headmen have advised us, "Don't give up! Get up and do it!" It's difficult to say what's the right thing to do.

The second reason for the association's diminishing momentum derives from its competition with state authorities—especially with Lewu Munyo and the local police. The association focused on curbing drug use and trade and on rehabilitation. These goals were likewise those of local official antidrug agencies spearheaded by the police. Occasionally, the association outshone the police in terms of the number of heroin users arrested. The patrolmen were also common villagers and members of specific lineages; they had access to insider information that the police, all Han Chinese or Nuosu from other areas, were unlikely to get. Aging parents of drug users might come to the patrolmen and ask them to take their addicted children away because they could no longer tolerate their depletion of already diminished family resources. The patrolmen could arrest users and enforce simple rehabilitation at the association's office. But the same parents might not wish to have their children detained by the police, fearful of long-term incarceration in intimidating state-run facilities. Every now and then, the patrolmen sent tough offenders directly up to the county police office. They bypassed the local township police because of the tense rivalry between these two organizations. And indeed, that rivalry only grew worse as high-level government officials continually praised the association as a grassroots model, at the implied expense of the local police.

Rumors and finger-pointing between patrolmen and local state agents became pervasive. These problems ultimately tarnished the image of the association, which in turn affected the relationship between it and Limu's drug control leader, Lewu Munyo. When, in mid-2005, I discovered that delegates from Muha Village were usually absent from the association's meetings, I asked those who attended for an explanation. An elderly man told me with a hint of hesitation, "That [Muha Village] is Lewu Munyo's territory. His political promotion was based on the successful drug control there, and he is now the deputy head of the township government. How can we control his village?" A founding member of the association, Lewu Munyo now kept his distance because of the patrolmen's controversial deeds and conflicts with the local police; the association had lost its original backer in the township government.

Thus the association lost its legitimacy, which had stemmed from either "traditional authority" or "official mandate." Its ambiguous condition—an ultimately untenable position between society and the state—meant that it drew criticism from peasants and local officials alike. Meanwhile, however, the association continued its operations and remained a positive model for grassroots antidrug campaigns in the eyes of high-level officials. The local government was not happy with the association but did not disband it because of its value as a symbol to the outside world. And local police continued to use the association's records to bolster Limu's drug control numbers.

Community interventionist experiences elsewhere, although not directly related to drug control, shed light on the association's predicament. Research in Africa has shown that indigenous, community-based coping programs may work well in the early stages of a chronic epidemic such as AIDS. Often, however, the implementers of these programs become overstretched and the community's social fabric is torn as the overwhelming reality worsens, leading to local people's disillusionment (Schoepf 2001).

A similar but less severe situation challenged Limu. The ambiguous position of the association as a community organization with law enforcement power—but lacking the legitimacy and funding of a normal government entity—put it in an unfavorable situation relative to both the local people and state agencies. The appetite of association members for drug control diminished drastically soon after the organization's launch. Some cadres left and tried again to deal with the drug problem in their own confined communities; others simply gave up, forswearing any future participation in drug control. The local means of coping with drug problems reverted to the individual village, *she*, lineage, or even families. As of this writing, the broad-based association initiative—acclaimed as the first grassroots antidrug organization in China—exists in name only.

The Political Economy of Traditional Authority

In the midst of the heightened tension between the police and the patrolmen, the Liangshan prefectural government launched a Three-Year War on Drugs (*sannian jindu zhanzheng*) in mid-2005. As the new war on drugs policy unfolded, the township government asked peasants to hold village drug control meetings again. Although the county government had instituted bans on levying fines, in these meetings the township government upheld the discretionary power of individual lineages and villages to establish their own penalty scales.

Fining remained a deterrent approach in Limu's drug control endeavors. Although all villages, under pressure from the township government, once again set up rules for levying fines, village cadres were demoralized by the mixed messages coming from the county and township governments, as well as by past experience. With no real alternatives, village cadres could only urge drug dealers to ply their trade outside their hometowns. "Die outside; live outside. Don't trade drugs at home and endanger your own kin and neighbors," a cadre who was also a headman preached at one village meeting.

Local efforts based on the mobilization of kinship organizations were effective only for a short time. This by no means implies that these organizations have completely lost their authority in Limu. Rather, what I want to underscore is that Limu's broader political economy conditioned the effectiveness of kinship-based social control there. As I will relate shortly, when the township government ordered all villages to reestablish drug control programs following the promulgation of the prefecture's new war on drugs, only one village offered a glimmer of hope in the second half of 2005. Again this was Muha Village, whose kinship-based authority was strengthened by a subtle manipulation of economic interests, and where Lewu Munyo was both the village party secretary and the township government official in charge of the campaign. But even here, the campaign yielded only some positive results, and they did not last long.

To sustain his village's image as a showcase for drug control, Lewu Munyo reformulated his village rules, bypassing the townshipwide antidrug association. Muha was financially better off than the other villages in the basin, having one cement factory and four hot-spring restaurants. With these income-generating enterprises, Muha's steering committee commanded considerable financial resources that could be used as instruments of discipline, something the other villages did not possess.

Lewu Munyo once again used his administrative power to coordinate with lineage headmen in a third wave of drug control. This time, they instituted punishments of even greater severity. In addition to fining individual users or dealers as before, the village steering committee would suspend the factory and restaurant jobs of the delinquents' kin for two or three months, a sanction that entailed substantial loss for the affected families. Muha's steering committee asked each lineage to assemble so that village cadres and lineage headmen could announce the new penalty policy on drug control. This tough new rule pressed lineages harder than ever to control their members.

I attended one such lineage meeting in July 2005. The Hielie lineage had about thirty households in the village, and each household contributed 40 yuan to the meeting organizers so they could buy an ox for the occasion. Approximately 100 lineage members attended. As the meeting began, the headman announced the severe penalties:

> From today forward, we set the rules to punish drug users and dealers. If violators are blind or disabled, we will only fine them. For healthy violators, we will dismantle their houses, confiscate their lands, and expel them from the lineage. . . . It's not that we headmen want to do it. We have to follow the state policy. You young people are all aware of the harm of using drugs. I don't understand why you want to spend a lot of money on it. [A contribution of] 40 yuan is nothing to you young people; but for us elders, 40 yuan can buy salt for a year. We elders don't take drugs but need to pay out compensation money for your misconduct!

A few days after the meeting, the village steering committee penalized the Hielie lineage owing to one member's disobedience. I later met a young man of this lineage who was an employee in the cement factory. He told me village cadres asked ten employees of his lineage to stop working for two months, in accordance with the new rule. The committee also levied a 1,000 yuan penalty on the violator. I asked the young man what he thought of this extended punishment, and he replied, "It doesn't feel fair. But we must follow our village rules. We cannot break the consensus."

To enforce the stringent decisions of the steering committee, Lewu Munyo decided to hold the village headmen's meeting every ten days. Sometimes in these meetings certain headmen might plead for the others' sympathy and a reduction of the penalty, but headmen of other lineages would generally reject such requests. As a headman argued in one meeting, "There is no way to curb drugs if we loosen the penalty. If we don't honor our agreement, I will no longer be involved in drug control. Thus, in the future, if my daughter becomes a drug user, I will not pay fines."

Because of the increased penalties in Muha, for a while drug-related behavior there declined again. Soon after, however, Muha's headmen discovered that their young members were going to other villages more frequently. The headmen wondered, "Since they don't have kinsmen in those villages, how come they go there so often? They must go for drugs!" The headmen began checking young men's bags and pockets upon seeing them return from neighboring villages.

In the beginning, the meetings of Muha Village's headmen were held regularly, but after one or two months the meetings became sporadic. Within a few months, the headmen no longer gathered regularly, and the third wave of drug control in Limu fizzled without explanation. I considered this failure to be reflective of a general pattern in local drug control campaigns: launched with hyperbole and great excitement, the local leaders hoped that the new deterrent program would produce immediate results and that their efforts would pay off in full. But when the measures brought no immediate or tangible results, the leaders soon became disillusioned and too tired or too busy to continue their interventions.

Nevertheless, not all local people became bogged down in failed antidrug campaigns. In 2006, Lewu Munyo gained yet another promotion and moved on to another township. The centralized power of the Muha Village steering committee subsequently diminished. Muha's status as a model village for drug control has faded away because it was the special product of a uniquely charismatic and powerful person's efforts at intervention. More important, the full complexity of Limu's drug problems had been overlooked; those problems far exceeded the capacities of local civilian actors.

Revisited Tradition, Contested Modernity

To comprehend the implications and significance of Limu's hopeful, then bitter, grassroots activism, one must examine the roles of the state and traditional authorities such as kinship organizations and situate them in the changing context of China's modernity paths. One may readily conclude that Limu's arduous efforts at drug control failed. I identify two problems with those unsustainable campaigns: first, the state's habitual top-down and simplistic "model" approach to social replication; second, the withering of traditional Nuosu kinship authority, which had been reconfigured under capricious state governance and the rising individualism that has come with the reform era. These problems set up the initial fleeting success and the eventual collapse of lineage drug control efforts.

The Socialist Model in Neoliberal Capitalism

The state, during the local drug control campaigns, co-opted local society; its antidrug program appeared to provide guidance but offered no real substance. While the state encouraged grassroots campaigns in the interest of ensuring the success of its own war on drugs policy, it proffered few resources to aid local people. The state handed local lineages the unfunded mandate to take care of social problems it could no longer manage directly. Local communities became an arm of the state's enforcement mechanisms, tackling social "delinquents" while remaining subordinate to state power. In other words, the state had neither the means nor the will to help local Nuosu communities function as autonomous and sustainable entities. Where local communities exceeded the bounds of permissible power, conflicts arose between the formal authority (state agencies) and the informal one (local kinship-based institutions). Through an analysis of the state's ambivalence toward this local crisis we can clearly see the ambiguity of the contemporary Chinese state, which is simultaneously socialist and neoliberal, no matter how incompatible these ideological strains may be.

The established way for socialist China to manage social engineering goals, either pragmatic or utopian, was to set up "models" for others to replicate. This model approach simplified the complicated social processes that underlay the path to state-sanctioned goals. This approach generally consisted of two distinct phases. The first was to identify or select a few exemplary models representing success in carrying out a specific task. Once the government identified these models, in the second phase the state's propaganda machines—in the collective era chiefly official newspapers—vigorously promoted them so that other state agents and ordinary people could emulate their practices. Soldier Lei Feng and the mountain village of Dazhai are the two best-known models glorified by the state in the collective era (Diamond 1983). Sometimes the state would even create its own models: for instance, to sustain the image of a model agrarian community, the state provided under-the-table subsidies to the tune of over two million yuan to Wugong Village in the North China Plain during the years of collectivization (Friedman, Pickowicz, and Selden 2005).

In the reform era, state agencies adopted the same approach to the Nuosu grassroots drug control campaigns. The first village in Limu whose kinship-based mobilization displayed a degree of effectiveness won the government's endorsement as a "model village for drug control." The leading cadre in this campaign, Lewu Munyo, was also designated a "model cadre." Owing to his model cadre status, Munyo enjoyed speedy political promotions at a time when other drug control efforts were fizzling. Higher-level government officials expected other villages in Limu to emulate this one-time success and achieve the same results, but they never investigated why this particular village or its lead cadre had been successful. They simply blamed either the local leaders or the peasants for the failure of attempts in other villages. These officials overlooked the broader political-economic contexts in which successful local practices were put to work and did not ask if they were transferable, a problem that Diamond (1983) pointed out as typical of socialist China.

The model approach has also been employed as a justification for state failure at large. This governmentality is similar to what James Scott (1998) calls "miniaturization" in authoritarian states: When grand social experiments fail, their planners retreat to a more easily manageable micro-order, such as a model village or demonstration project that is essentially detached from reality because it is a gross simplification and does not situate itself in a macrosocial context. The miniature model plays into a one-size-fits-all fallacy. The authoritarian state can overlook all local variations or, even after acknowledging variations, sacrifice them for the sake of uniformity. In Limu's antidrug campaigns we see clearly the "model approach" and the "miniaturization process" at work. This governmentality epitomizes the paradox we find in contemporary China: while embracing capitalist development, the state still intermittently resorts to practices entrenched in its socialist past.

The Reconfiguration of Kinship Authority

The second problem area in which to unravel the ramifications of Limu's drug control is that of the changing meanings associated with traditional authority. Traditional authority derives mainly from kinship relationships. Nevertheless, in China's reform era the moral economy of the kinship-based community has undergone a reconfiguration such that more factors mediate the relationship between the individual and traditional institutions.

During the nonstate era, lineage organizations constituted the principal Nuosu social and political institutions. After 1956, the Communist government consigned kinship organizations to obscurity so they would not compete with the state's official apparatus. Ironically, although the state drove Nuosu lineage organizations underground, the collective life worlds of the pre- and post-1956 periods actually had many characteristics in common: in particular, interpersonal relationships were mostly predetermined at birth or by prescribed political standing. During both periods Nuosu people's lives were organized through common rituals that were either religious or political in nature. These rituals celebrated certain social ideals in which group interests trumped individual interests. Under this circumstance, social mobility and voluntary contracts based on mutually agreed upon needs were limited.

With the market reform of 1978, a shift in the ideological paradigm ushered in major social changes. Ostensibly, kinship institutions soon resumed their former prominent status as the moral basis of Nuosu peasants' everyday lives. For example, when two Nuosu strangers meet, they will exchange information about their lineage ancestries to determine their proper relationship. Still, China's market reforms, gradually bringing society into line with neoliberalism, have incrementally altered the social meanings of Nuosu kinship. The free flow of goods, labor, information, and capital has turned the Nuosu people's ways of thinking outward to an expanded economic rationality. In their daily lives, market-based contractual relationships have gradually combined with—or even replaced—traditional kinship-based obligations (Heberer 2005; Liu 2007).

On the other hand, Nuosu kinship organizations may pit local society against state authority because these organizations can mobilize large-scale social activities and define codes of behavior for their members. Therefore, the state must simultaneously encourage and restrain indigenous institutions, depending on whether they help the state or challenge it. The state remains the foremost authority relative to the individual, although Nuosu kinship organizations have reasserted themselves and regained some lost authority. The role of the revived kinship organizations is thus quite delicate. As one village cadre, a respected senior in his own lineage, commented, "We Nuosu cyvi used to be very powerful. But now we can only follow the Communist Party and are no longer as united as before."

Given this delicate situation, the most common kinship-based activities in Limu nowadays are those related to kinsmen's mutual financial obligations, such as funerals, marriages, and accident indemnity, all in the name of lineage solidarity; these all fall well outside the state's major judiciary concerns. More strategically, local Nuosu can transcend actual lineage boundaries to form large support networks of fictive kinship, which expand their pool of collective resources, as mentioned earlier in this chapter. In short, revived kinship activities seem to concentrate on practical and nonpolitical affairs.

.   .   .

In conclusion, the promising rise and premature decline of Limu's community involvement in drug control illustrate the complicated and multilayered factors that entangle Nuosu peasants there. Those campaigns demonstrate the Nuosu's cultural resilience and creativity as well as the moral efficacy of their traditional institutions, but the campaigns' eventual failure points to conflicts of disparate practical interests that have overridden the concern for collectivity. The local community alone simply could not contain the problems that accompanied the trend toward China's increasing globalization—the drug flows, human mobility, and relentless individualization—through the efforts of bare-handed peasants.

This draws attention to the enhanced freedom of choice and increased risks for Nuosu youth, which arose unprecedentedly, took root in the 1980s, and manifested in their migration, drug use, and self-enforced drug control. All these activities point to the significance of individuality in an increasingly precarious world, a factor that certainly was salient but also silent in the local campaigns. Since 1994, the grassroots mobilization, law enforcement actions, and deaths of many young drug users have jointly contributed to a decline in the prevalence of heroin use in Limu. Nevertheless, it lingers on. Younger people continue to take up heroin, and small-scale drug dealings persist in Limu. The question I asked earlier, "As a form of social control, is the kinship institution anachronistic?" remains an open one.

Relationships between traditional Nuosu authorities and the individuals over whom they exercise power reveal yet another conditioning aspect of the revived kinship institutions. Yunxiang Yan (2003) argues that rising individualism has been an unexpected consequence of the collective era, when the authoritarian state successfully transposed individual loyalty from the family to itself. This gave individuals their first opportunity to experience life free from the strictures of the traditional patriarchal family, although they still had to submit to the rules of the socialist state. Yan's argument may not be completely applicable to Limu, however, which presents other historical and social complications. In comparison with mainstream Han areas, the significance of kinship ties remains deep-seated in the mind-set of nearly every Nuosu individual, even though the reach of Nuosu kinship authority has shrunk considerably. In addition, as I mentioned above, the Nuosu's basic way of life during the nonstate and collective eras was essentially the same; in both eras, the Nuosu individual lived within a confined community, a part of the ubiquitous collective body, and so was never truly "free." When Nuosu youth first migrated to cities, however, they entered a stage in Nuosu history that can be described as cultural and economic liminality. By their move from collective living into an urban market economy, they pursued a type of modernity that seemed both exciting and risky.

When asked their opinion of lineage-based drug control, nearly all the young men I talked with answered along the following lines: "Lineage control is useless unless you've already decided to stop." But none of these young men would deny the importance of having kinsmen's, especially their headmen's, support, even if only symbolically. To better illustrate the rising sense of in- dividuality—however ambivalent and vacillating—among the Nuosu youth, I will provide more intimate narratives shared by a few young Nuosu in the next chapter. These narratives about their dreams and troubles reflect the complex web of kinship ties, market forces, and personal will that they must engage in their lives in transition.

4 Contentious Individuality on the Rise

KINSHIP ORGANIZATIONS, religious rituals, and state authorities all played significant roles in Limu's drug control campaigns. My emphasis on structural forces, however, is not meant to diminish the importance of individual agency. A comprehensive analysis of Limu's drug control process is possible only if we fully take into account factors such as the rise of individualism among Nuosu youth. Individual agency was not unknown earlier in Nuosu society. The type of individuality we see among today's Nuosu youth, however, is distinct from that of the past. This emerging individualism is embedded in the political-economic conditions of the transforming Chinese state, moving away from the Nuosu's traditional kinship-based doctrine of a confined way of life. It is only in the era of capitalist modernity that individual Nuosu may perform their individuality, colored by Nuosu sociocultural particularities, in different social contexts. The active involvement of youths in social change is pivotal to the continuity and discontinuity of any authority, traditional or modern.

Research on the Nuosu tends to emphasize the importance of their kinship system while giving short shrift to individual agency.[1] Prior to 2005, my views were close to those espoused in two earlier studies that characterized Nuosu lineages as the most crucial cultural element in successful drug control (Zhang et al. 2002; Zhuang, Yang, and Fu 2005). Later I realized that the conditions described in these studies were not applicable to the Limu I observed. They did not reflect the dynamic social process through which individual youths engaged with lineage authorities and their political-economic constraints.

Today's young Nuosu were born or raised under the new social order of capitalist modernity; their behaviors and aspirations reflect the commercialized cultural norms acquired through mass media and the ever-expanding global market they are eager to take part in. In one important sense, the failure of drug control enforcement in Limu is at least partially attributable to the involved authorities' inability to comprehend or weigh appropriately young people's migration and drug use as an irresistible desire to be modern.

In this chapter, I examine this new individuality among young Nuosu through the stories of four affinal brothers and their sisters. Their lived experiences and personal narratives in large measure articulate the drug problem and provide an immediate sense of their transition from tradition to modernity. The role of young women in the local drug problem is also made evident in these stories. An analysis of their stories reveals how these young people have been drawn into local practices, national politics, and expanding markets as they grapple with forming new personal identities and pursuing shared dreams. They are trying to make sense of the rapidly changing world and create a meaningful life for themselves, even though it is a world over which they and the traditional authorities have little control. In short, I am trying here to situate the stories of these young men and women in wider social contexts so that we can better understand the kinds of individual agency, as well as their limitations, that are contributing to Limu's convoluted process toward capitalist modernity.

Four Brothers

The stories of these brothers showcase kinship solidarity and its limitations in relation to Limu's dual epidemics of heroin and HIV/AIDS. The four brothers' impulses to care, love, and help, together with their anger and helplessness, surface in their simultaneous yet ambivalent embrace of both traditional ways of life and the market economy. Their lives—which they lead in close connection with parents, sisters, wives, other brothers, relatives, and neighbors—illustrate the diversity of social responses to the drug crisis in Limu.

These four young men were among twelve first cousins who were the sons of four sisters from the Hxibi lineage, which originated in Lutu Township in the high hills (see Figure 6). In the Nuosu patrilineal kinship system, maternal parallel cousins are like true siblings even though they may belong to different lineages. These four brothers took different educational and career paths. All of them took or are still taking drugs, and one had tested HIV positive. They had been close since childhood, but between 1996 and 1998 had grown apart because they, along with others of their cohort, were struggling with drug habits. During

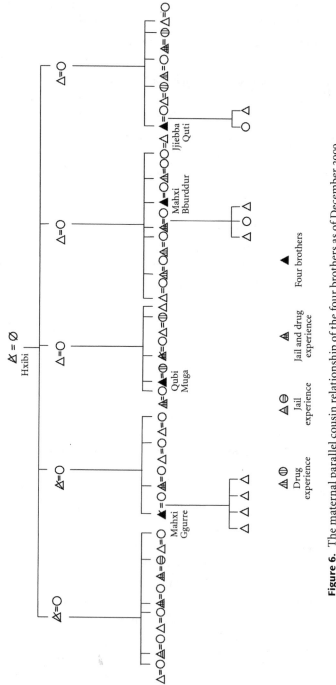

Figure 6. The maternal parallel cousin relationship of the four brothers as of December 2009

this period they did not care much about each other owing to their individual obsessions with heroin. Indeed, drug users' social bonds with family, friends, and even peer drug users are likely to diminish as heroin use increases (Pearson 1987; Pilkington 2006). It was only after several of these twelve brothers successfully broke free of heroin that their close-knit brotherhood was revived.

These young men created a watch group that monitored drug activities among themselves, supplementary to their respective lineage campaigns against heroin use. This represented an additional level of action within Limu's kinship-based efforts in drug control. At the time of my writing, one of them lived at home, one had just died of AIDS, one worked outside Liangshan, and the last was drifting in the city, stealing and taking drugs. As a result of their respective experiences of venturing out, they possessed various levels of fluency in spoken Han languages. The following stories follow their rank in seniority, based on Nuosu criteria rather than age.

Mahxi Ggurre

Ggurre was the oldest among the twelve brothers. He was thirty-three years old in 2005, married with four children. Ggurre was hard-working and well off, simultaneously running a brewery, a pork stand, and a roof-tile kiln. He was illiterate and relied on another brother to do the bookkeeping for his businesses. Even though he fared well, his wife often complained that he provided insufficient monetary support to his family. In this Ggurre was typical of young married men in Limu. They usually thought that a small amount of money should be sufficient for keeping their wives and children and spent the rest of their earnings on their own needs and pleasures with brothers, kinsmen, and friends. Ggurre drank every night with his brothers and male friends in the tiny room where he kept his mobile pork stand.

Ggurre was HIV positive, but none of the villagers discriminated against him. His brothers and neighbors all respected and liked him because of his generosity and easygoing personality. I first met Ggurre at a bimo ritual at Muga's home, where he was helping this brother prepare livestock for ritual sacrifice. It was there that Ggurre learned of my interest in AIDS. After that, on various occasions over the course of 2005, he told me about his experience and perception of the disease.

> I tested HIV positive in 2001. That year, all the adult villagers were called to have blood tests done at the waterfront of Riha Village. . . . A few days later, a

friend told me that my name appeared on the AIDS [HIV positive] roster at the clinic. At the time, I was working as a painter for the township government. The township government would not allow me to continue my work there because of my disease, so I quit. That night, my brothers and friends killed chickens and bought liquor for me. I cried. They said, "You are not acting like a man. How can you cry?" That year, a doctor said I had at most one year to live. Since then, I have lived my life without big expectations.

After becoming aware of his HIV status, Ggurre asked his brothers to buy liquor and kill a chicken for him every day. He told his brothers that he was going to die, so they tried their best to comfort him. On one occasion Ggurre sought treatment from a bimo for his HIV infection; a year passed, Ggurre was well, and no symptoms of illness had surfaced. After listening to Ggurre's story filled with twists and turns, I wondered whether his good physical condition had something to do with the high level of protein in his diet. Eventually, Ggurre declared to his brothers that he was completely cured and no longer had AIDS "in" him. In the same manner he told me, "Five years have already passed, and I am feeling good. I think the doctor misdiagnosed my disease. I don't have AIDS and I don't believe in AIDS." After that, Ggurre worked hard again and launched his pork stand because he wished to have pork readily available for meals: he had greatly enjoyed his yearlong diet of meat dishes. He became the first pork seller in Limu. This is unusual in rural Nuosu communities; usually people kill pigs only for special events such as social gatherings or treating visitors from afar. Before Ggurre opened his pork stand, meat in Limu was served mainly as a symbol of reciprocity among kith and kin.

Ggurre's HIV infection resulted from his heroin injections. He was the first of the brothers to undergo forced drug rehabilitation, administered by his oldest maternal uncle of the Hxibi lineage. This uncle was an important figure among these brothers with respect to drug control, although his approach did not always lead to success.

I first went to Chengdu for fun in 1992. An old auntie from Zhaojue County was selling heroin [yeyi]. That was the first time I saw the drug. Afterward, I spent most of my time seeking fun in Chengdu. At most, I would stay at home for ten to twenty days and then go out again. . . . Heroin was introduced into Limu in 1993. Nearly everybody went to Chengdu to seek fun at the time. . . . Many of my friends I had fun with in the 1990s have died.

In 1995 I began injecting drugs because I didn't have the money to secure enough drugs for smoking. One day in 1997, on my return home, my oldest maternal uncle found me and took me back to his home in Lutu Township. He borrowed a pair of handcuffs from the police to restrain me. He watched me during the day and bought liquor for me at night. Relatives from the Hxibi lineage and neighbors all came over to stay with me at night. My uncle did not allow the other brothers to come over and see me. He was afraid that they would bring me drugs. Five days later, I was clean. . . .

But a few days later at home, I relapsed. My uncle came to Limu and found me again. He confined me in my father's brewery for a day and a night. I broke down the door and ran away to Luja Village and then went to Chengdu. My uncle did not seek me out. But in Chengdu I decided to stop taking drugs. Then I came back home. . . .

I tried three more times to kick the addiction before I finally succeeded. I did it together with six brothers of my Mahxi lineage. We killed a pig that weighed over one hundred kilograms, and our lineage headman also came over to accompany us during the process. He wanted us to swear off drug use and stop drifting. He said that we were too addicted and inhuman. I felt ashamed to be scolded by our headman. But it was so easy to relapse into my habit whenever I saw others using. I forgot my own oaths. After relapsing, I would again want to stop using drugs, and my family would again call our headman over. I let him down many times, but he came over every time I tried to quit. But some other kinsmen did not come again because they were upset at my repeated failure. . . .

Eventually, I did it. But some of my brothers were still using drugs. So in 2001, I proposed a collective antidrug meeting to the other eleven brothers. It was held in one brother's spacious yard on a periodic market day. We bought a big pig that was as heavy as one hundred or more kilograms. Our sisters, married and single, and neighbors brought over twelve boxes of beer in support of our efforts. Aunties and uncles all came and joined us. Over forty people gathered together in the yard. In the meeting, I asked each married brother to contribute 100 yuan to the wife of Jjiebba Quti [a brother; see below]. Her mother had just passed away, and I suggested that we help each other out in the future. And we swore together not to use drugs any longer. We also agreed to send addicted brothers to the rehabilitation center in Zhaojue County for three months, and we brothers would share the rehabilitation expense of 350 yuan. . . . After this meeting, three of the brothers kept taking drugs. We tried to help them kick the habit, but they would always run away and escape our monitoring.

At the end of 2005, Ggurre began working as a foreman for a Han contractor. He took a few young men from Limu to Chengdu for a construction job. He earned double salaries: one for his basic construction work and the second for his work as the foreman of his Limu crew. This job made him happy and energetic. Before he left for Chengdu on this job, his brother Muga asked him, "You have AIDS, so are you sure you want to go?" Ggurre replied with surprise: "You still believe there is AIDS in me?"

Ggurre's naivety and optimism eventually surrendered to AIDS in July 2009. Two weeks before his death, another brother, who traveled with him to work in northeast China, called Muga to meet Ggurre in Beijing. When Muga saw Ggurre, he was already too weak to walk. Muga took him to a hospital in Chengdu that specializes in treating infectious diseases such as AIDS and tuberculosis. After examining him, the doctor advised them to leave without treatment because Ggurre had already reached the terminal stage of AIDS symptoms. Muga recollected Ggurre's response upon hearing the doctor: "This AIDS is real!" Ggurre soon could no longer speak and died a couple of days after Muga brought him back to Limu. Over 200 relatives and neighbors attended his funeral.

Qubi Muga

Muga, my key informant, was twenty-six years old in 2005; he was the most capable and enthusiastic among his twelve brothers. Muga was born in a bimo family and was supposed to take up being a bimo as his career, but he had different ideas about his future. Muga left and returned to Limu frequently to handle various kinds of business. He had many good Han friends beyond Liangshan, so he was sensitive to cultural differences between the Nuosu and the Han. He said that Han people were smarter in business and knew better how to eat diverse kinds of food and keep their houses clean. He wanted to make money and live a Han-style life, modern and hygienic.

At the same time, Muga was very traditional. Every time he returned to Limu, he held a bimo ritual for peace and welfare. He said, "My friends and brothers all think I must have made a lot of money outside so that I can afford to have bimo rituals every time I come back home. It's not true. I want to have bimo rituals regardless of whether I make money or not. Indeed, I might have spent too much money on rituals." Homecoming rituals were a common Nuosu practice to ensure people's well-being and household peace after completing a journey. Given the fact, however, that people come and go frequently nowadays, most

Limu people do not hold such rituals every time they return home owing to cost considerations. When I asked Muga what he hoped to achieve by leaving home in search of income and then coming back to spend the money he earned on homecoming rituals, he smiled in embarrassment: "It's hard to say. But I don't feel comfortable without a ritual after coming back."

Muga was born in the high mountains about 100 kilometers from Limu. He moved to the Limu basin at Ggurre's invitation. Ggurre wanted all his brothers to live close by so they could help each other. Muga moved down first and Jjiebba Quti (another brother) followed suit.

I never went to school, but not because my family was poor. No one in my birth village up in the mountains had gone to primary school; it was too far away. My [paternal] uncle's son went down to the basin area for schooling. I didn't dare to come down because I was afraid of Han people. I cried every time I saw Han people. . . . My father is a bimo. When I was twelve years old, he began teaching me Nuosu writing and bimo practices. In addition to learning to be a bimo, I shepherded some eighty sheep and goats owned by my family.

When I was about fifteen, my father came to Limu to work together with Ggurre's father in a brewery. So I came down from the mountains with him. My life began to change. I no longer wanted to go back to the high mountains. There was nothing to do there. Besides, it was extremely cold. . . .

At the age of seventeen, I stole some green beans from home and sold them at the Zhaojue free market to buy train tickets to Chengdu. I, along with a few Limu friends, wanted to have fun in the city. But our money ran out soon after we arrived in Chengdu. My brothers Ggurre and Bburddur, who had ventured out earlier, looked for me at Chengdu Railroad Station. They gave me money and told me to come back home. But ten days later, again I went to Chengdu. An uncle of my Qubi lineage gave me money to come home. Ten days later, I followed friends to Xi'an to steal for a month and then came back home for the Nuosu New Year. Afterward, I took off to Beijing to steal again. It was then that I began taking drugs. . . .

Eventually I was arrested with five grams of heroin, 8,000 yuan in cash, and four cell phones in hand. The police sent me to the Labor and Education Camp for over a year. The beatings in the camp were horrible! I was beaten for three days and three nights until a Han man I had known saw me. He was like a big brother among the inmates, so I was no longer beaten. Ah . . . but other newcomers were beaten badly and were allowed to eat only once a day. The labor in the camp was hard. That was the toughest period of my life. I was only twenty-three but looked much older when I was released over a year later. I called my Han friends and asked them to come get me at the camp, and their first words upon seeing me were "You look so old!" Later on, I ran a sheepskin and goatskin business with my brother Mahxi Aho in Inner Mongolia. . . . I no longer dared to steal. I was terrified of being arrested again.

Muga did not want to undergo his maternal uncle's method, which he described as "horrible," to break his addiction; he decided to quit by himself.

I decided to kick heroin after I was released from the camp. When I came home, my oldest maternal uncle came to my house and wanted to take me over to Lutu Township. He wanted to do to me what he had done with the other addicted brothers. I had seen him bind the hands and feet of other brothers, and I refused to put myself in such utterly dreadful conditions. I told him I wanted to go to Beijing to free myself from drugs. Drugs were readily available in Sichuan and Yunnan, but not in Beijing. So I went there.

I relied on intravenous drips in a hospital. I told the doctor that I hadn't taken drugs. But the doctor replied to me, "You clearly look like you've taken drugs. Don't worry. I'm not a policeman. If you want to break your drug habit, you have to take some painkillers, not just the drips." So I began taking painkillers. The doctor told me to take them at most twice a day. But the withdrawal symptoms were too painful, so I took the medication three times a day. The doctor scolded me for that. The first two days of withdrawal were the most difficult; the pain was all over my body. Later on, it became easier. I spent six days in the hospital and successfully controlled myself. . . . Then I went home, asserting that I was no longer taking drugs. My uncle did not believe me and still wanted to take me to his home for his brand of addiction breaking. I went with him to Lutu Township for three days and he never saw me taking drugs, so my uncle finally believed me.

Muga's success at breaking his addiction derived from a combination of his amazing self-discipline, the potent biomedical treatment, and his strong traditional beliefs. His level of self-control reflected his bimo training. He had strong beliefs in the power of animal blood and used it to control himself and his brothers.

I didn't attend the Qubi lineage meeting for drug control in 1999. I didn't want to be caught by our headman, so I left home. We follow lineage rules. But actually none of us young men think the lineage antidrug meetings are effective.

Many parents didn't have confidence that their sons could stop taking drugs completely, so they didn't dare to let their sons drink the concoction of chicken blood and liquor that was served at lineage meetings. We believe that drinking this concoction constitutes a serious oath and that all violators of the oath will die. Actually, many young men in Limu who eventually stopped taking drugs have done so without being part of this forced attendance at lineage meetings. You cannot force people to do or not to do something if they don't believe in it. Vows have to come from your heart.

When I came back from Beijing in 2003, I was afraid that I would take drugs again. There were so many friends using drugs at our gatherings in Limu. They always asked me whether I wanted to share drugs with them. So I decided to hold my own ritual to swear off the drug habit forever. I asked Quti whether he wanted to join me. I asked him because he is my brother. I wanted him to seriously think about whether he really wanted to kick the habit. I didn't want him to be sloppy about our private ritual. I told him he would die if he violated his own vow and I didn't want him to die. He considered my proposal seriously and decided to join me.

I called out my name and Quti's name when we mixed the liquor with chicken blood. I swore, "From today on, if Jjiebba Quti and Qubi Muga relapse into drug taking, we will die the day after. In contrast, we will be well and peaceful if we no longer use drugs." We believed in the chicken [blood], and we meant what we said, from our hearts. So since then, neither of us has used drugs again.

Muga often relied on bimo rituals to alleviate his difficulties, illnesses, and welfare issues. Although to my eyes he behaved and dressed in a very modern fashion, he was exceedingly traditional in his inner disposition. But he decided not to become a bimo.

In the year 2003, at the age of twenty-three, I decided not to work as a bimo. You could see that I had changed a lot then. When I was in Inner Mongolia with a few brothers from my Qubi lineage that year, we swore together that we would never take on bimo work as a vocation. We wanted to run a business and make money. Bimo eat and drink in an unhygienic way, and performing rituals is hard work. . . . My father was unhappy with my decision and said that our Qubi lineage is meant for the bimo vocation, so at least one of his three sons must work as a bimo. I gave up. My younger brother Yyhxox is out drifting for fun. My youngest brother Nyonyo wants to study in school and doesn't want to work as a bimo either. I don't know. I don't dare violate my father's wishes, but I don't want to do the job he has been doing his entire life. One of us three must do it, so perhaps Yyhxox can do it when he comes back, or I will resume it after I turn forty.

Muga's hope that his younger brother Yyhxox might undertake the familial bimo vocation never materialized. When I revisited Limu in October 2007, I saw a young man resembling Muga lying in the sun on the dirt ground by Muga's parents' house, in a manner commonly seen in Nuosu villages. I later learned that this was Yyhxox, who had just returned home after being lost to his family for two years and was seriously ill as a result of heroin use. I still remembered vividly how two years before, Yyhxox's father and Muga had had their hands full dealing with the kinsmen of Yyhxox's wife. They demanded that either Yyhxox make an appearance or his wife be granted a divorce with handsome compensation. At last, after months of negotiation with four ndeggu mediating, Yyhxox was divorced from his wife during his absence. This time, with Yyhxox finally back home, albeit ill and dirty, Muga and his father made plans to renovate Yyhxox's abandoned house in order to find him a new wife. Sadly, however, when I returned to Limu in July 2008, Yyhxox's mother told me, in tears, that he had fallen to his death in the spring of that year, leaving behind a small daughter for his elderly parents to raise.

Mahxi Bburddur

Bburddur was the main troublemaker among the twelve brothers. He was twenty-eight in 2005 and had attended primary school up to the third grade. He had been out drifting and using heroin since the age of sixteen and was the most addicted of the twelve brothers and even of most of the youths I came to know in Limu. His family members and brothers had tried many times to help him break his addiction but to no avail. I attended one of his drug-cessation sessions on a rainy night. Many of his brothers, sisters, aunts, uncles, and other kinsmen came over to keep him company. But the next day he found an opportunity and ran away.

One day in late 2005, he injured the muscle around his midriff while engaging in a burglary in Nanjing. He had seen the police coming and jumped from a window to get away. He returned home to recover from the injury. In earlier encounters when we met during his brief visits home, Bburddur had always maintained his distance, even though he was polite; apparently he feared that I was spying on him for the police or the government. It was during his longer than usual stay in Limu this time that I had a chance to talk with him at length. By now, he had heard good things about me from his brothers and neighbors, so in the course of our talk he lowered his guard.

> I began using drugs at the age of sixteen when I went out for fun. At the time, everybody did that, and I thought that's what men should do. So I also wanted to be a man like them. I began stealing the next year and was caught at once. Ha! I came of age in prison. Many young men like me all came of age in jail. The first time I was in jail, I swore I wouldn't steal again. I wanted to stay home and be a good son. But after I was set free and saw my friends migrating out, I simply forgot all those vows. The scenery away from home is better than at home. It's more fun out there. Even if I can't find money there, I still want to go. . . .
>
> I went to big cities to steal because it's not so shameful to steal when you are far away from home. I would feel ashamed if I stole near home. . . . I used to hang around the railway station in Chengdu. Every time I felt like using drugs but was out of money, I went out again to steal. I often injected drugs when I was away. But at home, I usually smoke because my family would get very unhappy if I were shooting up in front of them. . . . My lineage kin and brothers have helped me kick the drug habit about five or six times. They accompanied me day and night, and bought painkillers and sedatives for me. You also came once, I remember. Sometimes the Mahxi lineage headman also came over to watch me. But I have never succeeded in breaking my addiction.

Bburddur spoke fluent Mandarin Chinese with precise pronunciation and intonation, better than many other men who also frequently migrated to Han cities. His language ability suggests good survival skills in the city. However, he also shared characteristics with other Nuosu youths who moved out to Han areas, including their social gathering places and their practice of stealing. Their "ethnic" markers are evident in terms of behavior surrounding drug use.

> I've been to many places, but I have the most friends in Chengdu. I have many Han friends, but I never shared syringes with them. Nuosu and Han people don't use drugs together and don't share syringes. After a Han man uses his syringe, he will either keep it or toss it away, in the same way as a Nuosu. Even if I gave my syringe to a Han man, I don't think he would take it. . . . Why? Maybe he is afraid that we have diseases.

Bburddur was married but childless. He retained his youthful mind-set; that is, he was not ready to settle down and take on adult responsibilities. He said he might stop going out when he became too old to be energetic, probably around thirty or forty. Before then, he simply wanted to have fun.

> I will go out again once my muscle injury heals. Going out and stealing, to me, is just as commonplace as farmers working the farmland. This is my life, and I am used to it. I am accustomed to the life away. I don't have money at home, but there is plenty of money out there. . . . Of course, I'm homesick occasionally when I'm in the city. But once I come home and look in on my family, I miss the outside world again.

People could not restrain or discourage Bburddur from drifting out again and again. But neither his brothers nor other family members were ever hard on him. The strong kinship ties between troubled youths and their kin are their greatest resource once their footloose dreams have been dampened or ended for one reason or another. One month after Bburddur had recovered from his injury and slipped off again, he called Muga from a detention center in Hunan Province and asked for money. He had tried to stab a policeman during an arrest on burglary charges. As might be expected, the police beat him severely. He asked Muga for 3,000 or 4,000 yuan to pay for hospital treatment for his injuries. He had initially called his blood brother, but having no money, his blood brother asked Muga to help. Muga was angry at Bburddur but decided to help because, as Muga sighed, "He is still my brother, no matter how big a mistake he has made."

Jjiebba Quti

Quti was thirty years old in 2005, but he still counted as the "younger brother" of Muga, who was twenty-six, because Quti's mother is the youngest of the four Hxibi sisters. Quti was shy and reticent, so people thought of him as feminine. In contrast, Quti's wife was very "manly," with a robust body and an outgoing and hearty personality—characteristics that, according to Nuosu standards, were masculine. Quti's oldest aunt, Ggurre's mother, often teased him, calling him a henpecked husband. Whenever Quti was teased, he would leave without speaking, wearing a shy smile. I never saw him become angry.

Muga, however, considered Quti to be the most masculine of men in terms of his ability to perform hard work and his knowledge of ritual practices. During the Nuosu New Year, in November, many migrating young men returned home and killed New Year pigs for their families (see Figure 7). There is a specific way to kill New Year pigs, and people believe that any mistake made in the process is a bad omen for the coming year. Some young men who lived near

Quti's house had become accustomed to a Han way of life and were unfamiliar with traditional practices. These men all went to Quti for help whenever they had difficulty sacrificing their New Year pigs. Quti was the most welcome man in the village on such occasions.

Quti once asked me to teach him some Chinese characters. He behaved like a diligent pupil, holding his pencil earnestly. He gave me a broad smile when he saw his own persona become embodied in a few characters inscribed on a sheet of white paper. Even more touchingly, his eyes shone with affection at his daughter's written name. His joy at recognizing words, no matter how limited his ability, showed me what a wonderful thing literacy is to an adult.

> I never went to school because there was no school in the high mountains. In 1995 my big mother [the Nuosu expression for mother's oldest sister] called me down from the mountains to help her in her family's business. I did everything for my big mother—making corn moonshine, tending cattle and sheep, farming, and doing construction work. My big mother treated me well. She bought me clothes and gave me 200 yuan per month. But she put most of the money

Figure 7. Men killing the New Year pig bare-handed

aside in preparation for my marriage. I lived in my big mother's house. . . . In 1996 I spent 2,000 yuan for a bride and killed several sheep and oxen to marry my wife from Muha Village. In total it cost me more than 3,000 yuan!

Quti began taking drugs nearly three years after he came to Limu. He had his first taste of heroin because his big mother was involved in the drug trade. At that time, many people were trading drugs for money.

My big mother was trading drugs when I worked for her. One day, she handed a bag of drugs to me and asked me to dig a hole in the ground and hide it. The government's antidrug enforcement was tightening at that time. I was curious and tasted a bit of it. I fell asleep. When my big mother found out I had used the drug, did she chew me out! She said, "You did not come to Limu to take drugs." She wanted me to return to the high mountains, but I didn't want to leave. . . .

I began using drugs after that incident. Many friends were using drugs, and we all considered yeyi good stuff. . . . I didn't have money because my big mother kept all my earnings. I made some money by mediating between drug sellers and buyers. I never left Limu, so I had a pretty good idea where to buy it in town. And people coming back home from afar needed to know where to buy drugs. So I bought drugs for them and made a small profit. . . .

One day, my oldest maternal uncle came to me and asked, "Aren't you ashamed? You came from the high mountains to use drugs! You have nothing, no house, and no land. You've got to stop!" . . . It was about 1999 when I decided to kick my habit. Withdrawal pains were all over my body, but I overcame them by drinking a lot of liquor at night. My big mother chewed me out again when she saw me drinking like crazy. . . . I also took painkillers. Ggurre [the oldest of the four brothers] bought me painkillers in Zhaojue. He had already kicked his habit by then. My efforts seemed to be successful. Later, Muga asked me to swear permanent abstinence from drugs with him. That night, I lay in bed thinking sadly: I have nothing and my families still live in the mountains. I felt sorry for my big mother and my oldest uncle. I truly wanted to get off drugs. So I joined Muga and since then have never used again.

In August 2005, Quti followed a foreman from Limu to Chengdu to work on a construction project. He returned at the end of October, before the Nuosu New Year. The night of his return, Quti's brothers, sisters, parents, and I gathered in his shabby house and listened to him recount his urban experiences. He had worked in Chengdu for three months but returned home with only

100 yuan in his pocket. He told us he had spent the rest of his money on transportation, cigarettes, food, and some entertainment. He even spent 12 yuan on admission to the Chengdu Zoo. As he talked about the tigers, lions, and other animals he had seen there, everybody listened attentively because they have never seen such exotic animals. Quti's wife did not blame him for bringing back almost nothing; instead she was also quite interested in his adventures. Despite the lack of tangible monetary profits from this venture, Quti concluded, "It was fun out there in the city." From that time on, Quti continued to work construction jobs in the city.

.   .   .

These four brothers exemplify the experiences shared by most of Limu's young men. They are constructing the meanings of life for themselves under circumstances their kin simply cannot control. They experiment with novelty, pleasure, and new lifestyles and in the process change their personal identities and relationship with Nuosu traditional institutions and practices. These activities constitute a life-transition process that many people around the world have engaged in during their youthful years. Their pursuit of footloose experimentation clearly demonstrates what we may recognize as the deep-seated yearnings of individuality: the more constraints they face, the more eagerly they dream of living somewhere beyond Liangshan. These four brothers, like other young men in Limu, took the initiative in exercising their youthful agency. Certain of their Nuosu sisters followed suit. But the individuality and agency of young women have yet to attract the attention of Limu's lineages in their grassroots drug control efforts.

Locating Women in Local Development

Gender roles in Nuosu society are basically segregated, especially in public activities. Unlike men, young women have been overlooked in local drug control campaigns—not because young women played no role in the local crisis but because their social roles rendered them virtually invisible in kinship-based and male-dominated activities. The social invisibility of women in Limu created many obstacles to my already difficult entry into the field.

The Researcher's Gender and Its Implications

Being a woman, or more precisely, having a situated female gender role, may affect the experiences of anthropologists conducting ethnographic fieldwork in different research settings (Golde 1986). My interaction with male and female drug users or dealers has been influenced in great part by the gender role I played in various daily-life situations in Limu. Social construction and its processes are crucial elements in exploring gender issues. "That gender is not fixed in advance of social interaction, but is constructed in interaction, is an important theme in the modern sociology of gender" (Connell 1995, 35). Social interaction is entwined with broader patterns of meaning and power that intersect with other sources of stratification such as identity and status (Lewin 2006).

In Limu, I was categorized by the local Nuosu as an in-between gender. This liminality was at times advantageous, providing me a situation not dissimilar to that of Nader in Mexico and Lebanon, where she was respected as a woman and yet regarded as different from ordinary local women, and as such had access to local men's culture (Nader 1986). Although I did not intend to behave like or identify with local men, I was sometimes treated by them as an "honorary male" (Tedlock 2003). I unintentionally acquired this honorary male status because they saw me as socially different from their own women and hence accepted me in some of their activities and conversations that usually involved only men. As the local men often stressed, "[Local] women can't join [in this occasion], but you can." Owing to their generally inferior social status in many societies, woman ethnographers often equip themselves with a high level of empathetic understanding of vulnerable peoples (Tedlock 2003). Since I belong to a gender that is less intimidating to local young men, they felt less embarrassed to expose their weakness and ignorance in front of me than in front of local men and women. Despite the occasional frustration or unsuccessful effort, I and my research were generally respected and accepted by local Nuosu men.

What restricted my interaction with women in the field, however, was likewise due to my role as a "gendered knower" (Callaway 1992). Local cultures do not encourage women to pursue daring adventures, much less anything labeled as socially negative. In Limu I found that, unlike the men who were the main focus of my research, most of the young women began their involvement with drugs after heroin use had already morphed from being fashionable into being deviant. Therefore the stigma associated with involvement in drugs, together with women's generally inferior status, impacted the way in which they related to drugs as well as their self-perceptions, and this tended to make them reclusive. Oftentimes young women who were rumored to be involved with drugs did not welcome me the way their male peers did, and they tended to be more defensive and reluctant to answer my questions. Moreover, like other women and men in Limu, these women thought that I was really different from them.

In their eyes, I was better off, independent, and highly educated, seemingly knowing about both the Han and Nuosu cultures. And even worse, I was a mature woman yet had no children, a major deviation as compared to their own lives and expectations concerning adult roles.

My limited language skills plus the Nuosu's gender segregation further compounded the problem of gaining access to women during my field research in 2005. My Nuosu language skills improved as my fieldwork went on, yet they were still not sufficient for me to engage in conversations involving complex or delicate issues. The great majority of Limu women did not speak Han languages. Even primary school–educated young women could not express abstract ideas in rudimentary Han languages. This frustrated my ongoing search for female interpreters; I could find only male interpreters, who were wont to make comments and to engage in public discussions. My attempts to approach local women were thus further complicated: young Nuosu women were simply too shy and reluctant to talk with men, my male interpreters included, because of the strong sexual taboos and strict gender segregation. The socioeconomic gap, while not inhibiting my research relationship with local men, seemed also to make establishing a feasible relationship with local women more difficult. In the initial stages of my fieldwork, therefore, my attempts to make women visible and vocal were significantly limited.

Women's Invisibility and Their Yearning

Women have been playing an increasingly important yet overlooked role in Limu's contemporary development. Nuosu society seldom treats women as real participants in public affairs. As a rule, only women who have children may attend their husbands' lineage meetings. Married women change their lineage status to that of their husbands in accordance with customary law and after bimo ritual practice, although they maintain ties with their original lineages. Young and unmarried women generally do not attend lineage meetings. Even if women are present at this sort of public gathering, they usually cluster on the margins, listening to headmen and the other men talk without making any public comment. Men do not expect women to speak in public because, according to a headman's blunt explanation, "Women can only chitchat about insignificant topics, making no real sense. They don't know how to deal with important issues."

Given this gender-based exclusion, women typically acquire important information only indirectly. Occasionally men may pass something they hear in meetings on to their wives, and the wives may in turn pass it on to their daughters. The circulation of information in this manner is often contingent, incomplete, and subject to distortion. Take the causal link between drug injection and HIV infection as an example: Some women learned from their men—and believed—that HIV exists in the drugs themselves because "only drug users fell ill [i.e., became HIV infected]." Thus women's exclusion from health-information networks can have dangerous ramifications, since young women are also at risk of HIV transmission, from sexual contact as well as from their own drug use.

A growing number of Nuosu women followed their men into migration, drug use, and trade. The isomorphic subordination of women to men in these activities explains why women had yet to form their own gender identity in this life transition or attract the societal and official attention of drug and AIDS interventions. Furthermore, during my stay in the field most of the migrating women did not return home for long stretches. Thus my knowledge about young women on the move or involved in drugs was limited by the infrequency and brevity of their home visits. I had no success trying to get at and understand their lives in any comprehensive way until the later phase of my residence in 2005. Fieldwork is a series of trials and errors, with the occasional lucky break.

On the day I had a breakthrough, a woman drug user and Muga's close neighbor, Hlyjy Axi, had come back from Chengdu. Muga knew I was eager to talk to female drug users, so he took the initiative to approach this young woman and convinced her that I was harmless and friendly. She was persuaded and agreed to talk to me. Later on, with her help, I met another young woman, Hielie Aga, who happened to be home visiting her family for two weeks. Aga was married to a man in Limu and often went with him to Chengdu. I spent the entire two weeks with them and came to rely on Aga's language skills to mediate my conversations with still other young women, including another neighborhood girl and two sisters of the four brothers profiled above. Their narratives, mostly recorded in 2005, are brief but reveal their perspectives on local drug issues and the insufficient attention local and state drug control agents have paid to them. They expressed their confusion, fears, and desired options, which bear a certain resemblance to those of their male peers.

Aga spoke excellent Mandarin, partly owing to her extended stay in Han areas. She sold drugs in Chengdu with her husband, who was a heroin addict. To me Aga appeared to be smart, capable, and beautiful, and I assumed that she could have had a better life in Limu had she not been married to a drug addict. But this assumption turned out to be my own wishful thinking. Aga, like many of her male peers in Limu, wished to have a materially improved life with little concern for the legality of making this livelihood possible. She put it in a straightforward manner: "My family was too poor to allow me to continue my education in junior high school. . . . I wanted to make a lot of money and have fun. There's nothing [profitable] I can do at home." In fact Aga realized her dreams by following her husband. She was quite well off thanks to this profitable business, and she ostentatiously wore gold earrings and had gold rings on her pretty hands.

Other young women who stayed behind in Limu were similarly unsatisfied with their stagnant condition. "It's hard to be a woman here. We have to do everything, but men only need to earn money," declared eighteen-year-old Anyu Ayi. She uttered these words at a gathering where five young women and I were talking. Ayi, like most Nuosu girls, had been engaged during childhood, but she was reluctant to marry her fiancé. She complained, "His family owns a lot of farmland. If I marry him, all the work will be dumped on me alone. I can't take on so much hard labor. So I don't want to marry him." Ayi's fiancé was away drifting, but she could not break up with him since her family has already received the bridewealth during the childhood betrothal. In traditional Nuosu culture, children become engaged (actually, "married" by local standards) when the boy's family has paid the betrothal money. But the wife must not live with her husband until a few years later. There is no fixed rule as to the time of cohabitation by the couple, which depends mainly on their ages, bilateral familial obligations, and the woman's own will. Between the betrothal and cohabitation, however, the husband's family has the right to demand the wife's labor for farm work and other chores. This Nuosu custom is still widely practiced in rural Liangshan and this continues to grieve countless young people who have no affection for the spouses selected by their parents.

Ayi was not alone in complaining about her limited opportunities in life. Other girls growing up in Limu also wished to trade their rural lifestyle for a "modern" one. Muga's sister, Qubi Arryr, who was twenty years old in 2005, was married to her husband when her family still lived up in the high mountains. This marriage was in effect even though Arryr had moved down to the Limu basin with her natal family, which made Arryr more "modern" than the high-mountain dweller to whom she was engaged. She explained to me, "I don't like my husband's place. It's up in the mountains and living there is very inconvenient." Given the gap in their life experiences and expectations, Arryr divorced her husband in 2005, after having lived with him for just one year. Her divorce meant that 10,000 yuan had to be paid in compensation by her natal family. Jjiebba Nyonyo, twenty-three-year-old sister of Jjiebba Quti (one of the four brothers discussed earlier), divorced her husband for the same reason in 2004. Many years after moving to the Limu basin with their natal families, these young women adamantly refused to move back and live in the high mountains. Their commonsense view was that moving to cities was the goal to be coveted—the direct opposite of moving to a locality even "worse" than rural Limu. They also yearned to see the outside world, having heard their brothers' accounts of urban adventures.

These women never attended any of the lineage meetings about drug control. Neither did the kinship-based intervention efforts aim to reach them. Hlyjy Axi had been taking heroin for about two years. She picked up the habit at home while hanging out with young male relatives and friends who had returned from the cities. To sustain her habit Axi began dealing drugs, mainly in Chengdu but sometimes at home.

> In Chengdu, we buy drugs from Nuosu, never from Han people. We sell only to Nuosu. We are afraid of the Han, who might be informers [to the police]. Most drug dealers are women because men can do burglary and we women can't. . . . It's too difficult to get off drugs. Many of my [male] friends use drugs. So . . . I'm resigned. . . . It's fun to use drugs. With drugs, all my dreams are nice.

In the eyes of her neighbors, certainly, Axi was not a good girl. She was fun seeking, an extrovert, and had been dating men outside her marriage bond since childhood—characteristics of a loose woman by local standards. Presumably because of her unusually open style in Limu, Axi expressed her friendliness to me in a direct manner. She gripped my hands whenever she saw me, and chatted with me in Nuosu whether I understood her or not. She seemed lonely as she had to live with the tacit judgments of her lifestyle in the neighborhood. Axi often took heroin with her male friends, and her widowed mother could not control her. Axi's male drug-using friends described her to me as a "bad woman," implying that Axi engaged in sex in exchange for drugs. I heard of occasional sex trade associated with addicted women; but given the fact that many drug-using women had followed their male partners in these adventures, the sex trade had not become a significant means of getting by among Limu's young people.

It is hard to be lucky when one is involved with drugs. When I returned to Limu in the spring of 2009, I heard about Axi's most recent troubles. One day in the autumn of 2008, after toiling in the rice paddies for a whole day bringing in the harvest, Axi returned home with a few young men and they started using heroin together. The local police suddenly broke in and arrested them all red-handed. Axi was sent to jail, and I have not heard word of her since learning this news.

Not only "bad" girls used drugs or behaved erratically; even ordinary girls might get involved with drugs. Arryr and Nyonyo told me that they had once taken heroin behind their brothers' backs. Arryr admitted:

> I felt like using drugs when I saw my brother Muga take them. But I didn't dare to ask him for drugs. I was afraid he'd scold me. But I got into his drugs secretly three times. It was fun, but it also gave me a headache. I haven't used since Muga stopped taking them. I had neither the money nor the guts to buy my own [drugs].

Likewise, Nyonyo stole her brother Quti's drugs, although she was aware of their side effects. She had seen how her father tied Quti's hands and feet to force him to break his addiction, and she described the treatment as "terrifying." But the potentially deadly curiosity common among male Nuosu youths had grabbed her. Other girls told me privately that Nyonyo was still using drugs secretly, but she made no mention of that to me.

One day in early 2006, Arryr and Nyonyo disappeared. Eventually their families learned that they had traveled to the coastal province of Guangdong to work in a garment factory. A neighbor came across them by chance near the railway station and later told the families their whereabouts. In the summer of 2006, Arryr returned to Limu during my visit there, and I asked her about her experiences working in the factory. She told me that she and Nyonyo had followed a male friend who had contacts in that garment factory. Arryr worked there for four months, but she had no idea where in Guangdong Province it was. Four months later, she returned home and declared that she did not want to go out again:

> It's no fun. We had to work nonstop. No weekends. The monthly pay is 600 yuan. But I needed to pay 800 yuan to the guy who took me over there. The factory manager gave us toothpaste, a toothbrush, and chopsticks and then deducted the cost from our salaries. So I brought home only about 1,000 yuan after working for four months. There were over two hundred Nuosu boys and girls working in the factory. But we didn't have time to have fun together. Nyonyo is still there because she didn't make enough money to buy the train tickets back. She asked for too many days off, so the boss deducted a large portion of her wages.

Among these five young women, Anyu Ayi was the youngest and had never been involved with drugs or migration. But she also yearned to see the outside world and said that she would seize the opportunity if, someday, someone would take her there. Ayi is typical of the growing number of young women in Limu who are likely to migrate along with men and are at risk of picking up a drug habit or contracting HIV during their adventures. These problems have profoundly affected some young women but have remained below the surface in Limu's efforts toward drug control.

Becoming Independent and Endangered

To underscore the importance of human agency in migration, researchers have called for a gender-sensitive approach in migration studies (Willis and Yeoh 2000). Gender relations may shape the differences that separate female migratory motivations and patterns from those of men and they may be modified during and after migration. A gender-sensitive approach also reveals migration to involve both an ongoing process of constructing the migrants' gender and the unraveling of each gender group's everyday internal heterogeneity (Hibbins and Pease 2009). This line of argument offers a humanistic perspective on human mobility rather than merely focusing on economic motivations as traditional demographers have done.

Among the young women moving to the cities from China's vast rural areas, marriage and its implications seem to be an important concern. Pun (2005) describes how *dagongmei* (female migrant workers) who leave their rural villages to work in urban-based factories between puberty and marriage consider working in the city as a time to exercise "freedom" beyond their villages and even outside marriage. Hyde's female entrepreneurial informant opened her own business in a migrant town and decided not to marry because "marriage only makes women into chattel and slaves" (Hyde 2007, 175). These women took chances, experimenting with new ways of life once they had moved out of their traditionally confining circumstances.

Nuosu women's involvement in drugs is often influenced by their male partners, to whom they are supposed to be subordinate. This involvement, however, may lead these women to reflect on their own lives and their relationships with men. In other words, no matter who initiates the movement away from home and all that entails, these women's new engagement in life suggests experimentation to them. They may begin selling drugs in response to their men's pressure for financial support. At times, however, women may also use this profitable small business to become financially independent. Their desire for independence, socially and financially, is often associated with an intention to leave their men. Vugo and Ami exemplify this conditional individuality.

Vugo was twenty-seven and brought her two-year-old daughter to Chengdu's South Railroad Station to sell drugs. I spotted Vugo and her chubby baby girl near the station in 2007 when she smiled at me. She recognized me as someone who had spent a lot of time in Limu. Vugo's husband had been executed by court order in 2006 for trafficking 16 kilograms of heroin. When I asked why she was there, Vugo pointed to her daughter and said, "Her father died. I have no alternative!" As Vugo told me more about her decision to sell heroin in Chengdu, I sensed her desire for adventure and independence:

> After her [the baby's] father died, I didn't want to be transferred [remarried] to his lineage brother.[2] We have to live on. I tried to find a job at a construction site and made less than 5,000 yuan in five months. But others who sell drugs can make 2,000 yuan in a single month. So I wanted to follow suit.

Vugo was off to a difficult yet new start in the city. At my request, she led me to her temporary home behind the railroad station. It was an extremely shabby room located in a large and dilapidated housing compound. The Han owner had built a couple of makeshift row houses in the compound, and nearly all the tenants there were Nuosu. Vugo shared a room with another woman from Limu and each of them paid a monthly rent of 25 yuan. Despite its dirt, dimness, and shabby conditions, this room provided Vugo and her daughter with a new start in life, by means of which Vugo hoped to make money through drug dealing and escape the pressure to remarry.

I did not stay long with Vugo because she needed to get back to business, morning being the most active time for drug dealing around the station. Young Nuosu men who engaged in burglary at night or the pickpockets working in the early morning had just returned. It was time to trade food and drugs to these men for their newly acquired loot. While walking with Vugo away from her residence, I bumped into three Nuosu young men jubilant at their recent score. An hour earlier, the three pickpockets had made off with more than 2,000 yuan and one cellular phone downtown. They had just returned to celebrate. Vugo greeted them happily and together they withdrew from my sight to somewhere in the compound.

Likewise, Ami took off to Chengdu to leave her heroin-addicted and HIV-infected husband. Her husband had used up all their savings and property on heroin and often forced Ami to make money to support his addiction. When I saw Ami selling drugs at Chengdu's North Railroad Station in 2007, she had been there for almost two months. I was surprised to see her without her husband since, in my memories of Limu, she was a tiny and somewhat timid woman. More important, I knew that Ami was HIV positive, having contracted the virus from her husband. She began taking antiretroviral medication supplied by the China-UK Project in mid-2005. Her self-imposed removal from supervised medication worried me. Her response:

> I have no alternative. He [the husband] was still using drugs and beat me every day. I've got to feed my kids, so I followed relatives to do business here. I left the other kid with my parents. . . . [*looking at the daughter she holds*] No alternative. We both fled here. . . . I am still following the doctor's instructions for AIDS medication. You see . . . [*She showed me enough antiretroviral drugs for a month's use in her bag.*] We Nuosu will have a hard time getting a divorce. I don't have money to compensate [my husband] for the divorce. . . . I just don't want to go home. He beat me every day.

Ami had changed from a timid woman to a courageous one after two months in Chengdu. She had a cellular phone and had learned some Mandarin Chinese. As the income she made through drug dealing increased, she became assertive about pursuing her own life without her husband. Although Ami worked her drug trade under the aegis of a man from Limu, she represents the type of women who are ready to embark on their own journeys toward individuality and look forward to a better life ahead.

Unfortunately, a year after I saw her in Chengdu, Ami died, presumably of AIDS. One day in the summer of 2008, as her health was rapidly declining, the big-time male trafficker she worked with inquired about where he could find an "unlicensed" AIDS doctor in Chengdu. It goes without saying that he did not find one. Ami and her daughter were immediately sent back to Limu and she died the day after returning home.

The female side of the issues of drug use and AIDS has received only casual consideration in the context of local drug control efforts, and my treatment of this subject does not go far beyond that. From my limited opportunities to talk to a few women involved in migration and drugs, what I learned was insufficient for me to reach any definitive or analytical conclusions concerning their present and future life trajectories or the influence of their experiences on local gender relations. Still, despite the brevity of the discussion offered here, it is clear that young women's rising expectations and assertions of individuality, exemplified in these personal stories, will play a more than passing role in shaping these dual epidemics in the foreseeable future. I was told that, in September 2006, around sixty female drug users and dealers who had just returned from the city because of heightened drug enforcement there had been arrested in Limu. It appears that migration and drug involvement will become part of the life-course transition for young Nuosu women just as it has among male youths. Young women in Limu are gradually joining their male peers in an epochal transformation filled with opportunities and uncertainties.

5 Failed State AIDS Intervention

IN 1997, when local Nuosu people were engaging in their kinship-based drug control, Limu reported its first case of HIV infection caused by drug injection. The next year the state launched its investigation into the township's heroin-related HIV/AIDS problem. During the first stage of its investigation (1998–2000), the Liangshan Prefecture government worked with an international organization, Médecins Sans Frontières (MSF). After MSF phased out its operations in Limu, the China-UK Project was established there and in other localities in Sichuan and Yunnan provinces in December 2000. The China-UK Project was sponsored by the Department for International Development (DFID), an official British aid agency, in cooperation with the Chinese government.[1]

This project aimed at helping China curb the spread of HIV and upgrading its capacity to cope with future epidemics. Between 2001 and 2006, the China-UK Project was the leading AIDS intervention agency in Liangshan and in Sichuan Province as a whole, in terms of scale of funding and social issues covered. This project outshone Chinese government–funded AIDS projects and exerted great influence on HIV/AIDS prevention practices in the province (Lan et al. 2005). Still, five years after its first blood-test drive in 2001, as its programs were about to be phased out in Limu, the HIV/AIDS situation in the township remained grave. The project had yielded few positive results. The entire project team, from the prefectural officials down to the township health workers, all privately acknowledged that the project's intervention in Limu had been a failure.

Why did this well-intended and well-funded AIDS intervention project fail to improve local health conditions? This chapter delves into its local operations for an answer. More important, I will show that this failure cannot be located in the particulars of that single locality or its unique Nuosu characteristics but must be understood within the broader context of reforming China's multi-faceted global engagement.

The implementation of an international aid project in China is necessarily a highly politicized process. According to a bilateral memorandum, the China-UK Project was to apply successful international AIDS intervention practices in various branch projects in recipient communities. A premise of this proposal was that these practices would be applied in a manner consistent with Chinese conditions (China-UK 2000, 4). In other words, local implementation of the international health project would be contingent upon multilayered considerations, whether political or practical; in this sense it was reminiscent of the top-down bureaucratic operations the Chinese state had been using since the collective era.

In studying the Chinese government's responses to AIDS, Sandra Hyde points out that the state is not a monolithic or unified agency and must be "disaggregated into everyday dynamic practice in order to fathom the logic of disease control" (Hyde 2007, 23). My examination of the China-UK Project in Limu reveals the same complicated interactive patterns among diverse state agencies at different levels. In China, any foreign intervention, especially at the rural-local level, must be filtered through state agencies for approval and implementation. The Limu project was one of numerous state projects planned and implemented from the top. Needless to say, the way local state agents executed a project might not be in complete accord with what project planners at the provincial or national levels had in mind. Likewise, the higher-level state officials often implement and evaluate local projects in a generic manner, with little attention to local needs and conditions (Lan et al. 2005). These gaps between the various levels of state agents were detrimental to any project.

It was the lowest-level state agents who operated Limu's China-UK Project. Occasionally the project's national office sent high-level officials, such as externally recruited consultants or researchers, to local project sites for inspections and evaluations of project progress. To state agents at the bureaucratic bottom, whether the intervention was initiated by the Chinese government alone or in collaboration with international counterparts made little difference. Oftentimes, local project workers were not kept in the information loop. As one China-UK Project worker complained to the project's evaluators, "The project officers seldom passed on [evaluation results] to us. . . . I feel we are just coping with supervision and evaluation from above blindly" (Lan et al. 2005, 26). As a result, the frontline workers' practices followed entrenched patterns of the official work style at the local level.

This bureaucratically distorted or diluted process of implementing a project issued from the top is not uncommon. We must pay heed to the local politics that play a critical role in shaping a project's trajectories and its often unintended consequences. Morgan's research in Costa Rica provides another example, in that internationally funded health projects there bore only "a perfunctory resemblance to original international formulations" (Morgan 1993, 10). There, as in China, projects were likely to be filtered through the host state's bureaucratic hierarchy, whose domestic conditions and competing political interests significantly affected the project's implementation. The particularities of the China-UK Project in Limu were significantly affected by the Nuosu's peripheral position in the country. This sociocultural and political-economic marginalization is at play everywhere in state governance and state agents' practices at the local and everyday levels.

Based on my understanding of the political process, I attribute the project's failure in Limu to two critical problems: bureaucratic inadequacies and state agents' cultural incompetence. These two problems can be traced, in turn, to the shift of China's development paradigms from socialist modernity to a market-driven ideology. Bureaucratic inadequacy was an obvious problem of which many of the state agents involved were aware; after all, their work suffered from its consequences, too. In contrast, the harm caused to project implementation by state agents' cultural incompetence was not as apparent. State agents generally failed to be aware of that harm because of their dogmatic espousal of a commitment to "science," the officially sanctioned rationality that has dominated the periods of both socialist and capitalist development.

One episode in particular guided my investigation into the roots of this failure. One autumn afternoon I was sitting with several health workers in the courtyard of the Limu Township Clinic, just as I had done on many other days in 2005. The workers were playing chess and drinking beer to pass the time. Ddisse Munyo, the thirty-two-year-old head of the clinic, complained to me about the work orders he had just received from high-level government offices. He ascribed the China-UK Project's failure to government officials' ignorance of current health-work problems:

> How can we handle so many requests from above? They don't give us sufficient operating funds. We have to focus on treating patients in order to earn

our own revenue. As for public health education and vaccination, we can perform them only sporadically, depending on whether our budget can finance them and whether the superiors have requested them. . . . Peasants now have many muddled ideas. They may even accuse us doctors of malpractice if their children show some side effects after vaccination. They lack both *quality* and *knowledge*. . . . The high-level officials also want us to do extra work, like the China-UK Project, and write additional reports. . . . We don't have sufficient time and resources to accommodate so many demands. The county-level [official] agencies are at their best when they bully subordinates and hide their own inadequacy from the officials above them.

Munyo continued, in a tone of exasperation:

They [high-level officials] sit in their comfortable offices and do nothing but wait for our progress reports on the China-UK Project and on public health. What can we do? Just fabricate the data! Actually everybody [in the government] adds water to the data pool because no one has time to collect the real data the high-level office wants. As we add more water to the data pool, the water will carve out its own course [*shui dao qu cheng*]!

With even greater agitation, Munyo continued his comments, probably because I was paying close attention to him and he was encouraged by the other health workers' vocal agreement with his complaints:

In the past, health care service was a *political* mission. Cadres did it without considering any personal gain. Now it is a major source of *economic* revenue. Nothing can be done without money. The market reform policy has its positive and negative consequences, like two sides of a coin!

Shifts in Development Paradigms and Changing Health Care

The establishment of a socialist health care paradigm in Limu and its subsequent shift to a market-driven orientation has brought about not only science-based rationality but also drastic changes in social relationships. The first paradigm of modern socialist health care emphasized "prioritizing prevention" and "serving the people"; both practices provided political legitimacy to the state as it mobilized limited national resources and its vast population for promotion of the public good. The state organized rural areas into standard cellular communes and integrated health care into the overall collective way of life. Through medical

modernization and socialist collectivization the state attempted to replace traditional Nuosu health practices with science-based knowledge.

Since the market reform took off in 1978, however, the Chinese state has gradually and gently brushed aside its former commitments to egalitarianism and
the official prioritization of public health. This paradigm shift has turned health
care into an entity apart from local community life—a luxury. This transition
took place in part because China adopted strategies advanced by U.S. propo-
nents of privatized health care (Blumenthal and Hsiao 2005). The central government introduced financial decentralization and passed fiscal responsibility
on to local governments, from the provincial level down to the townships, in the
1980s (Tang and Bloom 2000). Since then, all state agencies have had to compete
for political credit and funding sources to support their own operations. The
social relationships among state agencies, which used to revolve around the central government's directives and resources, have since given way to the market
principles of competition and profit maximization. These changes have resulted
in the state's failure to mobilize its official agencies and common citizens for the
sake of the public good. The idea of a collective entity, whose well-being relied
largely on concerted action by citizens, has ceased to be a major concern among
many state agents, although the idealist slogan "Serve the People" is still periodi-
cally invoked in the party-state's rhetoric in order to legitimize its own existence.

In addition to changes in social relationships around community health
care, the state agents' condescending attitudes toward locals or local knowledge
further compound the problems of Limu's official health interventions, such as
the China-UK Project. In effect, state agents have little respect for local peasants
and are unlikely to engage them in joint coping strategies in the face of local
epidemics. Their dismissal of the important role that local social institutions
can play in intervention has led them to mechanically transplant their projects
to Limu without making adjustments to suit local circumstances. This is precisely the situation that James Scott has commented on: "A mechanical application of generic rules that ignores these [local] particularities is an invitation to
practical failure, social disillusionment, or most likely both" (Scott 1998, 318).
Although state projects may aim at improving local living conditions, Scott
stresses, they often fail owing to the gaps between the scientific knowledge espoused by state agents and locally situated knowledge.[2]

Even worse, as research has demonstrated, developers often blame their intervention failures on traditional culture. Claiming the latter to be a crucial barrier to development reveals the developers' unwillingness to reflect on their own

harmful detachment from local knowledge and practices (Appadurai 1996; Crewe and Harrison 1998). The same pattern applies to Limu. The dichotomy between "backward tradition" and "modern science" has become the excuse to which officials resort whenever they face project failures. I am not suggesting that during the collective era state agencies always respected local knowledge or took it into account when making decisions. My point is this: in the reform era, when effective realization of the public good must be built on consensus and compromise, state agents' general ignorance of local knowledge and their categorical rejection of traditional practices have insidiously compromised health interventions.

In the following section I outline the major changes that have taken place, from collectivism in the late 1950s to the current market reform, in relation to health work in Limu and Liangshan at large. Through an analysis of these paradigm shifts we may better understand the bureaucratic competition and ideological conflicts in which state agencies and local people become embroiled. This improved understanding will enable us to disentangle, in the specific setting of Limu, the intersecting factors that ultimately led to the China-UK Project's failure.

Socialist Medical Modernization

The introduction of biomedicine into the Liangshan region began in the late Qing Dynasty (Kuangxu 27th year, or 1901), at the instigation of Western missionaries (Song and Tian 1995). But the reach of modern health care in those early days extended primarily to ethnically mixed areas such as current Xichang City and Huili County, where most of Liangshan's Christian churches were located. In 1947 a British missionary doctor, Anthony J. Broomhall (Hai Hengbo), established a clinic in the current county seat of Zhaojue County, with the permission and assistance of the local nuo, and began offering medical services there. He left China in March 1951, when the People's Liberation Army entered Nuosu-dominant Liangshan (Ma and Diehl 2001). It has only been since the establishment of the socialist regime that modern medicine and its practices have been introduced into the Nuosu core area of Liangshan. Other approaches, including political mobilization of the masses and the communal health network, were also deployed to achieve socialist medical modernization.

The Introduction of Biomedicine

Beginning in 1951, the Communist government gradually introduced biomedical health care into Nuosu-dominant areas. Limu was one of the first Nuosu-dominant localities to be equipped with a modern medical team. The Limu

Township Clinic officially opened its doors in August 1957 as the Democratic Reform got underway (Sichuan sheng 1999). Bringing biomedicine to Liangshan was both a necessity and a pragmatic strategy for the People's Liberation Army, which was charged with bringing the state's socialist modernization to the remote and hostile (to the Han majority) Nuosu region. "The main health work at that time was resolving difficulties in the health situation and promoting the good of liberation among minority populations," noted the retired Han doctor Zhang Guifa, superintendent of the Prefecture Hospital located in Zhaojue County in 1955 (personal interview). To establish a better relationship with the local people and encourage their acceptance of biomedicine, many army doctors lived with the Nuosu and learned their languages and cultures (Gao 2002). These practices attracted many new army recruits and gained much positive publicity for the new regime among the Nuosu populace.

Demystification of the indigenous ritual healings was part and parcel of socialist medical modernization from the 1950s through the 1970s (Sidel and Sidel 1982). The state labeled traditional Nuosu healing practices and beliefs "superstitions" and banned them (X. Liu 2001). To the Communists, medical modernization meant not only introducing sanctioned knowledge and technology to localities like Liangshan but also changing local concepts and even worldviews associated with health.

The first corps of Han Chinese doctors who came to Liangshan trained indigenous health workers. The government chose young Nuosu to be paramedics because of their support for the revolution and their willingness to serve their people. The government sent them to Ya'an Hygiene School, which belonged to then Xikang Province. Xikang was administratively abolished in 1955, and thereafter Liangshan was incorporated into Sichuan Province. Four years later, in 1959, the Liangshan Hygiene School opened its doors and functioned at the same level as a senior high school. The Nuosu health workers (locally called "doctors") who were trained in the school in the 1950s and 1960s became the backbone of biomedicine and public health services in Liangshan.[3] Many of these health workers went on to serve as high-ranking officials in health-related state agencies in the ensuing decades.

Mobilizing the Masses

Since the founding of socialist China, the state has integrated health work into its political movements. Mass mobilization for disease control was the principal means by which the Communist Party legitimized its control over the vast countryside and mobilized its scarce resources to improve rural health (Sidel and Sidel 1982; Tang et al. 1994). A famous talk given by Chairman Mao on June 26, 1965, articulated the rationality of socialist health care policy, including the oft-quoted slogan "In medical and health work, put the emphasis on the rural areas!" (Sidel and Sidel 1982, 4).

Mao's call for a reprioritization of national health care programs led to a mass mobilization of China's health personnel and resources during the ten years of the Cultural Revolution (1966–76). The state forced medical personnel to relocate from cities to the countryside, where they served as health workers, paramedics, or other types of workers, a policy that was associated with the training of over a million barefoot doctors—mostly local peasants and sent-down educated young people (Hesketh and Zhu 1997).[4]

From the outset, the Limu Township Clinic had been home to these sent-down doctors and a training center for Nuosu barefoot doctors. A former barefoot doctor who was conscripted at the clinic in 1968 recalled the difficult conditions of their training:

> We all sat on the dirt ground for classes. All the teachers were Han doctors. Initially, we didn't understand a word of the Han writing. But gradually, we picked it up. We students worked first and received training later. We followed our teachers out to visit patients and pick therapeutic herbs in the wild. Our jobs were mainly in health promotion, such as separating the living areas of humans from those of livestock, digging latrines, performing inoculations, and presenting hygiene education.

By the end of the 1970s, as the policy of sending down urban intellectuals continued, Limu's clinic boasted dozens of Han Chinese doctors trained in well-known medical colleges in Shanghai and elsewhere. At that time, the clinic was a remote facility in a mountainous region and, in fact, ranked only as a secondary-level facility within the three-tier health-referral network (i.e., county hospitals, district/township clinics, and village dispensaries, in descending order). Nevertheless, the Limu clinic was a well-equipped medical establishment that could even perform certain surgeries such as appendectomies and gastrostomies.

The Communal Health Network

Foreign researchers generally marveled at socialist China's achievements in public health: by the 1970s the country had established a well-organized and mul-titiered health care system (Bloom 2001; Chen 1989; Lee 2004; Tang et al. 1994;

World Bank 1997). Among China's health care achievements in the collective era, the system of barefoot doctors in rural China, including trainers and trainees, gained worldwide recognition for its success in reaching a vast number of poor peasants. The Chinese model even inspired the World Health Organization's Primary Health Care initiative at the 1978 Alma Ata conference (White 1998).

The success of the barefoot-doctor system rested on a collective way of life in which every individual was an integral part of a commune (Hesketh and Zhu 1997). The practice of barefoot doctors operated in tandem with the Cooperative Medical System (*hezuo yiliao*), which was organized as part of the collectivization of rural society. Barefoot doctors were commune members and provided primary health care to other members almost free of charge. The commune compensated them with workpoints. Under this system, the state had clear regulations regarding the exchange of goods and services in the communes, all based on workpoints.

This self-reliant collective way of life, in which the Cooperative Medical System played a key role, lasted for about twenty-five years. By 1979 approximately 27 percent of China's medical personnel served 20 percent of its urban population, and approximately 73 percent served the remaining 80 percent in rural areas. These figures indicated a diminishing rural-urban disparity, although disparities in the quality of health personnel and health care facilities remained (Lucas 1982, 158).

This blossoming of rural health improvements soon suffered a serious setback as China made a drastic turn toward capitalist modernity after 1978. In the ensuing years, the dismantling of the rural communes put impoverished areas at risk.

The Marketization Paradigm

From 1977 until the early 1980s, Mao's successor, Deng Xiaoping, changed China's development trajectory and began to reorient the country's medical establishments. The objective of this wave of medical modernization was to correct previous policies, which had emphasized the *quantity* of medical personnel without adequate regard to the *quality* of their professional training, particularly in rural areas. Health care training that de-emphasized professionalism and specialization during the collective era soon gave way to a new policy that called for the upgrading of professional expertise and advancement in China's scientific and technological fields (Lucas 1982). This change in health care policy has had significant consequences: the retreat of rural health personnel and the decentralization and privatization of health care. These changes, in turn, have affected the morale of frontline health workers. The party-state has insisted on only one fundamental guideline espoused in the previous period of medical modernization: that of a science-based rationality and practice.

The Retreat of Rural Health Personnel

With the onset of this new directive, the entire country once again experienced the redistribution of its professionals, who this time moved mostly from rural to urban areas. The national government called for "the homecoming of techni-cal personnel" (*keji renyuan guidui*).[5] Sent-down intellectuals and professionals employed their personal networks and material resources to gain official permis-sion to return to their families and original institutions in cities. In Limu, at least thirty well-trained sent-down doctors and nurses had left the township clinic by the mid-1980s. They left behind complicated medical equipment such as an X-ray machine and dental-care facilities that no one who stayed on knew how to use.

In the meantime, the Cooperative Medical System was gradually phased out as the farmland redistribution policy dissolved the communal system. To satisfy the new modernization policy, which mandates better-quality health workers, the government instituted a qualifying examination program for former barefoot doctors. Only a small percentage of them passed the exami-nation and were awarded the new title "country doctor" (*xiangcun yisheng*). Out of the eight villages in Limu, only three of the former barefoot doctors received the official "country doctor" status, which entitled them to a stipend of approximately 25 yuan per month for their work.

Numerous barefoot doctors lost their jobs overnight (Tang et al. 1994). Oth-ers became private health practitioners without license or supervision. Most villages in remote areas now have no certified health workers, and vaccination programs and outreach health services have steadily declined. Nationwide, when the communal system ultimately collapsed in the mid-1980s, approxi-mately 900 million peasants lost access to health care service programs (Blu-menthal and Hsiao 2005).

Decentralization and Marketization of Health Care

As market reform has progressed along neoliberal lines, the state has decentral-ized its social welfare programs, and the ability of local governments to main-tain health care facilities has increasingly hinged on local financial conditions. Some research shows that health care in better-off coastal areas did not suffer decline in the early years of reform (e.g., Huang 1988). But overall, the health care system of the vast interior suffered devastating reductions. Nationwide, the percentage of the government's contribution to local health care annually fell from 28 percent to 14 percent between 1981 and 1993 (Bloom 2001; World Bank 1997). According to the 2000 World Health Organization report, China ranked 188th out of 191 countries in terms of the fairness of the state's financial contribution to health care.[6] Since then, individual citizens' ability to participate in the market economy, measured by their earning power and level of wealth, has become the sole criterion determining their access to health care (Chen 2001).

Health workers' behavior, inevitably, is shaped by prevailing cultural and political factors (Bloom, Han, and Li 2001; Segall 2000). In the reform era, knowledge and expertise are valued as privately owned commodities, in contrast to the collective era when state ideology dictated the higher priority of public service. As marketization continues, the state can no longer expect health workers to do as much as they used to if the state does not appropriately reward them with tangible benefits. Owing to the dual factors of the declining financial commitment to public health on the part of the state and the increasing profitability of privatized health care, many health workers see public health work as a burden. They, especially the well-trained ones, have either transferred from the public sector to profit-making private business or have gradually shifted their work from disease prevention to more lucrative curative treatments and technologies (Bloom, Han, and Li 2001).

Rural patients have suffered most from these drastic changes, as their incomes are spiraling downward in comparison with urban industrial workers. To increase their own incomes, local health workers often engage in unethical practices, such as accepting kickbacks on the sale of certain drugs, requesting under-the-table payoffs, or overprescribing drugs and health services (Bloom 2001). Charging fees for supposedly free services, such as childhood vaccinations, is also a commonplace practice that recognizes such payments as subsidies for rural health workers and incentives for them to meet governmental immunization targets (Tang et al. 1994, 47). As a consequence of all these developments, the number one factor in China's rural poverty has been the enormous increase in health expenditures (Liu, Rao, and Hsiao 2003). In a 2001 survey, 21.6 percent of rural households had fallen below the poverty line owing to their medical expenses (Kaufman 2006, 57).

In addition to these direct effects on patients, decentralization and market competition have led to another detrimental impact on rural health care programs: decreased coordination among state health agencies. The sharpened competition among poor local agencies for funding, power, and political credit has compelled them to act in their own interests and consequently constrained their ability and willingness to jointly cope with public duties. The Chinese disease control agencies have become vertically organized in parallel yet separate networks, making collaboration and information sharing more difficult (Kaufman and Meyers 2006).

The Predicament and Passivity of Rural State Agents

As market reform progresses, the provision and quality of rural health care have correspondingly declined, as has the staffing of health clinics in far-flung rural areas. For example, most of Limu Township's isolated villages, as well as many of the townships in the high mountains, still have no health workers. Most skilled and experienced health workers are concentrated in the administrative centers of major townships and cities, and their services focus on profit-making disease treatment. Health workers are reluctant to go to more remote areas to serve the have-nots, and typically it is the new graduates from hygiene schools who are sent to the remote areas that seasoned health workers avoid. As a result, these relatively inexperienced health workers must deal with the most destitute populations. The isolation and lack of better opportunities for frontline health workers have contributed to their low morale since the change in health care policy.

When I resided at the township clinic in 2005, I had many opportunities to observe and talk with health workers about their lives in Limu. Because the Limu clinic is also the district clinic, it is staffed with more health workers than ordinary township clinics, which usually have a staff of between one and three. During that one year, the number of health workers in the Limu clinic fluctuated according to turnovers in personnel. In total, I met fourteen health workers—seven Nuosu and seven Han, eight females and six males. Most of them were in their twenties or early thirties. Except for four health workers assigned particular duties, the rest were divided into two shifts and handled patient treatment. On an ordinary day, at most eight health workers were on duty at the clinic, and their work schedules generally were from 9 a.m. to 3 p.m.

At the township and village levels, health workers are supposed to provide both primary health care and public health services. Nevertheless, as White (1998) points out, preventive care priorities such as sanitation and environmental health issues have been overlooked even though the state has continued to emphasize preventive medicine in rural health care in the reform era.[7] Public health at the clinic and in Limu at large was in peril. My traumatic experience of using the unimaginably filthy clinic latrines (on a par with those elsewhere in Limu) made me wonder how sanitation at the clinic and throughout the township could ever be improved. A sprawling open garbage dump fronted the clinic, close to the primary school and the local government offices. During my year in Limu, I never saw this dump cleared. People tossed in all kinds of trash, and children, dogs, and pigs rummaged through the heap in search of odds and ends or whatever could be chewed on. The garbage dug up by the children and animals would spill over into the sewage ditch between the clinic and the dump. A water pipe, buried shallowly in the ground, extended along the polluted ditch. The so-called tap water was always mixed with mud and other impurities—perhaps contaminants from the sewage ditch.

Limu health workers often complained about the local peasants' lack of hygiene and the poor living conditions. To my mind, their complaints lacked justice as grounds for blaming the local residents. The inner courtyard of the clinic, where health workers and their friends gathered, was always littered with cigarette butts, leftover food, and discarded snack packages; flies were everywhere, as well as fleas and pests I did not recognize. None of the state agencies or government offices seemed to consider sanitation a serious part of their duties, nor did local peasants seem concerned about the situation. People's apathy about sanitation made the already tough rural environment even more unpleasant, not only for me but for everyone living there.

The quality of health workers' training was also suspect. Not every worker in the Limu clinic could handle even the most basic skill of giving hypodermic injections. Each health worker had a specific assignment, such as child inoculation, dispensary management, patient treatment, or casework for the China-UK Project. Of all these responsibilities, patient treatment was the most lucrative. Most of the clinic's earnings came from installing intravenous injections or drips. Peasants often came to the clinic for injections for whatever illness they might have. The clinic director usually assigned the female nurses who were skilled at giving injections to handle this type of treatment. Sometimes, when the skilled nurses were not around, I saw other health workers try and fail to inject a patient two or even three times; finally they would call for help from a former barefoot doctor who was working as a handyman in the clinic. Peasants sometimes joked, "Many drug users' injection skills are better than the doctors'!"

Health workers seemed less concerned about primary health care or public health work than about enhancing their personal specialties. To explain their poor injection skills, some of them told me that their professional training did not include nursing. Some had graduated from the hygiene school with a specialty in dentistry, radiology, or anesthesia, but the clinic did not require these more specialized services. The most common complaint was that the clinic offered its staff no opportunity to improve their expertise. Moreover, with their low levels of medical training—the equivalent of a high school education—most health workers had few opportunities to find better jobs in the private health sector and leave the rural township. Occasionally some might successfully arrange for a promotion and transfer out to bigger health agencies in the county seat, but this reflected their *guanxi* (interpersonal relationship) networks in the bureaucracy. Some might choose an entirely different career in order to leave the clinic. Those who stayed behind, dejected and apathetic, performed their jobs in a lackadaisical manner.

Overwhelmed by professional apathy, most of the clinic's health workers were reluctant to live in Limu. They commuted between the township clinic and their homes in the county seat. They clearly did not intend to integrate themselves into local social life, and Nuosu peasants in return did not see them as friendly and trustworthy members of the community. The Maoist ideal of an integrated organic society in China's rural areas no longer existed, if indeed it ever had.

Chen Li, who served as the head of Limu Township Clinic in the 1980s, remarked on the differences between the health care of the collective era and that of the reform era. His comments eloquently summarize China's bygone socialist dreams of rural health:

Mao Zedong said in 1965, "Emphasize health work in rural areas!" He called for intellectuals to go down to the rural villages. At that time, every commune had a cooperative health care unit, with money, medicine, and health workers. A few years after Mao died in 1976, the central government issued a document that abolished the clinics in rural villages and criticized the low quality of barefoot doctors. Our state seemed to have just awoken. Our dreams died. It's not easy to return to the dreams. Now peasants are worried. They can't afford being sick. In the past, sick peasants thanked Chairman Mao for the availability of medical facilities for their treatment. Now they can resort only to Amitabha [the Buddha] to avoid illness.

To sum up, three critical problems in health care that have arisen from market reform over the past two decades have received the greatest research attention: the disparity between rural and urban areas, the overall malfunction of the health care delivery system, and the ineffectiveness of the health care apparatus for epidemic control (Blumenthal and Hsiao 2005). These problems epitomize what I saw in Limu and constitute the context in which the China-UK Project was implemented. The effects of market reform on China's health care have featured prominently in many studies (Bloom 2001; Bloom and Gu 1997; Bloom, Han, and Li 2001; Blumenthal and Hsiao 2005; Hesketh and Zhu 1997; Hsiao 1995; Kaufman 2006; Lee 2004; Liu and Mills 2002; Liu, Rao, and Hsiao 2003; Tang and Bloom 2000; Tang et al. 1994; White 1998). Few studies, however, have examined the deteriorating quality of health-related practices at the local and everyday level as a result of the shift in the development paradigm. The China-UK Project shows how a well-intended program can fail in the face of this larger dysfunction.

Looking into the China-UK Project

My analysis of the failed China-UK Project in Limu focuses first on the social arena in which the project was implemented. This understanding can help us dissect the problems within state agencies and in their difficult relationship with the local community. Later, I will discuss five cases developed by the project to critically highlight specific practices. My analysis points to bureaucratic shortcomings and the state agents' cultural incompetence, which I consider to be the overarching reasons for the project's failure.

Competition and Information Blockage Among State Agencies

At the outset of my stay in Limu, I was confused by the inconsistent information I received from state agencies involved in local AIDS intervention. I had to rely on a good deal of guesswork as I tried to determine the reliability of the information. The confusion derived, first of all, from what I learned from competing offices at the county level.

The China-UK Project office in Zhaojue County fell under the jurisdiction of the Bureau of Health, not the more dynamic Anti-Epidemic Station that in mid-2005 was incorporated into the county's Center for Disease Control (CDC). This arrangement was unlike similar projects run in other counties in Liangshan Prefecture. By and large, the Bureau of Health is an administrative office in charge of a few specialized units such as the county's hospitals and its health personnel.

The Anti-Epidemic Station is charged with preventing and controlling infectious diseases, so it tended to be more active in its operations. Initially, the China-UK Project was housed under this station, but when the official responsible for the project received a promotion to deputy director of the Bureau of Health, he took the project and its considerable funding with him to his new office. After that move, disease control personnel had little involvement in the project.

Since market reform has compelled most local agencies to focus on their own interests and has made securing funding an end in itself, the considerable budget of the China-UK Project certainly slaked the host agency's thirst for funds. Precisely how an agency and its officials used project money was in many cases kept secret, even from the sponsors. Limu's China-UK Project had a five-year budget that, according to one county official, was less than 200,000 yuan (US$25,000 in 2005)—a meager sum for a comprehensive intervention project involving a population of approximately 4,000 people in three extended villages. I must note that I had no access to information about the budget allocated to Limu's China-UK Project; the county's project office kept the actual amount a secret. Township officials and health workers were also out of the loop. From what I could discover, the county health office spent nearly 80,000 yuan (US$10,000) of the project's budget just on meals and entertainment in the year 2004. High-level officials criticized the county office for its wasteful conduct but could do little to prevent such abuses. Likewise, the project's provincial evaluators reported that a large percentage of the budget was used for "supervision and evaluation," which included transportation, receptions, and meals for high-level officials visiting local project sites. Lack of financial transparency and insufficient supervision were common problems in the various local programs carried out under the aegis of the China-UK Project (Lan et al. 2005).

Accompanying the problems related to funding was a decline in coordination among state agencies. Oftentimes a local agency that collected important information would not share it with another agency at the same level or lower; different agencies had their own assignments, approaches, priorities, and credit to be won. The differences in HIV/AIDS statistics generated by different agencies are a case in point. Disease control offices, police and military units, and reproductive health departments collected AIDS-related data following their own criteria and targeting specific populations. State agents in different offices proceeded with their own work without genuine collaboration with other relevant offices. That each state agency did its work in its own way must also have reduced the sharing and use value of the data collected (Lan et al. 2005).

The China-UK Project's own statistics reflected what Biehl (2005) calls "technologies of invisibility," in that state and medical agencies neglected unregistered HIV/AIDS cases and therefore failed to frame the planned intervention appropriately. The project counted only registered HIV-infected people as its intervention targets and ignored unregistered HIV cases. When I first visited Limu, I learned from township officials and health workers that the number of cases of HIV infection found in the project's blood testing was sixty-eight in 2002 and that it had increased to ninety-six in 2003. I later heard that because of confusion or errors in testing, the 2003 figure of ninety-six had been inflated. In 2004, sixty-one confirmed cases of HIV infection had been registered in the three monitored villages. A few registered HIV-infected patients had passed away over the years, and a few previously unregistered HIV-infected drug users had been added to the project roster. The clinic's China-UK roster at one point in 2005 listed seventy-eight HIV-infected people. Officials and health workers told me that the actual number of cases of HIV infection was significantly higher in Limu. One high-level health official revealed to me some unpublished figures for 2005: "The annual rate of increase in HIV/AIDS cases in Liangshan as a whole is 46 percent. Among carriers, 90 percent are Nuosu, 90 percent are males, and 90 percent are drug injectors. Who knows what else is out there?" Local state agents tended to lump HIV and AIDS cases together in their statistics. Not until mid-2005 did the China-UK Project seriously begin to assess whether registered HIV-infected people had developed AIDS symptoms. Before then, estimates had largely been guesswork, based on health workers' surmises or clinical judgments.

The Center for Disease Control of Zhaojue County posted its own figure of eighty-seven cases of HIV infection in the eight villages of Limu in March 2005; this was nine more than the China-UK Project roster and contained many names not on the latter's list. The CDC list reported information from the mandatory blood tests drawn in drug-rehabilitation centers, detention centers, and prisons. These incarcerated populations were the most common base from which the Chinese government at all levels acquired data on HIV infection and constructed the HIV/AIDS trajectories in China as a whole (Weng 2002).

Unlike the two agencies discussed above, which targeted mainly male drug users, the Maternal and Child Health Bureau (MCHB) of Zhaojue County focused on women. After 1997, women who attended antenatal clinics were also included in the state sentinel surveillance for HIV (He and Detels 2005). Zhaojue County's MCHB established an annual health checkup (*funü san cha*) that covered all women between the ages of eighteen and forty-seven. The main purposes of this checkup were to ensure the success of China's birth-control policy and improve antenatal health: it assessed pregnancy status, the presence or absence of intrauterine devices, and possible sexually transmitted diseases. In recent years, these annual health checkups also began to investigate HIV among targeted women. At the end of 2005, Zhaojue County reported its first case of a pregnant woman who was HIV positive.

The three above-mentioned state agencies had different statistics that reflected their different sources and purposes. There were no integrated figures, by specific population or for the entire county, to provide a road map for overall strategies and actions among state agencies and workers involved in AIDS intervention. Needless to say, their collaboration was starkly inadequate, if not completely lacking. Moreover, the data pool could be compromised if the responsible agencies needed to inflate their achievements or downplay the severity of the crisis locally. State agencies at the prefectural or provincial levels might have the authority to organize otherwise fragmentary data and the needed resources for effective epidemic control, but their efforts could be hampered by unreliable data sent from subordinate offices or by competition among agencies. In the reform era, such dysfunction among health agencies has had a significant consequence: No matter how well intended or well planned intervention projects may be at the national level, they are enormously difficult to implement at the local level. Various state agencies entertain distinct political and economic agendas that often take priority over public health (Kaufman 2006, 60; Kaufman, Kleinman, and Saich 2006b).

The Malformed State-Society Partnership

To effectively implement projects, all the social relationships surrounding intervention practices must be considered, rather than focusing on only one set of stakeholders such as developers or beneficiaries (Crewe and Harrison 1998, 19). In theory, the China-UK Project officials, whether at the national or provincial level, should have demanded a thorough investigation of community relationships and practices before implementing any local plans (China-UK 2002). The actual conduct of the state agents at the local level, however, made this goal unattainable. The China-UK Project focused mainly on individual participants and failed to take into account the complicated social networks in which these individuals were embedded. As a result, state agents encountered considerable cultural and social barriers and only haltingly muddled through the entire intervention period.

Why was there no engagement with local knowledge and social relations? As my understanding of Limu grew, it became clear to me that state agents had no intention of forming partnerships with local society for any common undertaking. I have a twofold explanation for their reluctance. First, state agents, if they were to establish such a partnership, would have needed to spend a considerable amount of energy and time to acquire cultural competence in local knowledge. Their reluctance to stay in rural areas suggests that they preferred to apply so much effort to other interests or perhaps to nothing at all, since they did not consider staying at the Limu clinic a long-term career plan. Second, state agents generally held the opinion that the local peasants were "backward." Since the 1980s social scientists researching China have become increasingly interested in the contested state-society relationship (e.g., Perry 1994; Pieke 2004; Rosenbaum 1992; Solinger 1999). For instance, Pieke (2004) argues that the state's influence on society, or on the state itself at the local level, is an ever-changing product of both local and supralocal cultural struggles. In this light, officialdom's dismissal of local knowledge and practices is not a surprise; it simply reflects the marginality of Nuosu peasants in the eyes of the state.

Five Cases

To further illustrate the implementation problems of the China-UK Project, I will examine five kinds of practice whose stated purpose was to assist HIV-infected people in Limu. These involve pig raising, opportunistic-infection treatment, planting Sichuan peppercorn (*huajiao*) as a cash crop, needle exchange, and providing antiretroviral (ARV) treatments. In addition to these practices, the project occasionally provided AIDS education. These practices were initiated by the County Health Bureau and supervised by the project's prefectural office. Limu Township officials and health workers manned the front lines.

Case One: The Pig Raising Program   My understanding of how HIV-infected participants perceived the China-UK Project was inspired by Crandon-Malamud's (1991) classic ethnography of medical pluralism in Bolivia. She characterizes medicine as a "primary resource"—in the same category as monetary or social capital—through which one gains access to a "secondary resource" (such as hierarchical relations that one may need to achieve vertical social mobility or material privileges) that is more significant than medical treatment per se in local social life. What seems clear is that health care produces and reproduces social relations.

The people of Limu were encouraged by the China-UK Project to treat AIDS as a "profit-making" disease. In its first two or three years, the project team gave certain sums of money, such as 50 yuan, to registered HIV-infected persons on major seasonal holidays and between 5 and 20 yuan to peasants who participated in blood tests or monthly AIDS follow-up sessions at the clinic. This sort of tangible benefit made project participants consider their disease a source of privilege. Here is an example: one HIV-positive man asked an official, who had come out from Beijing to assess the project in Limu in June 2005, "Are AIDS people also entitled to have a greater number of children [than ordinary people]?"

The China-UK Project initiated the pig raising program as a way to help HIV-infected people support themselves. Ideally, participants would raise the project's piglets and later sell the grown pigs for profit or raise more piglets as a livelihood. But many of Limu's healthy people were poorer than the HIV-infected ones and eager to have a share in the sudden bonanza. So some healthy locals went to doctors and requested "AIDS certificates" in hopes of receiving free piglets and other charity goods earmarked for the project's participants. They were envious of the privileges that came with HIV-infected status.

Further, the participants' personal relationships with project officials resulted in the differentiation of registered patients into distinct categories of "favored" versus "less favored." Following old bureaucratic habits, the local project team demonstrated its achievements by showcasing model patients selected from the registered participants, while ignoring the project's less promising cases. These model patients accommodated the needs of the project team whenever high-level officials arrived to assess the work. In return, they received more or better resources, such as regular medical treatment, donated clothes, or piglets.

Mahxi Ggurre, the first of the four brothers described in Chapter 4, received three piglets, even though he was comparatively well off. He owned a roof-tile kiln and a brewery. Owing to Ggurre's financial ability to feed his project pigs, they grew nicely and he became a model for the pig raising program. The local team appreciated Ggurre's visible achievements and even awarded him a "China-UK" recognition plate that hung over his house entrance. Peasants who did not have enough food for themselves, let alone for pigs, were not able to raise the profile of the pig raising initiative. Moreover, some impoverished registered patients killed the piglets for food or sold them to buy necessities. Predictably, they failed to attract attention and support from the project team.

The pig raising program had another unintended effect that also derived from the habitual top-down approach used in government projects. Following the international protocol of informed consent that governs the implementation of an AIDS- or drug-related project, the China-UK Project requested that its participants sign an informed-consent form upon receiving piglets, despite the high illiteracy rate in Limu. This document provided instruction on how the pig raising program should be run and what its purpose was. Usually, health workers or other officials obtained "signatures" from the recipients by signing on their behalf and then asking them to mark their fingerprints on the agreement form. Peasants in Limu called this agreement the "AIDS *shoujü* [receipt]," because only HIV-infected persons could receive the free piglets. These receipts were of course useless to the recipients. Most peasants could neither read nor remember the document's detailed instructions. Nevertheless, AIDS receipts could come in handy for drifting drug users and dealers, who used them to avoid jail terms, as the following example illustrates.

A few days before the Nuosu New Year in November 2005, I was surprised to see a particular man strolling in his village—as far as I knew, he had been arrested for theft in Taiyuan, Shanxi Province. At a gathering of young men in the village, I later learned that he had had with him an AIDS receipt borrowed from an HIV-positive friend. He had put his own fingerprint over the original fingerprint and pretended that he was the HIV-infected person. The Taiyuan police station placed a phone call to the Limu clinic and confirmed the HIV status of the person whose name appeared on the receipt. Police usually do not detain HIV-infected persons for long, either because of fear of AIDS or because of the lack of medical support in detention centers. He was released right away and had returned home in time for the holidays.

Case Two: The Opportunistic-Infection Treatment Program   The opportunistic-infection treatment program was initiated in large part as a way to promote drug users' participation in voluntary blood tests and to ensure registered patients' attendance at the monthly AIDS education sessions. Only people on the project roster were eligible for this free treatment—basic antibiotics and at times intravenous drips for whatever symptoms the patient had. Health workers admitted that this treatment was merely "consoling," without any proven therapeutic effect on AIDS symptoms, and they often considered HIV-infected people who requested this treatment to be "troublesome."

The conflict between the county and township health agencies over financial responsibility for these free treatments ultimately led to the dissolution of the program. The County Health Bureau ordered the township clinic to provide free treatment, even as it withheld promised funds. Unable to first secure the needed money, the clinic head was reluctant to provide the service for fear of depleting the clinic's own revenues. Therefore the free treatment was not always readily available, and the program completely failed to accomplish its goals of assisting HIV-infected people and promoting voluntary blood tests. Sometimes when I met ill people who were drug users or whose spouses were HIV infected, I suggested that they take blood tests at the project office to get free treatment if they were infected. They typically replied that the treatment was useless and not always available, and so they did not bother.

Case Three: The Sichuan Peppercorn Program   The Sichuan peppercorn program provides a vivid example of a malformed state-society partnership. The local community united to conceal facts from "ignorant" state agents in hopes of obtaining an avalanche of "public good." This program was not treatment related, so township health workers were bypassed during the program's planning and implementation stages, as was also the case with the pig raising program. The responsible county official, a Nuosu who had grown up in the city and did not speak the Nuosu language, designed the program and allocated the funding on his own. Ignorant of local social relations, he doomed the program to failure; the program began in 2004 but had fizzled out by the following year.

The peppercorn is a widely popular spice in Sichuan cuisine and hence a cash crop. According to the county official in charge, the peppercorn program had contracted about 90 mu of the village's collective land for its experiment. He told me that the project had spent approximately 50,000 yuan (US$6,250) and planted 12,000 peppercorn saplings. He expected to harvest the peppercorn two years later (i.e., 2006) and to divide up the earned profits from the harvest into two parts: 80 percent would go to the project's registered patients and the remaining 20 percent would be split among ordinary people who resided in the village where the plantation was located. But what he had not reckoned with was the fact that Limu residents had never grown cash crops, and no clear arrangements had been determined for the division of labor to tend the plants.

The official in charge believed he had an ideal plan that would result in program success. But some Nuosu health workers and officials from other localities in Liangshan argued that it would take more than three years to raise the peppercorn to harvest. They sneered at the program as a bad joke or an easy way of stealing official money. As Munyu, the head of the clinic, commented, "This Sichuan peppercorn program is of no use. By the time the fruit can be harvested, the HIV-infected people will probably have all passed away. How can this program help them?"

On an early 2005 visit with a group of health workers and officials to a part of the field, I saw very few peppercorn saplings. On subsequent visits I made to the project land on my own, I saw seasonal crops being grown there. More surprisingly, the villagers who were growing these crops insisted that the field actually belonged to individual villagers rather than to the village collective. They said that the township and village cadres involved in the land contract jointly concealed the truth from the county official in charge. In doing so, all parties involved got kickbacks in various forms. By the end of 2005, project officials privately acknowledged the failure of the planting venture but offered no explanation.

Case Four: The Needle Exchange Program   Needle exchange was first initiated as a way to reduce the transmission of hepatitis B among drug users in Amsterdam in 1984. The following year, New York City expanded sterile-needle access for drug users to reduce the transmission of HIV. Over time more and more countries have adopted needle exchange as a harm reduction approach. Many of the adopting governments have had to struggle to convince the wider public that needle exchange programs are an effective public health initiative rather than a criminal justice issue (Singer 1997; Vlahov et al. 2001).

Given the legal and moral complexities, a successful harm reduction must include well-coordinated education, effective information dissemination, accessible facilities, government support, and community consensus (Hammett et al. 2006; Page 1997). Hasty implementation of such a project inevitably neglects essential negotiations with and education of all involved parties, especially the police, and will likely encounter obstacles. Limu's China-UK Project did not learn lessons from similar projects—whether successful or failed, international or domestic—and as a result the needle exchange program in Limu failed miserably, an outcome that surprised few.

Limu's needle exchange program was based on a total of just one week's planning in April 2005. The planning period was cut drastically short because prefectural government officials declared that they wanted to assess the program—even though it had not yet been implemented. Such an unannounced inspection was not uncommon for the China-UK Project at large. They often disturbed local work plans and exhausted local state agents (Lan et al. 2005). To cope with this particular inspection, the county office had no choice but to order township health workers to meet the demands from above. With no time for negotiation, the project team in Limu managed to select two registered patients as peer educators in each of the monitored villages, build a small open-air incinerator at the edge of the clinic courtyard, and make boxes for transporting needles and syringes. The boxes bore the logo "China-UK." With these preparations, the needle exchange got under way.

As usual, the project team did not consider consulting with traditional Nuosu authorities and village cadres for local knowledge and practices that might facilitate the needle exchange. Nor did the team hold public education sessions for villagers. The reasons for this negligence in the case of the needle exchange program likely derived from the time constraints as well as from the agents' habitual dismissal of local custom. Not surprisingly, the provision of free sterile syringes and needles to drug users encountered resistance almost immediately.

The first wave of opposition came from the family members of drug users. They accused the plan of supporting addicts' continued heroin use. This is one of the most common responses to such programs worldwide, although the accusation has often proved contrary to the facts (Page 1997). Another objection was more particular to local Limu culture: people questioned who would take responsibility should any deaths occur owing to drug injection with the distributed needles. Their question stemmed from traditional Nuosu judicial concerns over assigning liability for a life-and-death event. Nuosu peasants who deliberate the causes of an injury or death believe that the most recent or immediate factor contributing to the incident is accountable for its consequence. (I will discuss further the issue of Nuosu legal liability in Chapter 6.) In response, state agents angrily accused Limu peasants of being "backward and irrational" for raising such an objection; it did not occur to them that their own practices were rooted in thoughtlessness.

Once again, state agents circumvented these problems with a bureaucratic formality—the signing of informed-consent forms. The form used for the needle exchange program was also prepared in haste. Drug injectors who wanted the free and disposable syringes and needles had to sign—or imprint their thumbs on—a sheet of paper. The major significance of this informed-consent form was that it would absolve the project team of any liability should a death occur among drug users who used the distributed needles. Obviously, the demand for signatures or fingerprints was a violation of confidentiality, and many drug users eventually would not participate in the plan because they feared self-disclosure. In the meantime, the program made little effort to educate the local people or work with the family members of drug users, and the latter's criticisms of the program continued to mount.

The needle exchange program in Limu also illustrates the particularly poor coordination between health and penal agencies. When the first incident took place five days after the implementation of the program, it became clear that none of the officials involved had even considered the role of the police.

On a cool and quiet day in early April, I stood in front of my residence at the clinic pondering where to go for my exploration that day. A health worker in charge of the China-UK Project rushed to the clinic and exclaimed, "There is no way to continue needle exchange! Our peer educators have been arrested by the police!" According to his account, two peer educators who were carrying needle-exchange boxes printed with the "China-UK" logo were arrested by the police soon after stepping out of the clinic. The police found in their "China-UK" boxes clean needles and syringes and accused them of using illicit drugs. Limu health workers reported this incident to the project's county office and asked for assistance. Five days later, when I saw the two peer educators coming to the clinic, their heads had been shaved. They smiled at me shyly and explained, "They [the police officers] shaved our hair right after sending us to the detention center." They had tried to explain their line of work, but the police did not believe them.

After their release, the two men said they would not continue their work. They could neither convince the drug injectors' families of the importance of needle exchange nor justify their liability should a death occur. Even worse, they remained at risk of being apprehended by the police for doing this job. So they decided to quit, with the additional explanation: "We earn less than 100 yuan a month for this work, but we may have to pay a fine of 2,000 yuan to the police if we are arrested."

Later, one China-UK official told me that his office had negotiated with the police. The agreement they reached was this: The police would continue arresting drug users because of the state's war on drugs policy; they were simply carrying out their official duties. But as long as the project team was willing to bail out its peer educators, they would be released the next day and there would be no need to pay the penalty.

In their research on similar harm reduction programs in China and Vietnam, Hammett and his colleagues have pointed out that in these two nominally socialist states, tensions existed between state agencies over policies that treated drug use as a "social evil" worthy of harsh punitive measures. They describe the coexistence of confusing policies and the legal environment surrounding drug use and harm reduction intervention in the two countries as "schizophrenically progressive" (Hammett et al. 2006, 219). Without delicate arrangements, rigorous education, and balanced give-and-take among various government offices and between the state and the local society, any harm reduction program is doomed to failure, creating a public fiasco that yields only meaningless political rhetoric and ineffective health intervention.

Case Five: The Antiretroviral Treatment Program   The antiretroviral (ARV) treatment program was the last of the China-UK Project's undertakings in Limu, and it was the only one that the prefectural government promised to continue after the project ended in early 2006. The ARV treatment program began in the middle of June in 2005. The program selected two patients who would receive the first round of AIDS drug treatments. The selection was based on the patients' CD4 cell counts (under 200) and liver condition. One of those selected was a woman who had contracted HIV from her husband, and the other a male drug addict who was still taking heroin.

The project team treated these experimental cases differently. It believed that the woman would comply voluntarily with the ARV treatment, so health workers asked her to come to the clinic for her medications once a week. What the team did not anticipate was, as recounted in Chapter 4, that this woman would migrate to Chengdu two years later to trade drugs and die, presumably of AIDS, without supervised medication in 2008.

In contrast, seeing the male patient as likely a problem case, the project team promised a village cadre 60 yuan per month to supervise the man's daily ARV medication. The recruited village cadre later complained that the county official had arbitrarily reduced the monthly amount to 30 yuan and that he had in fact never received any payment.

Before long an incident occurred that resembled the arrest, two months earlier, of the peer educators. Police arrested the man who was receiving ARV treatment; he had been caught with half a gram of heroin in his possession. As could be expected, health workers reported the arrest to the county health office, which again tried to negotiate with the police to gain either his release or permission to send him additional medications in jail. The police initially refused both requests because the formal prosecution of his case was already under way. Still, a week later the drug addict was released. He told me that the police chief had beaten him until he bled; the chief only stopped beating him because other police officers reminded him of the man's HIV status. The addict argued that the illicit drugs did not belong to him: he had been at the wrong place at the wrong time. Although the project workers did not believe him, they could not afford to lose their test case—a potentially successful ARV treatment.

This ARV case is yet another example of the chaotic discordance among various state agencies surrounding drug use and AIDS interventions in Limu. On one occasion, I asked the health official in charge of the China-UK Project why the project was based at the County Bureau of Health rather than the Anti-Epidemic Station as in other counties. He replied, "The China-UK Project requires coordination among all government offices. Only the Bureau of Health can do that work." Theoretically he might have been right, but in fact such coordination never happened.

. . .

In the foregoing sections I have examined various reasons behind the China-UK Project's failure in Limu. In a report written for the project's provincial office in 2005, evaluators identified a few major problems facing the implementation of the project at the local level that are very similar to what I have shown above: for example, questionable financial decisions, lack of coordination among state agencies, antagonism between high- and low-level state agents, and finally, low morale and exhaustion among frontline workers (Lan et al. 2005). The messy and sometimes absurd practices that occurred in Limu's China-UK Project did not come from nowhere. I believe these problems are traceable to many interwoven structural problems rooted in the drastic change in China's health care paradigm.

With market reform, the state commands only a watered-down political legitimacy with which to mobilize workers and ordinary people for the public good in the absence of material incentives. Increasingly market-oriented social relationships have not only created blowback that has constrained the state's commitment to equality but also influenced state agents' morale and ethics in doing their work. In the case of Limu, the project team's position was sandwiched between high-level state agents and peasants, as well as between the imperative to make a profit and the mission of public service. This position further aggravated their already condescending attitude toward working in this poor rural area, and hence deepened their ambivalence and passive resistance to any extra work such as that presented by the China-UK Project. Still, given the general orientation toward profit making, any involvement in a foreign-aid project was an opportunity to advance their private interests. Under these circumstances, state agencies and agents would be competing to secure as much money as possible through the project. This prioritizing of private interests over public health may explain the lack of interagency coordination and inadequate local footing of the top-down policy planning and implementation we have seen during the period of the Limu programs. The failure of the project points generally to the predicament public health efforts in China's rural areas face in the reform era.

Engagement in the Cultural Domains

Of the two explanations I have provided here for the project's failure—bureaucratic inadequacies and the cultural incompetence of state agents—I see the latter as a crucial problem at the local level and would like to elaborate on its significance to the China-UK Project. In addition to their ignorance and dismissal of local culture, state agents selectively seized on local culture to justify their failures. One such "cultural barrier" was Nuosu taboos about sex, which were often blamed as an obstacle to delivering health education.

This putative cultural barrier was used by the project team as a pretext for brushing aside sex education as part of its AIDS interventions. The reluctance among Nuosu health workers and officials to provide sex education, which they nevertheless considered necessary for long-term effective HIV prevention, stemmed from strong Nuosu taboos against talking about sex and the body. One China-UK Project official recalled a lecture he gave to a group of Limu people about the relationship between unsafe sex and HIV transmission. "Many women spat at me after the talk, saying, 'Are you not a Nuosu, and don't you feel ashamed to be talking about that?'" Another Nuosu health worker delivered a health education session to Limu primary school children and teachers about the five major infectious diseases in Liangshan (i.e., cholera, tuberculosis, leprosy, snail fever, and AIDS). He emphasized the linkage between drug injection and HIV transmission, only lightly touching on the issue of sexual transmission in a single sentence: "AIDS [HIV] can be transmitted between husbands and wives." Upon my inquiry as to why he skirted around the issue of unprotected sex and its risks for everybody, he admitted, "There is no way to talk about sex in public. It's too embarrassing!"

Talking about sex in public was indeed disapproved of in Limu. To an extent I could understand and sympathize with these health workers' complaints about the local condemnation of sex education. I personally encountered similar problems. I first realized the grave consequences of talking about sex or body-related topics publicly when I asked a pregnant woman, in the presence of two other women, when her due date was. This woman had been very friendly to me, but immediately after my question she stood up and left without saying a word. I was taken aback and asked the woman beside me what I had said wrong. This woman was hesitant to reply at first, but after a long silence she finally told me not to ask such a question in public again. She said, "She [the pregnant woman] is shy and afraid that others, especially her father-in-law, might hear your question." The pregnant woman's sister-in-law eventually told me that even her mother-in-law [i.e., the grandmother-to-be] had no idea when she was due, even though they lived in the same house at that time. I later came to understand that the Nuosu have an exceedingly strong taboo on sexuality that prevents people from talking about issues perceived as commonplace in other societies. Another example: Many young women confided to me their shock at first experiencing their monthly periods; mothers simply did not talk to their daughters about menstruation. I consulted three female elders about this matter, and they all told me that it was embarrassing for both mothers and daughters to talk about it. Usually mothers simply left their daughters to learn about their periods from older peers or by themselves.

If it is true that Nuosu culture raises barriers to the state's AIDS intervention, the question then becomes, is the "cultural barrier" unchangeable and therefore to be blamed for the Limu project's failures?

Reckoning with "Cultural Barriers"

AIDS interventions in many other localities around the world have shown that culture is never static or unresponsive to changing conditions. The removal of barriers to positive behavioral change depends in great part on the willingness of the interventionists to build a partnership with local society—for example, seeking out local authorities as consultants or employing local young people as advocates—and to provide health workers with proper advice, instruction, and training. For instance, Pigg's (2002) research in Nepal demonstrates how an innovative approach can engage young people in sexuality-related discussions about HIV prevention even in a society where open discussion of sex is taboo.

The China-UK Project was launched in 2001. A few years later, health workers noted that the project's registered patients had gradually become more receptive to the health education provided at the monthly AIDS follow-up sessions, where health workers routinely asked whether the attendees used condoms for sex with their wives and then distributed condoms to them upon request. Many of the drug users unhesitatingly replied "yes" to the inquiry, although health workers doubted the truthfulness of their answers; at least the attendees were no longer embarrassed by the question. Although this progress could be seen only in the case of particular individuals, it demonstrated that Nuosu culture is not monolithic and unchangeable with regard to sex education or changing sexual behavior. This glimpse of change, however, seemed invisible or meaningless to the state agents who continued to entertain the idea of local cultural barriers.

Limu's China-UK Project did not foster a sound partnership with the local community. The main obstacle to forming the necessary working relationship has been the party-state's own culture, which has promoted science-based modernity and rationality since the 1950s. Even though state agents were aware of the Nuosu's employment of bimo ritual in their grassroots drug control programs, state agents avoided, at least publicly, communicating with religious healers because they considered state clinics to be official and scientific institutions, while the indigenous healers were "superstitious" (X. Liu 2001). One health worker's comment epitomizes this attitude: "Bimo ritual is not real therapy. New China does not believe in ghosts."

State agents' condescending attitudes toward Nuosu culture reflect national modernization goals. "Modernity, in this sense, is quite literally a worldview: a way of imagining both space and people through temporal idioms of progress and backwardness" (Pigg 1996, 163). This worldview was extended by state agents to dismiss many cultural elements that might have been useful in their interventions.

Modern Myth, Traditional Efficacy

The China-UK Project team, because of their ignorance and dismissal of local culture, failed to involve critical Nuosu authorities in mediating between the state and local people. In Nuosu society, mediation has long been institutionalized not only for conflict resolution but also in all the lived domains of kinship, ritual, worldview, healing, and social interaction. Traditional authorities occupy the roles of priest (bimo), shaman (sunyi), traditional judge (ndeggu), and headman (suyy), and each assumes specific mediation functions. Suyy mediate disputes among kin. Ndeggu mediate disputes between individuals who come from different lineages. Bimo and sunyi mediate between living humans and the dead (Bamo 2003, 70). State agents could have included these traditional authorities as facilitators in the project by appropriately negotiating and planning with them.[8]

Allow me to return to the issue of sex education to discuss how we might productively engage Nuosu authorities in interventions. These Nuosu carry out their socially recognized assignments in practical social settings that may concern any issue, including even sexuality-related disputes or illnesses. According to one popular ndeggu in Limu, the most common cases he has mediated have involved conflicts between couples. I once attended such a mediation. The case involved a woman's request for divorce and her claim that she should not be required to pay compensation to her husband. I learned that her complaint derived from her husband's sexual dysfunction. Other sex-related themes surface frequently in bimo rituals. In other words, sex-related issues are not entirely excluded from social discourse if they are culturally contextualized or mediated by the proper authorities.

Social problems in everyday life involve both men and women. In this regard, it is important to recall that bimo and suyy must be men, while many sunyi are women and women may occasionally serve as ndeggu. Regardless of the sex of these traditional authorities, their socially recognized roles allow them to broach sex-related issues to their fellow Nuosu under certain circumstances. As one well-known ndeggu explained to me: "Even though women may feel embarrassed about something, they must still speak about it to ndeggu; otherwise, we [ndeggu] cannot help mediate their problems. We are like medical doctors and must ask certain questions for our investigation."

On the whole, the China-UK Project team roundly blamed the local culture for what was chiefly its own failure. The state agents involved confined themselves to delivering condescending and monotonous lectures to the locals. The situation was akin to that described by Mark Nichter: intervention workers often present health education as a formal and instrumental medium through which those who "'know' can inject messages in those 'who don't know'" without enhancing the community's capacity for problem solving (Nichter 1989, 300).

In sum, gaining local footing is crucial for an intervention project's success. People do not simply passively accept—or resist—imposed interventions aimed at changing their behavior and culture; they may also actively reformulate their beliefs and practices by adapting elements introduced from outside in "willful and creative ways" (Harper 2002, 180). The Nuosu people have exhibited their enduring resilience and creativity in response to the drastic and dramatic changes that have beset their communities since the era of socialist modernity. The agency of local society, if appropriately supported and mobilized, may yet prove a resource for the state's AIDS interventions. Nevertheless, when state agents insisted on the dichotomy between "tradition" and "the modern," dealt with individuals to the exclusion of local society, and administered the project exclusively within the existing bureaucratic culture, their interventions became ineffective and generated unintended negative consequences. In the next chapter I will address other unintended consequences, as I examine how the decontextualized and mechanical implementation of international AIDS intervention protocols inadvertently instilled fear and the stigmatization of AIDS in a community where AIDS-related stigma had previously not been an issue.

6 AIDS and Its Global Stigmatization

WHEN I FIRST VISITED LIMU in 2002, I was greeted by slogans painted along the roadside in huge red or white Chinese characters: *yuanli dupin* (Stay Away from Drugs), *yufang aizibing* (Prevent AIDS), or *jieshen zihao* (Conduct Yourself Appropriately). After passing the "greeting" slogans at Limu's entrance, down toward the township center, I noticed a sign hung above the township office compound that read *aixin jiayuan* (A Beloved Homestead). Farther down the road, about 100 meters beyond several paddy fields and a row of shabby houses, another prominent message ran across the walls of people's houses and the township clinic: *shenchu ni de shou, gei aizibing bingren yifen guanhuai* (Reach Out: Give AIDS Patients Your Care and Support). These awareness-raising slogans about AIDS, drugs, and care seemed to be ubiquitous and informed visitors like me that this agrarian community in the middle of the rugged mountains was engulfed in these problems.

These slogans seemed further to suggest that the community must be stigmatizing people with HIV/AIDS, caring so little for their general well-being that the government had to intervene and preach compassion to remedy the situation. This assumption derives from a practice commonly seen across China: if slogans appear concerning a particular issue, that issue must be a real and pressing problem.[1] As my research on heroin use and AIDS in Limu progressed, however, I realized that my initial impression was at odds with reality. AIDS-related stigma was rare in Limu, if not nonexistent. So the issue became: Why were these huge warning signs painted along the road, and why was their message conveyed in such a preaching tone? Who had them painted and for what purpose?

These questions led me to explore how the Nuosu in Limu perceive AIDS and the members of their community affected by the disease. In this chapter I argue that, until the government's implementation of certain kinds of AIDS-awareness programs, the situation in Limu did not fit the overall pattern in the rest of China—and indeed in much of the world. Prior to state interventions, local Nuosu did not view this disease as a reason for discrimination. Yet, without first gaining an understanding of the local situation, China-UK Project officials mechanically transplanted a global anti-AIDS agenda that was supposed to increase the local public's tolerance of people with HIV/AIDS. Ironically, this intervention has only promoted fear and stereotyping of AIDS and its victims, a phenomenon previously unknown in the local Nuosu community.

Scholars have argued that an intervention regime reflects the planners' conceptualization of AIDS-related stigma in a specific society (Parker and Aggleton 2003). Seen in this light, the mottos emblazoned around Limu in fact reveal the interventionists' own attitudes toward drugs and AIDS, their habitual dismissal of local Nuosu culture, and their reliance on uninformed countermeasures to address local problems. AIDS-related stigma, like other social values and morals, is likely to be complex and exhibit a high degree of diversity in its conception and expression cross-culturally. With the rapid global spread of HIV, however, people have viewed this new disease with alarm, and the resulting sense of urgency has created a globalizing discourse around AIDS-related stigma that, in turn, may brush aside preexisting local perceptions of the disease. Interventionists often employ ready-made and portable tools and discourses, known as "briefcase concepts," to deal with such globalized problems in diverse cultural contexts (Eves and Butt 2008, 6). In consequence, as Green and Sobo (2000, 11) point out, people "tend to take as self-evident the claims of discrimination, related social losses and a resulting shrinking of the social networks of PHAs [people with HIV/AIDS]. . . . AIDS is not necessarily as socially destructive as it is reputed to be."

In Limu, the practices of state agents inadvertently initiated the stigmatization of AIDS. Their interventions teemed with illogical, biased, and culturally inappropriate practices, which unfortunately are characteristic of many interventions: "They far too often are part of the problem; they become iatrogenic" (Kleinman and Kleinman 1997, 9). To examine the process of AIDS-related stigma construction in Limu, I will first provide a brief review of research on AIDS stigmatization in hopes of drawing new insights for our understanding of the Chinese and global contexts in question.

Deviance, AIDS, and Stigma

The term "stigma" derives from the Greek and refers to bodily signs connoting unusual, and especially bad, moral characteristics of the person in question (Goffman 1963). A stigma is by definition a socially constructed label and can vary from place to place and over time: "Stigma involves not so much a set of concrete individuals who can be separated into two piles, the stigmatized and the normal. . . . The normal and the stigmatized are not persons but rather *perspectives*" (Goffman 1963, 137–38; emphasis added).

In other words, whatever constitutes "abnormal" is imbued with specific social characteristics and meanings. Stigma may signify "abnormal" physical attributes, such as bodily scars or deformities caused by severe leprosy;[2] but it may also refer to nonphysical attributes, as does the designation "slave society" that has been applied to the Nuosu. Stigma is a label imposed by others on the stigmatized, and the process of stigmatization represents the construction of "abnormality" or "deviation" from the socially accepted and "normal" (Alonzo and Reynolds 1995).

Link and Phelan (2001) identify five components of stigmatization that are useful for our understanding of this social process: First, society identifies human differences and labels people accordingly. Second, dominant sociocultural beliefs associate labeled people with preexisting undesirable characteristics. Third, the label dispensers separate the negatively labeled people from "us," the normal ones. Fourth, people who carry negative labels experience status loss and discrimination. Fifth, dominant social, economic, and political powers in society formalize and facilitate the attachment of stigma. When these interrelated components converge, stigma exists.

AIDS-related stigma does not occur autogenously. With reference to earlier research on stigma associated with illness and disease (Goffman 1963; Jones et al. 1984; Katz 1981), researchers have concluded that the most common reasons for the construction of AIDS-related stigma are three: the disease's close association with "deviant" behavior (e.g., drug use, prostitution, or homosexuality); the implication that carriers of the virus are irresponsible (e.g., have engaged in unsafe sex or drug injection); and the threat of contagion the virus poses (Alonzo and Reynolds 1995; Green and Sobo 2000; Herek 1999). From the outset, people with HIV/AIDS have been stigmatized by moral judgment marked by the signification of "deviance." This stigma matches or mixes with certain preexisting negative stereotypes regarding physical or nonphysical characteristics.

In dissecting the process of stigma construction, we may further ask: What constitutes "deviance" in a society where diverse groups live in variegated local cultures, as do the different ethnic groups in China? We may assume that these groups possess distinct criteria for identifying deviance rather than one monolithic concept of normality. "Stigmatization takes shape in specific contexts of culture and power" (Parker and Aggleton 2003, 17). In China, unfortunately, under both socialist governance and the globalizing effects of market capitalism, modernization has engendered a hierarchical order based on political and economic status, in which the hegemonic state and its bureaucratic elite usually hold most of the power to determine what constitutes deviance. It is evident worldwide that in general, people categorized as deviants do not have the power to define themselves; as a result, agents who oversee policy making and policy implementation may dismiss the voices of such so-called deviants. In AIDS interventions, project planners and practitioners may reproduce or create negative local meanings, thereby increasing the disparity in power between the "deviant" and the "normal."

The pattern just described was manifest at the onset of the HIV/AIDS epidemic. When awareness of this new disease took hold in the United States in the early 1980s, the earliest AIDS-related stigma fell upon specific categories of social minorities—gay men first, soon followed by intravenous drug users—both of whom were already stigmatized groups (Herek and Glunt 1988). In 1983 the U.S. Centers for Disease Control and Prevention (CDC) defined for the first time four "high-risk groups": homosexuals, Haitians, hemophiliacs, and heroin users (Farmer 1992, 211). Stigma was soon attached to people who belonged to these groups. Many observers criticized the negative consequences of this labeling practice, the Haitian case in particular. In 1985 the CDC formally removed Haitians from the list of high-risk groups, for two critical reasons: the CDC's concession that it lacked the data to justify this label for Haitians, and local and international condemnation of the CDC's discriminatory policy (Cohen 1999, 139). However, the "blame-the-victim" mentality persisted and underpinned many follow-on responses to AIDS interventions in Haiti (Farmer 1992).

The production or reproduction of difference through labeling of "high-risk groups" has contributed to social effects that go beyond the mere epidemiological purpose of calling attention to the high incidence of HIV infection among certain populations. Stigma arises when the public links the label "high-risk" to preexisting negative stereotypes. When the general public considers a group of people "culturally" predisposed to a particular type of problem, they

may also consider them unworthy of intervention or an investment in resources (Lock and Nichter 2002). Under these circumstances, the "at-risk" label
may then place individuals or groups at further risk, owing to a fatalism that
commonly arises after the withdrawal of external support (Hahn 1999).

The negative consequences of stigmatization soon prompted many anthropologists to criticize the labeling of AIDS-related risk groups (e.g., Frankenberg
1993; Glick Schiller 1992; Glick Schiller, Crystal, and Lewellen 1994; Marshall
and Bennett 1990; Treichler 1988). They have argued that the label has little to
do with the labeled people's lived experiences and have called for a contextualized understanding of these people to shed light on the fact that "it takes power
to stigmatize" (Link and Phelan 2001, 375). Some scholars have even proposed
the concept of "structural violence" as a referential framework for analyzing
AIDS stigmatization caused or contributed to by the "at-risk" label (e.g., Castro
and Farmer 2005; Farmer, Connors, and Simmons 1996; Parker and Aggleton
2003). Possible forms of structural violence include racism, sexism, poverty,
political oppression, and other social inequalities that are rooted in the historical and socioeconomic processes that also shape discrimination against people
with HIV/AIDS.

Ever since its emergence, AIDS-related stigmatization has become a human
rights concern. The United Nations and other international organizations often
stress the urgent need to counteract stigmatization as part of the worldwide
fight against the disease (Castro and Farmer 2005).[3] International or, more precisely, Western-derived organizations have been crucial in formulating the ways
in which AIDS is conceptualized and combated. Wherever these organizations
have circulated or imposed discourses on AIDS worldwide, human rights have
become a major issue (Altman 1998). Despite the differences in motivation and
practice among international agencies, they have acted in concert to establish
a universal antistigma agenda and coping strategies for combating the disease.

The international campaign against AIDS-related stigmatization began in
the United States and spread to the rest of the world; it even shaped the planning and practices of state intervention in a remote corner of southwest China.
By and large, international AIDS-intervention protocols underscore that all
local values and meanings are cultural constructs and all services and interventions should be locally appropriate (e.g., UNAIDS 2000). In many situations,
however, the notion of "culturally appropriate AIDS intervention" is an empty
promise because of policy makers' or practitioners' ignorance of cultural difference and power inequality (Pigg 2002). In other words, the antistigma interven-

tion agenda is often based on the assumption that "intervention specialists . . . know the truth about what is needed" and that they can simply impose an intervention program that will "increase empathy and altruism" or "reduce anxiety and fear" on a target community (Parker and Aggleton 2003, 16, 21). Limu is a real-world case that challenges this assumption. The moral assemblage regarding AIDS and its negative impact exhibits a different set of "facts" that have traveled across the globe (Nguyen 2005). At best the state's application of an externally developed antistigma agenda was mechanical and failed to adjust to the situation on the ground.

Transplanting a Global Antistigma Agenda

The involvement of international institutions in shaping the trajectories of recent AIDS interventions in China has been well documented (He and Rehnstrom 2005; Kaufman, Kleinman, and Saich 2006a). The Chinese central government began HIV/AIDS surveillance in 1986. Official reports of HIV infection became mandatory at all levels of government in 1989. In 1995 the World Health Organization supported China's Ministry of Health in establishing 42 sentinel surveillance sites (in drug-rehabilitation centers, prisons, border outposts, and karaoke bars) in twenty-three provinces. By 2002 the number of sentinel surveillance sites had increased to 158, covering all thirty-one provinces (He and Detels 2005; Wu, Rou, and Cui 2004). The China-UK Project was launched in 2000. The Global Fund to Fight AIDS, Tuberculosis and Malaria began operations in 2005. That same year, the U.S. pharmaceutical giant Merck signed a contract with China's Ministry of Health and promised $30 million for AIDS intervention (Lan et al. 2005). These are just some examples of large-scale international AIDS collaborations, not to mention the involvement of many other UN agencies, foreign government aid organizations, and international NGOs.

From the outset of the HIV epidemic in Yunnan Province and China's adoption of the international practice of labeling "AIDS high-risk groups," Chinese public health officials have targeted certain populations—drug users, migrants, and sex workers—for surveillance and screening, whether they have exhibited a high incidence of HIV infection or not (Hyde 2007). Since 1995 the list has included clinic patients being treated for sexually transmitted diseases and long-distance truck drivers. Since 2003 men who have sex with men have also been targeted for surveillance (He and Detels 2005).

Power and preexisting stereotypes concerning people are crucial to our understanding of state AIDS interventions in China. For instance, the designation of "high-risk groups" is not only a medical issue but also a moral, legal, and po-litical one (Hyde 2007). As in many countries, the label connotes personal mis-conduct or characteristics that can be classified as "deviant," but in China the state also considers deviance a threat to public security and a challenge to gov-ernment authority. The label carries preexisting moral connotations the state has associated with certain populations since the founding of socialist China. Among these "high-risk groups," drug users are seen as the primary target be-cause China's HIV/AIDS epidemic was reported to have begun among needle-sharing heroin users. Targeting drug users is additionally part and parcel of China's war on drugs, an important component of its modern nation building (Zhou 1999). For the Nuosu, the state's derogatory classification of them as a backward "slave society" has defined them and their culture as deviant in rela-tion to its science-based, Han-centered governance. The current prevalence of heroin use and HIV/AIDS among the Nuosu has only earned them more nega-tive stereotypes. As both a fatal infectious disease and "an epidemic of significa-tion," AIDS has exhibited "a continuum . . . not a dichotomy, between popular and biomedical discourses," as Treichler (1999, 15) puts it.

Under the circumstances, it is no surprise that AIDS-related stigma and dis-crimination have become a major problem across China (He and Detels 2005; Wu, Rou, and Cui 2004). Some provinces or cities have even instituted explicit discriminatory practices against people with HIV/AIDS (Davis 2003). In 1999, Chengdu, the capital of Sichuan Province, enacted a law that prohibited HIV-infected people from applying for marriage licenses (Hyde 2007). Policy re-searchers have frequently noted the degree to which Chinese health workers and officials ascribe stigma to HIV/AIDS, as seen in their reluctance to work with HIV-infected people (Wu, Rou, and Cui 2004; Yang et al. 2005).

Researchers and international organizations working with the Chinese gov-ernment have all emphasized the importance of preventing the formation of such stigma and have proposed various plans to minimize it (e.g., China-UK 2001; Kaufman and Jing 2002; UNAIDS 2001). This call certainly has merit and urgency, especially for people living under the shadow of discrimination. How-ever, few studies have actually identified the social relevance of AIDS stigmati-zation in China. One exception is research conducted by anthropologist Sandra Hyde (2007), who argues that Yunnan provincial public health officials have based their approach to AIDS-related stigma on preexisting stereotypes about local minority populations. Another exception is a study conducted by anthro-pologist Jun Jing, who, in his study of AIDS panics in China, stresses the importance of understanding them as culturally constructed phenomena resulting from the local media's criminalization of people with HIV/AIDS (Jing 2006).

My own research points to how health officials in Limu have incorporated their own brand of AIDS-related stigma into interventions that were set up to counteract an imagined stigma among the local Nuosu. The case of Limu demonstrates that the government-sponsored scheme was a self-fulfilling prophecy: it first created and then opposed a stigma that was much more limited by local factors than had been assumed. In the process, it actually engendered a local public discourse at odds with its initial intervention goal.

The China-UK Project, like other international AIDS programs, called for antistigma efforts to protect the human rights of people with HIV/AIDS. Internationally, antistigma interventions aim mainly at increasing public awareness and acceptance of people with HIV/AIDS. This objective is based on the assumption that ordinary people blame or have negative emotional responses to people with HIV/AIDS (Parker and Aggleton 2003). The project team working in Limu received similar directives from above and proceeded on that assumption. Predictably, the project team adopted the state's practice of using public slogans as key instruments of policy dissemination.

Even locally, the posting of the eye-catching slogans was not without controversy. Several state agents debated their merits—on the basis of either their consciousness of AIDS-related stigma observed elsewhere or their own fear of AIDS. When the China-UK Project had these slogans painted on walls across the town, certain county government officials were unhappy because they felt the slogans would deter visitors from coming to Limu, either for economic investment or for entertainment at the hot springs. The targeted Nuosu peasants remained largely indifferent to the slogans. One reason is that local people tended not to stigmatize people with HIV/AIDS, so they did not need to be "corrected" for these nonexistent prejudices. Another even more obvious reason was Limu's high level of illiteracy; the great majority of local Nuosu could not read these messages or other similar political slogans, especially those written in Chinese characters.

These slogans, simultaneously condemning heroin use and AIDS and promoting care for people with HIV/AIDS, revealed, as much as anything, the state agents' own fear and unease about AIDS and its victims. They served more as a declaration of the China-UK Project's authority and altruistic efforts than a message for public education.

To illustrate the gap between the state agents' intended messages and the local social reality with regard to the stigma of AIDS, I will show how the Nuosu in Limu perceived AIDS by way of an analysis of their moral world. In recent discussions of the formation of stigma, scholars have emphasized using the lived experiences of the local moral world as a vantage point from which to understand its production and transformation in a culturally specific context (Yang et al. 2007). A local moral world, according to Kleinman (1999), is a circumscribed domain where daily life is seen as the expression of moral tenets. The term "moral" here, following Kleinman, may be defined as locally specific codes of reasoning and judgment about acceptable or unacceptable personal qualities or conduct in the social arena. In contrast to ethical discourse, which is conducted by elites and intellectuals, both global and local, a moral code is the ideational component of everyday experience; it is "always about practical engagements in a particular local world" (Kleinman 1999, 365).

My exploratory questions concerning AIDS and stigma in Limu are these: What constitutes deviance among the local Nuosu? What moral tenets or worldview underlies this referential framework? Furthermore, what social factors in recent years have contributed to changes in Nuosu moral perspectives? I use Geertz's (1983) "experience-near" approach to construct an ideal-typical explanatory model for the Nuosu moral world. My analysis aims at filling the conceptual gaps between Limu peasants' and state agents' ideas about AIDS. It is necessary to point out that my description and discussion of the local moral world are not chronological but topical; the aim is to highlight the coexistence of contradictory phenomena and demonstrate the dynamic process of changing moral codes in the everyday lives of the local Nuosu.

The Nuosu Moral World

Driven by their antistigma concerns, health workers and government officials involved in Limu's China-UK Project were puzzled by the general absence of AIDS stigma among the local people. This phenomenon is manifest, for instance, in the story in Chapter 5 of the Nuosu who, unconcerned with the AIDS label, wanted to be included in the project roster to receive state resources. The state agents came to believe that the peasants lacked adverse feelings about having the disease because of their ignorance about its fatality. This belief, however, is inconsistent with reports indicating that simple misunderstanding or limited awareness about the emerging epidemic has often led to hypervigilance among the public and created hostility toward people with HIV/AIDS (Green and Sobo 2000).

To fully explore the deep-seated factors underlying Limu's situation, I examine four facets of the Nuosu culture: kinship relationships, disease etiology, the Nuosu theory of the causality and liability for death, and the taxonomy of death. A discussion of indigenous Nuosu reasoning may help explain why local people generally have only a vague perception of AIDS as a disease and do not harbor prejudice toward its victims.

Stigma in a Kinship-Based Society

In rural Nuosu society, individuals can barely survive emotionally without the support of kin; the most dreadful punishment for an ordinary Nuosu is to be expelled from one's lineage (Bamo 1994). Prior research has reported that HIV-infected Nuosu in Limu and elsewhere in Liangshan continued to participate in lineage meetings and share food and drink with healthy kinsmen, who seemingly had no apprehension about their participation (Hou et al. 2003). This inclusive kinship principle, with its central concern for the general well-being of all kinsmen, undermines the centrifugal forces of stigmatization, as we saw in the story of Mahxi Ggurre, one of the four brothers presented in Chapter 4.

The kinship principle is the bedrock of the Nuosu social milieu in which AIDS is situated, but it alone cannot account for the general absence of stigma in Limu; local Nuosu generally do not stigmatize people with HIV/AIDS outside their kinship networks either. Turning this reasoning around, we find that they do *not* automatically accept all kin members unconditionally. In other words, Nuosu *do* have cultural criteria—or discriminatory conditions—that facilitate their identification of difference and labeling of deviance in opposition to normality.

In Nuosu society, deviance and major social stigma are associated with breaching established norms and precepts that originate from within the kinship universe. Most non-disease-related stigma arise from socially unacceptable conduct judged to be in violation of preexisting social relationships. For instance, anyone who steals from other lineage members or engages in sex that violates the incest taboo (even among lineage members as remote as up to twenty or more generations) can anticipate facing strong stigmatization, possibly even the death penalty, or at least ostracism from kinship networks that extend beyond the local community.

As for disease-related stigma, the most serious attaches to people who live with leprosy, tuberculosis, or nauseating body odor. On the basis of their worldview and etiology, the Nuosu consider these three conditions "hereditary." As a consequence, intermarriage with people bearing them is taboo because Nuosu people fear that these marriages—through reproduction—will spread the illnesses or symptoms within the lineage. People even express strong aversion to the kin of a person with such symptoms, a sort of "courtesy stigma" attached to "normal" people related to the stigmatized person (Goffman 1963). In the past, in order to protect lineage members from contagion and preserve the reputation of the lineage, kinsmen would kill anyone with these symptoms, lepers in particular; at the very least he or she would be sent into exile in the wilderness. But AIDS, while a disease, has not been identified or categorized as "hereditary," and hence it has yet to jeopardize kinship relationships the way these other, stigmatized diseases do.

Nuosu Popular Knowledge of Disease and Illness

In all societies sickness requires interpretation, which is a culturally informed process. Such interpretation is embedded in the fabric of people's daily lives and is often linked with their religion and worldview. Kleinman (1980) proposes an explanatory model to distinguish between the objective and subjective natures of sickness that is useful for cross-cultural research. The centrality of "culture" that Kleinman underscores is key to the difference between a disease and an illness. A disease is a physiological malfunctioning of the organic body that incapacitates the patient. An illness, on the other hand, is a disease symptom that is defined by the culture as "sick" according to established norms. In other words, "Disease . . . represent[s] the medical model, illness . . . the native's point of view" (Treichler 1999, 159). Following this explanatory model, we may argue that the biomedical fact of AIDS as a new disease has yet to be incorporated into culturally established categories of illness by the Nuosu.

According to traditional Nuosu culture, most illnesses are caused by ghosts or the loss of the patient's soul (Azi 1993; X. Liu 2001). This etiology still dominates Nuosu peasants' daily life to a considerable degree. In complex societies, medical pluralism is the norm rather than the exception (Durkin-Longley 1984). Since the 1950s, when the state began championing science-based medicine as the only legitimate—that is, nonsuperstitious—approach to disease treatment, Nuosu peasants have practiced a kind of medical pluralism. Given greater freedom of choice in the reform era, rural Nuosu people have increasingly relied on more than one therapeutic system, simultaneously or in succession, to treat an illness. In other words, their diagnoses and treatments of illnesses mix science-based medicine, religion-based ritual healing, and occasionally a whole host of herbal, mineral, or animal potions that, functioning as medicine, have either been developed by the Nuosu themselves or introduced from Han or

Tibetan sources. Although in some cases rural Nuosu people may agree that biomedicine has the most potency for treating certain physiological problems, especially those involving acute conditions, they may still reckon the "actual" or "original" cause of the illness through their own cultural lens. One study shows that Nuosu peasants in Zhaojue County spend roughly the same amount of money on ritual healings as they do on biomedicine (Shi et al. 1999). In 2005 I observed or heard about various healing rituals in Nuosu villages almost daily.

Bimo have a body of knowledge about human misfortune that derives from their predecessors and ritual texts, by means of which they categorize sickness into culturally recognizable illnesses and prescribe treatments for them. AIDS has yet to be classified as a distinctive illness in this tradition. A bimo who once held exorcism rituals to treat two HIV-infected patients explained to me how he conceptualized AIDS:

> I don't know anything about AIDS. I just treat their illnesses and identify what the problems are in their body and in their relationships with specific ghosts, with the help of our bimo ritual texts and instruments. All disease symptoms are recorded in the texts. There is no AIDS ghost.

Indeed, many AIDS symptoms are quite similar to what Nuosu have already experienced in the rural environment in which they live, where inadequate hygiene, nutrition, and medical services are chronic problems and common diseases are prevalent. There are many recognized types of illness in their everyday lives. People are familiar with symptoms such as fever, fatigue, diarrhea, coughing, rash, and external infections. They can recognize the symptoms and diagnose such diseases as tuberculosis, liver disease, and skin disease, although they may not use biomedical terms to describe them. In short, local people may link many AIDS-related symptoms to their established knowledge of illness, for which reason they do not need to identify and explain AIDS as a "new" illness.

During my casual conversations with Limu people, they often asked me what AIDS "really" is or whether there is an AIDS disease. Many people did not believe that the disease existed at all. Mahxi Ggurre, for example, attended the AIDS sessions regularly and often played the role of "model patient" for the China-UK Project; but until he finally surrendered to the disease in 2009, he did not believe that untreated AIDS is fatal.

> I don't feel the disease in my body. I feel good. Sometimes I have colds, but I still eat a lot and work strenuously. Several years ago, two foreign doctors along with

the township clinic doctors said I would die within a year. Their words scared me to death! But later nothing happened to me, and I have lived for more than two years since then. I am feeling well. So they must be wrong. I don't have the AIDS disease. There is no AIDS disease. I no longer believe in doctors.

Some of the China-UK Project's registered patients accepted the biomedical status of HIV infection, especially if the insidious progress of the illness affected them in obvious ways; but their knowledge of AIDS remained vague. At times they continued to explain their illnesses, which were probably due to their weakened immunity, through a cultural lens. One day at the Limu clinic I saw an HIV-infected couple coming in for the wife's treatment. Upon seeing me, they invited me to visit them that evening, when they would be holding a bimo ritual. I asked them the reason for the event and the husband replied, "We Nuosu believe that there must be ghosts for our unknown illnesses." I was curious and asked, "But you know you are HIV infected and why you are sick. So why do you need the bimo?" The man explained:

> I know my AIDS comes from my drug injection. And my wife's AIDS [virus] was transmitted from me. So we don't rely on bimo for treating our AIDS. But my wife coughs endlessly and has had bad diarrhea lately. We think that these are caused by ghosts, and we want the bimo to find out which ghosts.

Sometimes local Nuosu people followed health officials' diagnoses, but at other times they relied on their own explanations. Their remarks suggest the extent to which local people consider AIDS to be an amorphous disease. It has yet to carve out a niche in their traditional universe of illness.

The Nuosu Theory of Causality and Liability

The Nuosu have a general theory of causation that provides a rational scheme of culpability in life-and-death events, and this can further help explain how their moral convictions resist the formation of AIDS-related stigma. When deliberating the causes of a person's bodily injury or death, Nuosu people typically single out the most recent and most immediate contributing factor. This reasoning is comparable to the causality-and-liability theory that the Jalé in New Guinea hold: "Jalé's reasoning deduces jural liability from a doctrine of effective action that does not distinguish between intent, negligence, inadvertence, and accident as aggravating or extenuating circumstances" (Koch 1974, 86). Occasionally the Nuosu may consider a culprit's motivation in an accidental or unpremeditated killing, and the factor of motivation may lead to other forms of compensation. In a murder case, however, a culprit's shirking of the death penalty (that is, collectively demanded suicide) will generally lead to disrespect in the community (Qubi and Ma 2001).

A Nuosu proverb best reveals the doctrine of direct and immediate causation: *Gene torruo masuwe, syne orruo masuwe* (In wrestling, the one on top wins; in death, the one at the bottom wins). This means that the dead person always merits compensation regardless of his or her previous conduct, and the person who "causes" the death is liable regardless of his or her intentions or circumstances. For instance, if person A identifies person B as a thief and subsequently B commits suicide out of shame, person A will be held responsible for B's death, regardless of whether B had actually stolen or not. When a death is involved, ndeggu frequently quote the proverb above when dispensing justice. This sort of death is called *nga sy ne bby*, literally "I give my death to you," signifying B's most effective method of protest against A.

As a rule, local Nuosu do not express their negative feelings toward someone directly to his or her face. In light of this Nuosu judiciary doctrine, should someone humiliate an HIV-infected person and "cause" him or her to commit suicide, the person responsible for the humiliation will have to compensate dearly. This doctrine also explains why an old woman felt she could do very little to intervene in her son's drug habit. She was unhappy about her son's drug addiction and scolded the dealer for selling drugs to her son. Later, when speaking to the son, the dealer had expressed his anger at her scolding. The son, in turn, complained to his mother that she had humiliated the drug dealer. He warned her not to risk bearing the responsibility should something bad happen to the dealer. This doctrine also explains why Nuosu drug dealers never sell to users in front of others: they want to avoid the perception that they had anything to do with any subsequent drug-related accident. Nuosu ideas of cause and effect are thus a crucial factor in people's reluctance to humiliate others.

The Taxonomy of Death

By and large, local Nuosu do not avoid preparing and attending funerals for the HIV-infected dead. I saw female kin and relatives stay beside or touch the face of a newly deceased victim to express their affection. Male kin prepare the cremation of the dead the same way they do for those who died of "ordinary" causes. Kin, relatives, friends, and neighbors come from near and far to mourn the dead as common courtesy. I observed that the Nuosu cremator burned HIV-infected bodies in the same way that other dead are burned, as a group of kinsmen waited on-site for the completion of the cremation. Upon my asking what they thought of HIV-related deaths, local Nuosu usually responded, "They died of AIDS, just as other people die from normal sickness."

The Nuosu have their unique way of distinguishing between normal and abnormal deaths and performing different commemorating rituals. Normal deaths include those from *na* (illness) and *mojji* (senility). *Bbyssy* (abnormal deaths) are caused by murder, suicide, or accidents. Each category has its distinct mortuary treatment. For example, the bodies of the "abnormally" dead cannot be burned on a hillside near or in the woods as can those of the "normally" dead. The abnormally dead must be burned next to a stream, and immediately after cremation the ashes must be washed away in the running water. For abnormal deaths, a series of bimo rituals must be performed immediately after the funeral to expel evil spirits, but the family of the normally dead need only hold a simple bimo ritual for the general well-being of all.

The Nuosu's taxonomy of death is strictly related to their general theory of causation. People point to the most recent and most direct factor as the "real" killer when deaths are associated with multiple causes. For example, when someone's death involves drugs, people reckon the death as normal if the person falls ill for a few days after injection. In contrast, the death is reckoned as abnormal— an accident—if it occurs immediately after the injection.[4] In line with this reasoning, people who injected heroin using contaminated needles, contracted HIV, and eventually died of AIDS symptoms were viewed to have had a normal death.

Thus far, I have examined Nuosu kinship ties, traditional beliefs and rules regarding disease and death, and their approaches to determining legal liability. Their practical reasoning helps answer why, early on, Limu's Nuosu did not assign negative labels to AIDS or its victims. In a nutshell, the elements Link and Phelan (2001) have suggested to be crucial to stigmatization did not appear in a significant way among the Nuosu.

In recent years, however, I have begun to notice changes. During my initial visit to Limu in 2002, I never observed or heard of any AIDS stigma. I interviewed a young man who married that year; no one from his or his wife's family objected to him because of his HIV status. In 2004, I visited a young male drug user who was reported to be HIV positive. His sister-in-law had just been transferred (married) to him earlier that year after his elder brother had died. She made no objection to this transfer. But by 2005, most young people I spoke to clearly rejected the possibility of marrying anyone with HIV/AIDS. Although local Nuosu retained their earlier perceptions of AIDS and generally did not stigmatize its victims, the fear of AIDS seemed to be creeping in. Some locals, with new concerns taking hold, were beginning to modify their interactions with people with HIV/AIDS. The stigmatization of AIDS has grown perceptibly in people's daily lives, in sync with Limu's changing political economy.

Contention over State Interventions

International public health priorities intersected with Nuosu moral codes as state AIDS interventions introduced a new sense of stigma among locals. At this juncture, we can study the local politics of stigma embedded in the mixed influences of state practices and the encroaching global market economy.

Since 2001 the China-UK Project had made similar interventions in other localities in Liangshan and had identified the Nuosu as the most volatile and epidemic-prone population in Sichuan Province. State agents circulated the image of a diseased community and a high-risk population, which the mass media transmitted to the general public, exacerbating old stereotypes held by the state agents and encouraging their condescending treatment. An ironic nickname used for the area, "The Five Golden Flowers" (*wuduo jinhua*), illustrates Liangshan's unfavorable position on China's road map to hygienic modernity. Public health officials in Liangshan and elsewhere borrowed the title of a classic 1959 film, which celebrates the socialist state's romantic and exotic image of its ethnic minorities and the mobilization of national masses to pursue the ambitious goals of the Great Leap Forward, for the local epidemics. In recent years, public health officials have added AIDS to an existing four-item list of major infectious diseases in Liangshan (cholera, leprosy, tuberculosis, and snail fever), and now these five afflictions jointly constitute the "Five Golden Flowers" of ethnic Liangshan. In the eyes of state agents, people in Limu and other HIV-impacted localities in Liangshan fit the old stereotypes of the Nuosu. In addition to their marginality as peasants and ethnic minorities (Cohen 1993; Litzinger 2000), HIV-infected Nuosu now bear a third stigma.

In consequence, unsurprisingly, the project's promise to engage local knowledge and practices remained an empty one. Its fight against AIDS-related stigma was implemented unthinkingly and so state agents simply translated their assumptions into the habitual use of slogans.

Unfortunately, the warnings and painted slogans did convey the message of a fearsome new disease to one local demographic group, the mostly educated state agents—government officials, health workers, and primary school teachers. In their conversations with me, they often expressed moral condemnation of AIDS and its victims. By exploring these negative responses, coming from people who should have known better, we may trace the steps of Limu's developing stigmatization of AIDS.

My own attitude toward Limu's health workers can be best described as ambivalent. At times I sympathized with their unenviable professional situation: the state assigned them to perform critical and complicated public health work but failed to support them with sufficient resources. On other occasions I was irritated by their exaggerated fear of and stereotypes about AIDS and its victims. Some health workers, for example, suggested that all HIV-infected people be quarantined in a separate locality so there would be no further transmission. Another told me, as we were walking to the hot-spring bathhouse for a shower, "AIDS is too serious here. Now I don't dare to take a bath in the hot-spring pool." I argued, "You won't get HIV by taking a bath in the pool." She replied, "I know. But the feeling is no good." She also told me that many of her friends in the county seat would not come to the hot springs anymore owing to their fear of AIDS. As mentioned in Chapter 5, health workers sometimes questioned registered patients' entitlement to the project's free treatment of symptomatic illnesses; one commented, "Why should we care for the infected drug users? It's a waste of time and money. They should not have used drugs in the first place. They reap what they sow [*zizuo zishou*]!"

Other state agents involved in the project entertained yet other myths about AIDS. Some complained that their work exposed them to the risk of HIV transmission, even though they had no direct bodily contact with HIV-infected people. One said to me, "We [the project team] are under a lot of stress. Think about the risks we run *facing* these HIV-positive people everyday! I don't want to do this work. It's too risky!" In reality, his main project-related duties were delivering charity goods and presenting lectures to registered patients—hardly risky activities by any medical standard. This sense of repulsion stands in ironic contrast to the idealistic China-UK Project proclamation "A Beloved Homestead" (*aixin jiayuan*), hung at the entrance to the township government building.

Fear of AIDS can be contagious. The driver for the China-UK Project did not want to get out of his vehicle anytime he drove officials over to Limu for inspections because, he maintained, "Here [in Limu] it's horrifying. I don't want to contract AIDS!" A Nuosu primary school teacher who lived in the township clinic screamed in fear when she realized that she had just touched a piece of embroidery made by a local HIV-infected woman. She cried out, "What can

I do [to remedy my exposure to the disease]? I haven't gotten married yet!" I can imagine how instructors with this type of negative attitude teach AIDS-related stigma to their pupils. These episodes took place in 2005, fully eighteen years after the early myths about AIDS circulated in New York City, where for two weeks a mailman refused to deliver mail to an AIDS task force because he feared catching the disease (Herek and Glunt 1988).

When talking to me or in my presence, most educated state agents in Limu tended to withhold their negative opinions about HIV-infected people. I gathered this was because they knew of my willingness to accept people with the disease. Like many local peasants who were interested in my activities, the state agents also gossiped about me. I usually did not know the content of their gossip unless someone voluntarily informed me. In one such conversation, a local official confided, "We think you are strange. It's meaningless to spend so much time on peasants. And you hang out with drug users and people with HIV/AIDS every day. Aren't you afraid?"

The China-UK Project provided the people of Limu with many forms of AIDS education, from propaganda posters in the township clinics to mass lectures delivered at the local schools and during township and village meetings. Even years after the project's intervention, most Limu people still could not make sense of what the state agents had told them about AIDS. As Munyo, the head of the Limu clinic, concluded, "There is no AIDS in the minds of our Nuosu peasants. It's hard for us doctors to teach them about AIDS." Failing to convey accurate knowledge about AIDS to the local Nuosu—in part because their own understanding of the disease was so vague—state agents resorted to lecturing peasants on the dreadful characteristics of AIDS in hopes of promoting awareness and prevention. Officials or village cadres who attended the project's AIDS-education sessions, in turn, passed this message on to the ordinary peasants. One cadre informant said to me:

> We are all afraid of AIDS. The AIDS education has taught us that. Being [HIV] infected means you have at most fifteen more years to live, just like probation from a death sentence!

On another occasion, I heard a township official at a village meeting give the following warning:

> Don't use drugs. Behave well. Or we Nuosu will become extinct because of AIDS. Han people are not afraid of leprosy but of AIDS. But you are scared of leprosy, not of AIDS. It's no good. You should be afraid of AIDS. It's fatal and incurable!

By continually lecturing on AIDS and, in particular, by conveying its horrifying effects through a mixture of biomedical assertions, half-truths, and a
degree of guesswork, state agents overcame initial obstacles to instilling in the
local Nuosu an uninformed conception of AIDS as a fearsome disease. Acceptance of this conception of AIDS was more pronounced among people who interacted more with state agents or who lived adjacent to the clinic, the primary
school, or the township government office.

One day in September 2005, Jjiebba Quti, one of the four brothers described
in Chapter 4, squatted in front of his house; he had bruises and scratches on his
face. Quti lived by the township government office and had had a big fight with
his robust wife the night before. His wife had learned from others that AIDS
was a frightening disease and had scolded Quti about his infection. The previous year a China-UK Project worker had informed Quti of his HIV positive
status but did not later ask Quti to attend the project's monthly AIDS sessions;
so Quti thought his "AIDS" had been cured. Unbeknownst to Quti, his name
was not listed on the project roster of HIV cases, even though he had acquired
the official AIDS label in 2004. When his wife blamed him for having the disease, he replied, "I am cured. I don't have AIDS now." But she refused to believe
him and beat him out of fear and anger. A few days later, Quti's wife asked me
privately, "Is there *really* AIDS?" I told her that there is indeed an AIDS disease
but it is often preventable if people follow simple and appropriate protection
procedures, such as the use of condoms. I also suggested that she consult health
workers about her concerns. But she abruptly ended our conversation by asserting, "I don't believe in AIDS. People say it doesn't exist."

The disparity between the professional and vernacular perceptions of AIDS
underscores the characterization of AIDS as "an epidemic of clarity, a disease
of confusion" (Setel 1999, 183). Moreover, such ambivalence about AIDS shows
how messages emanating from the state make their way into the minds of local
people. This local demographic difference in conceptualizing AIDS reveals
how its stigmatization has taken shape along lines of power, from international
and national levels through state agents to local educated people and gradually
throughout the entire community.

The Emerging Stigmatization of AIDS

In Limu, local Nuosu generally did not stigmatize people with HIV/AIDS. But
with continuous exposure to messages about the horrifying effects of AIDS,
they began gradually to consider AIDS special. Over the course of my stay in

Limu, I observed that local people responded to AIDS in contradictory manners: some exhibited little concern, while others expressed serious concern. Despite this ambivalence, local people's negative perceptions toward AIDS and its victims have grown in frequency and intensity.

Labeling is a crucial step in stigma construction (Goffman 1963; Jones et al. 1984; Link and Phelan 1999). In Limu there was no secret as to who was HIV positive because of the China-UK Project's broad-based blood tests and the charity goods distributed to registered patients. Oftentimes, as people introduced or described someone who was HIV positive to me, they would mention the person's "AIDS" along with the lineage name. Once I attended the funeral of a woman who had died the day before. One of her elder kinsmen, who was receiving guests at the entranceway, led me into her one-room house. Inside, I found her body facing the house entrance beneath the television set that was mounted up high on the wall. There were twenty to thirty women, young and old, sitting by her side or against the wall watching the flickering screen. Knowing that I carried a camera, the man glanced at the dead woman and said to me, "AIDS. Take a picture?" Several women in the room laughed and looked at me expectantly.

That the kinsman of the dead woman identified her cause of death as AIDS was intriguing. My local knowledge told me that Nuosu people do not readily disclose a case of shameful or stigmatized death, particularly to an outsider like me. In addition, the kinsman's matter-of-fact suggestion that I take a photograph of the body shows that he did not object to a visual record of the AIDS death. During my fieldwork, people often asked me to photograph them or their activities. But I was aware that locals objected to visual records of stigmatized people or deeds. For instance, I interviewed a cured leper in Limu and, after the interview, the old leper did not ask me to photograph him.[5] His family and neighbors around us did not prod me to photograph him either, as people normally would. Since the Nuosu consider leprosy a stigmatized condition, their avoidance of having him photographed made sense. Moreover, the women who overheard the kinsman's suggestion that I photograph the woman's body laughed out loud. Their response contrasted sharply with the silent response of the leper's family and neighbors. In brief, numerous AIDS-related episodes suggest to me that while locals still do not consider AIDS to belong in the category of abnormal diseases, they have gradually come to identify it as something unusual, whose exact nature has yet to be defined.

The long-term negative consequence of labeling is stigmatization, which develops incrementally rather than all at once (Link and Phelan 1999). Moreover, the distribution of stigma may not be uniform or even: for example, young people may be more receptive to new ideas than the old. As local Nuosu have learned that AIDS is to be feared and categorized as a special disease, some have begun to act on these ideas in their relations with AIDS-labeled people. One day, I invited several young men to lunch. One of them did not attend because, as he privately confessed to me later, he did not want to eat with another guest, who was HIV positive. He was not alone; another man, who attended the lunch, said to me afterward, privately: "I was a bit worried. Since you seemed not to be concerned, I just followed suit. But was it really all right to be eating with him?"

The growing concern about AIDS is also finding expression among infected people themselves. Several HIV-infected Nuosu told me that when they sought treatment for other ailments at Zhaojue County Hospital, they never volunteered information about their HIV status. They were aware of and uncomfortable with the stigma with which residents in the county seat regarded people with the disease. One young HIV-infected man made me especially aware of this "stigma consciousness" (Pinel 1999). During my fieldwork, men liked to shake hands with me as a way of expressing their welcome or friendliness. This man did not offer his hand upon my arrival. I assumed he was just shy, so I extended my right hand toward him. He hesitated and said, "I have AIDS." At that moment, it dawned on me that he had internalized others' fear of his disease and himself. As the gap separating labeled people from others widens, the appearance of stigma seems to be an inevitable development.

This development may be vague and amorphous in its early stages. For this reason we should not be surprised that, side by side with the emerging stigmatization of AIDS in Limu, HIV-infected men still joined lineage meetings, participated in social activities such as mediation and negotiation sessions, drank together with kinsmen on these occasions, and enjoyed leisure time with friends and neighbors; they also continued to labor with others in the fields, in the cement factory, and on construction projects beyond Liangshan.

Two days before his death in July 2005, I visited thirty-three-year-old Qomo Furmur, whose AIDS symptoms, especially ascites, had become evident. Although the China-UK Project workers had sent him to the county hospital for treatment, this had not helped because his immune system was in a state of seemingly irreversible collapse. When I visited Furmur, he was in bad shape. His father and neighbors had just carried him out of his father's dim and damp house for a bit of sun. His wife had been away working in Chengdu because his drug addiction had exhausted virtually all the family's assets a few years earlier. She was angry at him and did not wish to return. When Furmur had first fallen ill, his father took him in and cared for him. Every day, Furmur's father bought him cane sugar and dissolved it in water for him to drink; local people believe this potion is good for health. Sugar water was all the basic nutrition the poor father could afford for his sick son. During my visit a group of neighbors, adults and children, chatted and played around the sick Furmur. Sometimes as they were playing, the naked small children grabbed at his face from behind Furmur's back. I saw no expressions of concern on the faces of their parents, nor did anyone stop the children from playing with him.

But something else drew my attention in Furmur's case. Two days after my visit he died, and unlike the funerals of other young HIV-infected men, which normally attracted over two hundred people, only a handful of people attended Furmur's, most of them his neighbors. I wondered whether the small attendance was because Furmur had few kin. Muga explained, "This isn't the case. Furmur had many kinsmen, but Furmur's father couldn't afford to buy pigs and sheep to serve to funeral attendees. If Furmur and his father had the money, more people would have come for his funeral. People don't come to the funerals of the poor now."

Another HIV-infected man and his family in Limu were living in abject poverty. The family had many kinsmen in the area because they belonged to one of the largest lineages in the basin, but the family received no assistance from their kin. In recent years, they had rarely attended public affairs and local people seldom visited them; they lived in isolation. This family's situation and Furmur's case show that, among the Nuosu, social isolation of HIV-infected people may also stem from reasons other than stigmatization of the disease.

Many of the episodes mentioned above—the concern about eating with an HIV-positive man, the HIV-positive man hesitant to shake hands with me, Furmur's funeral, and the isolated family—made me aware of an additional factor that should be taken into account in studying the growth of AIDS-related stigma. In each of these cases, the HIV-infected person was extremely poor. I knew many relatively better-off people with HIV/AIDS who had not encountered comparable social isolation or discrimination. Stigmatization as a social process surely takes shape along the fault lines of inequality and power disparity (Castro and Farmer 2005; Link and Phelan 2001; Parker and Aggleton 2003; Yang et al. 2007). The emergence of AIDS-related stigma in Limu demonstrates that the local moral world is "a social space that carries cultural, political, and economic specificity" (Kleinman 1999, 365). As Limu takes strides toward a market economy in China's reform era, its traditional moral economy is changing in sync with its capitalist development (Heberer 2005; Liu 2007).

The Political Economy of Stigma

The social process of stigmatizing AIDS in Limu has revealed itself to be a complicated and delicate issue bound up with the local moral world, the state's AIDS-intervention practices, and the overarching political economy. Both state agents and local peasants participate in this process. In a time of rapid change, it is important to understand both local knowledge and its socioeconomic underpinnings in order to contextualize people's evolving lives and values; this is especially so in Limu as it accommodates itself to and creates its own version of capitalist modernity.

The changing moral landscape in Limu leads me to ponder general issues related to deviance and stigmatization among the Nuosu. Recent changes in the moral values attached to indigenous Nuosu social strata are especially provocative. In 2005 the traditional social hierarchy, which divided people into four social strata, still governed the worldview of the local Nuosu to a considerable degree and informed their practice of discrimination regarding those categorized as "slaves." But in Limu's everyday life these rigid divisions have in fact been collapsing, as is evident in certain common practices.

Marriage and social division provide one example. Traditionally, it was considered shameful for a Nuosu to marry someone from another ethnic group, including Han Chinese, or anyone from a lower Nuosu social stratum. Even now, many Limu people are still opposed to interethnic marriage in principle. Since the Democratic Reform, however, the Nuosu have grown accustomed to the view promulgated by the state that Han Chinese are culturally more advanced; and since the debut of market reform, the Nuosu have grown similarly accustomed to the view that Han Chinese are more materially prosperous or financially adept. Gradually, owing to this belief, the Nuosu's interactions with Han people have changed, including their increasing acceptance of Nuosu-Han marriage. This phenomenon has been obvious among the Nuosu who live in ethnically mixed areas or who work for various government offices. Now, in poor rural areas like Limu, more and more young people choose their spouses based not on their ethnic identity or social stratum but on general socioeconomic concerns.

The out-marriage phenomenon in Limu illustrates this shifting concern. Many Nuosu women who are descendants of "slaves"—and hence who had no prospect of marrying Nuosu men of good social standing—have chosen to "return" to their origins and marry Han men. At one time, government officials and local scholars saw the phenomenon of Limu's Nuosu women marrying out as evidence of stigma against local male drug users. Alternatively, one researcher called the phenomenon of marrying out a form of "human trafficking" (Hou et al. 2003). I do not know the circumstances under which these conclusions were reached; perhaps these phenomena indeed existed. However, my own understanding of Limu's out-marriage in recent years presents a totally different picture. When some of those Nuosu women returned to visit their families and kin in Limu, they were greeted with compliments such as "You've grown white [i.e., of light skin color] and plump. Life must be better in Han regions than here." A recent research project has reported an incident in which a Nuosu woman who had presumably been "trafficked" to a Han village refused to be "rescued" because she had never thought of her marriage to her Han husband as problematic. Instead, she was content with her much better livelihood away from Liangshan (Wei 2006). The researcher provided no detailed information about the woman's Nuosu social standing. My interpretation of this case is that material living conditions seem to have gradually become more important in marital considerations.

In the same vein, wealthy Nuosu men who come from "slave" roots may marry poor Nuosu women who come from the higher social category of "commoners." I attended a wedding in Limu in which the bride was from an important lineage and the groom was from a "slave" background. The groom was rich and the bride's family poor. She and her mother (her father had passed away) were happy about this marriage because of the financial security it offered. However, many of her kinsmen sneered at her "falling to a lower rung in the hierarchy" and thought that the marriage had disgraced their lineage's reputation. Most of her senior kinfolk, including her maternal uncle, were absent from her wedding owing to their disagreement with the union. Only young relatives accompanied her to the groom's home.

The changing moral landscape in Limu overall reminds us that stigmatization of AIDS is necessarily a multifaceted process. The devastating effects of this immunity-compromising disease are not the sole contributing factor to its stigmatization. Its stigma is being formed through a local social process that may also involve premodern social divisions, the state's modernity drive, and wealth differentials that have come with the expanding market economy of the reform era. Above all, the state's intentional and unintentional practices have played crucial roles in this negative development.

The findings I have presented in this chapter suggest that the Nuosu people's fear of AIDS originated, in large part, with the messages delivered by state agents in their intervention programs. The AIDS-related stigma that is gradually taking shape among the Nuosu likely will have an impact on the local moral codes. As one village cadre put it:

> We knew nothing about AIDS until the China-UK Project came here. Now everybody is afraid of AIDS. But we don't stigmatize AIDS patients. . . . It's hard to say whether there will be [AIDS-related] stigma in the future.

Preventing or removing stigma is truly important in any AIDS-intervention project. Yet such projects should be based on a prior understanding of the issue of stigmatization among any given people or society. By skipping this essential step, the project team introduced their own negative attitudes toward the Nuosu peasants and AIDS into the global antistigma agenda and transplanted it to a culturally unsuitable locality—Limu—where previously no such stigma had existed and would most likely not have developed without the state's programs. Although research including mine has shown that globalization has contributed to the problems of drug use and HIV/AIDS and concomitantly brought awareness of their risks, "it has not made people the same the world over" (Eves and Butt 2008, 5). We may see diverse interpretations and responses among people across cultures. The global "AIDS industry," however, has gradually made AIDS the engine of one form of globalization, "namely the dissemination of western-derived discourses to other societies" (Altman 1998, 233). The epidemics of heroin use and HIV/AIDS are ongoing in Limu, and no definitive end to them seems within reach. Both in this and in previous chapters, I hope to have illuminated how and why the interventions meant to alleviate a local health crisis in Limu have gone awry.

Conclusion

The implications of my research can be extended far beyond the landlocked Nuosu community. To understand the causes and spread of the epidemics that have devastated Limu, I have lifted my eyes "from the local dramas of a small village" to external conditions and the multistranded developments in the wider world (Farmer 1992, 253). Since China's historic plunge into the capitalist market, Limu's young men have constructed a new life trajectory, a process characterized by several stages—something I have called a "rite of passage" for the marginalized. Meanwhile, the long journey toward understanding them and their suffering has been my own rite of passage to becoming a professional anthropologist situated in the thought-provoking era of globalization.

My knowledge of and concern with AIDS in China expanded dramatically in 2000. That year was marked by a critical event that accelerated global awareness of AIDS in rural China: the *New York Times* ran a devastating feature story about an AIDS outbreak caused by unsafe blood collection practices in Henan Province (Rosenthal 2000). Soon the image of an HIV/AIDS pandemic in China was broadcast to the rest of the world. Even before this event unfolded, international agencies and the Chinese government had begun collaborating on AIDS intervention, in a low-profile and limited sort of way. Soon, however, the international agencies began to push full throttle for the Chinese government to acknowledge the titanic crisis it faced with AIDS (UNAIDS 2001) and to increase its acceptance of international assistance to curb the spread of the disease. A five-year plan (2001–2005) for AIDS prevention and control was implemented, and beginning in mid-2003, the Chinese government became significantly more open and progressive in tackling the problem (Kaufman, Kleinman, and Saich 2006b).

The HIV/AIDS epidemic in Limu and Liangshan becomes relevant and significant in this national—ultimately global—context. I first went to Limu as a
graduate student in the summer of 2002 with an applied AIDS research team
organized by Professor Hou Yuangao, a Nuosu ethnologist from Beijing Central
University of Nationalities, whose project was funded by the China-UK Project
beginning in 2001. At that time, to my knowledge, this project was one of the only
three anthropological studies, among the numerous China-UK–sponsored projects, that had been strenuously championed by Chinese anthropologist Jun Jing.
As a guest participant in this field project, my precise role was unplanned and my
knowledge of the Nuosu practically nil. Before we boarded the train for the two-
day journey from Beijing to Liangshan Prefecture's capital, Xichang, I was told
that Limu was the epicenter of the HIV/AIDS epidemic in Liangshan and that in
Sichuan Province, Liangshan was the region most devastated by the disease. I was
further told that the disease had been introduced by heroin users sharing needles.

That summer project inspired me to explore this poor and isolated community, which could only be reached by a nearly ten-hour bus ride from Xichang
during the summer rainy season. Part of the transportation problem at that
point was the result of construction along the main road connecting Xichang
and its adjacent rural areas. But the very difficulty of access made a deep impression on me and aroused my curiosity about the alleged crisis in Limu: How
could such an out-of-the-way community have come under the dual assault of
devastating heroin and HIV/AIDS epidemics?

After that summer I returned to Columbia University and reoriented my
dissertation research to focus on heroin and AIDS in Limu. In the following summers of 2003 and 2004, I visited Liangshan again, both times inde-
pendently, with the assistance of a few friends and scholars whom I had come
to know during my first trip to the region. On those visits I sought chiefly to
establish local contacts as well as to collect available documents or published
works on Nuosu culture and history. With the groundwork thus prepared, in
December 2004 I embarked on my year-long dissertation fieldwork in Liangshan, in high spirits and with the eagerness any graduate student experiences
on venturing into the field.

At the outset my application for local police permission to conduct unin-
terrupted long-term fieldwork in Limu encountered obstacles. I was told that
no foreigners had ever stayed in rural Liangshan for more than a month, nor
could I. Then in February 2005, after I had spent two months in limbo, my luck
changed. Through the assistance of various friends and officials in Xichang and

at Sichuan University in Chengdu, the local police finally assented and I was allowed to reside in this rural township on a long-term basis. My extended residence in Limu enabled me to establish daily contacts with villagers from all walks of life and develop intimate knowledge of everyday life there.

My induction into life in Limu culminated in the fruitful yet heart-wrenching year of 2005. During that year I often found myself preoccupied with gnawing ethical and emotional pangs due to the human suffering I witnessed in this poverty- and epidemic-stricken community. I spent many tearful nights alone in my shabby room in the township clinic, saddened by the sudden demise of friends from AIDS, drug overdoses, or other causes, or by the blatant injustices local peasants had to contend with, or suffering from itchy flea bites and the other hardships of the daily life I endured in the cold, impoverished mountains.

Between 2006 and 2009, I had opportunities to make several postfieldwork trips back to Liangshan. I felt ambivalent about these short trips. On the one hand, I was happy to see old friends in Limu again. I surprised many of them; they had not believed I would return to visit them again and again because outsiders rarely returned. On the other hand, I was inevitably saddened by my visits. The situation there remained dire, as I had expected, and Limu's incessant dirge for its departed youths refused to fade into the background. Each time I returned I heard about the deaths of more friends, and these losses took hold of me instantly and intensely. Having settled into a comfortable and secure living environment as a professional anthropologist in Taiwan, I am even more sensitive to the marginality and suffering that are the daily reality in Limu than when I shared their difficult lives in 2005.

Throughout the course of this research, my personal life trajectory—first in economically bustling New York as a graduate student, then in impoverished and peripheral Limu for fieldwork, and finally in cozy hometown Taipei as a professional—characterizes a life course that is not uncommon in the age of globalization. The mobility I have enjoyed and the differences and commonalities among the social and development inequalities I have seen in various localities are crucial to me: these not only shape my lifestyle but also my professional perspectives as an anthropologist who works "here and there." These personal experiences and disciplinary awareness have impressed on me the importance of studying beyond one's cultural confines to understand the epochal context in which one's own social being is embedded. My concern with Limu and the Nuosu in general is related to my own sense of self, both as a participant in the globalization process and as an anthropologist viewing it through a critical lens.

The Nuosu youths' new rite of passage reflects China's tumultuous initiation en masse into global capitalist modernity. What I learned from them convinces me that I must position their heroin and AIDS problems in the context of a transitional political economy, both Chinese and global, that is continually moving toward modernity. Modernity, as a goal-oriented drive for social change, has defined the transformation undergone by both the Chinese state and the Nuosu, from initially tentative experimentation in the twentieth century to a wholehearted embrace in the twenty-first.

In underscoring the importance of modernity to Limu's predicament, I am reminded of a quotation from François Delaporte, a scholar in the history of medicine, who maintains that "'disease' does not exist. . . . What does exist is not disease but practices" (Delaporte 1986, 6). His stark assertion does not deny the existence of bacilli that caused France's cholera epidemic of 1832. Instead he explores the interface between biomedical and political forces and from there endeavors to understand the life course of the disease and social responses to it, both of which were shaped by power relations in France at the time. Similarly, I have not just focused on drug use and AIDS per se but have emphasized marginality, inequalities of power, and ill-advised government practices, all of which have shaped responses to these dual epidemics among the Nuosu.

The twists and turns of China's drive toward modernity over the last half century have been manifested in a schizophrenic form of governance that alternates between localized regimentation and market fluidity. At the macro level, since 1978, China has changed its national economic development paradigm from socialist modernity to a capitalist one. This ideological shift, however, has hardly engendered a Western-style liberal democracy. The Communist party-state and its bureaucracy still command immense authority to monitor people's daily lives. In terms of local practices, as we have seen in Limu, the state has curtailed its funding for local social-welfare programs while continuing its strong-arm practices of political mobilization and demanding that Nuosu peasants carry out its unfunded mandate of public involvement in epidemic control. Because of this arbitrary governmentality, as Limu's experience showcases, peasants are always on the losing side of any development project. They can neither achieve genuine local empowerment through grassroots mobilization, owing to state control and intervention, nor compete successfully in a market economy, because of their inadequate training, education, and lack of state support.

Modernity has a Janus face: it is both constructive and destructive, "its victims . . . as numerous as its beneficiaries" (Hall 1996, 17). Capitalist modernity has accelerated global economic growth, yet it has also given rise to the spread of HIV across the globe, affecting most drastically the marginal regions where local people have inadvertently become stranded in the midst of social change. The Limu story, a prime example of this scenario, provides a grounded case for deciphering the multilayered processes of transition in the globalizing world.

Globalization on the Ground

Contemporary capitalist modernity, under the aegis of neoliberalism, has gone global, shaping and reshaping the development trajectory of what Dirlik (2007) has dubbed "global modernity" since the 1990s. Globalization as a paradigm has been altering the ways in which we envision the world. As far as the Nuosu are concerned, their encounters with different brands of modernity over the past half century, be they socialist, capitalist, or global, have been externally imposed and drastic, seeming to occur in blindingly rapid succession. The dual epidemics of heroin and AIDS in Liangshan began in the 1990s and continue to this day, inscribing deep scars in the collective experience of the Nuosu people as they continue to take part in the current modernity drive. In this regard, two additional questions concerning their future arise as my ethnographic account draws to a close.

The first question is temporal in nature: Is globalization the beginning of a truly unprecedented historical change, or is it merely a continuation of the past social development trajectory known as "modernization," a fashionable and influential concept from the middle of the last century? This question has been debated by scholars who study global development from the era of modernization to the current period of social and economic transformation (Dirlik 2007; Edelman and Haugerud 2005). If we consider socialist development a part of the modernization drive and regard its collapse as an epiphenomenon of the unrestrained forces of globalization, then similar questions about continuity or rupture between the recent past and the present have also been raised by scholars of postsocialism (Hann 2002; Verdery 1996). On the whole, these scholars all agree that the changes the world has experienced in the last few decades cannot be considered as a complete break from the past, and yet these changes have introduced unprecedented elements engendered by the whirlwind of globalization. The categorical and hierarchical classification of peoples and regions we saw in the modernization projects of the last century, such as developed versus developing, First World versus Third World, urbanites versus peasants, and so forth, often influences how people's everyday experiences are framed today.

As Dirlik (2007) puts it, global modernity perpetuates "past inequalities while adding to them new ones of its own" (7).

A comparative analysis of the rapid spread of HIV in the postsocialist landscape prompts us to confront old inequalities wearing new faces (Lee and Zwi 1996). Anthropologists of postsocialism often find that their subjects are more directly exposed to, while being less prepared for, the forces and paradoxes of globalization (Kalb 2002). Globalization has brought many postsocialist states into a new living environment that is fundamentally different from their recent experience of regimentation and restricted mobility—both geographical and social. People in such states had long been constrained in their freedom of choice and expression and lived under a social hierarchy that could not be challenged in the face of coerced political conformity. Given this, "what comes after socialism?" has been the critical question since the demise of the Soviet Union and its Eastern European allies in 1989 (Burawoy and Verdery 1999; Humphrey 1998; Mandel and Humphrey 2002; Verdery 1996). The answer is anyone's guess, but surely it is far more complicated than simply "capitalism triumphant" (Verdery 1996, 37).

During the current global transformation, not only have consumer goods, information, money, and humans become part of accelerating global flows but so also have illicit drugs and contagious diseases. Drug use and HIV have emerged as unintended consequences of this process; these new scourges mercilessly threaten ordinary people as they pursue—sometimes recklessly—lifestyles in which novelty, for better or worse, exerts its utmost influence. Like China, Vietnam launched its economic renovation (*doi mai*) in the late 1980s, shifting the country from three decades of centrally planned socialism toward a market economy. Before long, in 1990, the first HIV infection was reported there. By December 2005, the total number of reported HIV cases had reached more than 100,000; drug injectors constituted 50 to 60 percent of the reported infections.[1] Likewise, Eastern Europe and Central Asia (both formerly part of the Soviet bloc) have also been drawn into the fast-growing HIV/AIDS epidemic. Before 1994, neither region had a significant number of HIV infections (UNAIDS 2002, 32), but by 2005, the number of people living with HIV had reached an estimated 1.6 million out of a population of 474 million—an astonishing increase in ten years.[2]

In China, the first AIDS case was reported in 1985, but the first HIV outbreak among drug injectors in Yunnan Province was not recognized until 1989 (He and Detels 2005; Wu, Rou, and Cui 2004). Reported HIV infections grew at an estimated rate of 30 percent annually from 1995 to 2000, reaching 58 percent in 2001. The rate of HIV infections rose by 122 percent in the year 2002–3 (China Center 2004; cited in He and Detels 2005). By the end of 2007, an estimated total of 700,000 people were living with HIV/AIDS in China (UNAIDS 2008).

In China's momentous political-economic transition, one immediately notices that groups and individuals have unequal capacities to manage the challenges of globalization. Growing disparities between haves and have-nots, as well as between the center and the periphery, are often heightened by other social divisions, such as ethnic, gender, religious, and geographical distinctions. Some groups suffer disproportionately from the negative consequences of social change. A glaring example is the occurrence of HIV/AIDS among the diverse categories of people in China, where rural residents account for 80 percent of the infections (Wu, Rou, and Cui 2004). More males (71.3 percent) are infected than females, and 70 percent of the infected population is between twenty and thirty-nine years old (State Council 2007). The disease also disproportionately affects China's ethnic minorities, who in 2002 constituted only 8 percent of the entire population but made up 36 percent of HIV infections (Kaufman and Jing 2002).This chilling fact has aggravated existing stereotypes concerning ethnic minorities, as the state has attributed the HIV/AIDS problem to "part of a small group of ethnic minorities that engage in illegal, unhealthy, and unsafe practices" while refusing to acknowledge that China's unprecedented economic growth in the reform era might be a contributing factor (Hyde 2007, 19).

Hence modernity in the age of globalization unfailingly presents two faces, promising certain types of emancipation for some as it creates new forms of economic and political marginalization for others (Dirlik 2007, 22–23). As this ethnography has demonstrated, the expanded opportunities for Nuosu youth in space and time both for livelihood and for expanding their imaginations, together with increased individual freedom of choice, have been made possible through their participation in China's modernity drive. Yet the uncertainty brought about by the paradigm shift from socialism to capitalism has cast a deep shadow over their long-marginalized and -stigmatized communities. The outcomes of these changes are inevitably shaped by a combination of past and present conditions. To the Limu people, "the future is now" (Dirlik 2007, 3). Whether their transition will result in a bright capitalist modernity in some radiant globalized future or a return to the semifeudal inequality seen in post-socialist Eastern Europe (Verdery 1996) remains an open question.

The second question I would like to raise in this connection is spatial in nature: How should we treat local particularities in the face of the seemingly invincible and uncompromising forces of globalization? How important are those particularities for dealing with global problems on the ground? The forces of globalization are far reaching if not entirely irresistible, and their consequence has been "the simultaneous fragmentation and unification of the world" (Dirlik 2007, 20). The dialectic between the global and the local has been an important concern in contemporary scholarly research, particularly in anthropology, insofar as understanding the local has always been a central focus of the discipline.

Anthropological research since the 1980s has been critical of the hegemonic forces emanating from the political-economic centers of the world to local social actors at the terminal end of the reach of power (e.g., Wolf 1982). Since the 1990s, as globalization has emerged as a paradigm, the "local" has become even more prominent in anthropological research (Lewellen 2002). "The more things come together, the more they remain apart" seems to characterize our globalizing era (Geertz 1998; cited in Kalb 2000, 12). The globalization narratives embrace both institutions and innumerable local actors, who perceive and respond to global trends and issues in diverse ways. Thus one cannot really speak of a monolithic manifestation of globalization, just as "modernity" has become increasingly articulated and dissected over the past century.

The Limu case is telling in this regard. Limu may appear to be an insignificant microcosm in the broader ethnoscape of the gigantic Chinese state and an emerging global society. The trajectories toward heroin use and the HIV/AIDS epidemic there, however, illustrate the significance of local particularities in grappling with problems that are global in scale. Through what we have seen of the Nuosu youth and their new life experiences, as well as local state agents' imitation of international AIDS intervention practices, we can grasp how critically important local contexts are in a general portrait of globalization.

Researchers have pointed out that discussions of globalization sometimes neglect the role of the state in mediating between individuals or the local and the global, especially when it comes to transnational flows of goods, information, or technology (James 2006). Likewise, other scholars suggest bringing the state back in (Weiss 1998; Yeoh, Charney, and Tong 2003). In the Chinese context, a dismissal of the state may be fatal in envisioning the development of the country. Internationally, China has claimed to have established a development model that is an alternative to neoliberal capitalism. It emphasizes China's national particularities over Western-centered power and its global hierarchy. Ironically, the party-state's sensitivity to national particularities does not seem to extend to its domestic development agenda. The Chinese state continues imagining itself a unitary colossus and exerts its ethnocentric governance in what is in fact a multiethnic nation. The state remains central to shaping opportunities and constraints for ordinary citizens, rural people in particular, as they pursue new livelihoods, try to preserve their traditions, and deal with social problems. Where the people of Limu might be heading afterward hinges on how they deal with, or are dealt with by, their particularities.

The issue of identity is likely to be the next major challenge young Nuosu and their society must face. The problems of heroin and AIDS have been shaped not only by the Nuosu's particular marginal position in China's modernity drive but also by their choice of local and individual identities. Many young Nuosu have begun to think more reflexively about their own culture and society and to make decisions about cleaving to or distancing themselves from their tradition. How will Nuosu ways of life be carried on after the cruel destruction wreaked by heroin and HIV/AIDS? These epidemics will inevitably influence the future outlook of local Nuosu society. Global modernity continues to shape young Nuosu as their cultural particularities are dismissed and devalued; their identities are likely to "become detached—disembedded—from specific times, places, histories, and traditions, and appear 'free-floating'" (Hall 1992, 303). The uncertain future of what it means to be Nuosu and the identities of Nuosu youth are thus anchored not only in the fortunes of individual actors but also in the crucial role the state plays in delineating what development paths are available to them.

By situating local particularities—of both the Nuosu and the Chinese state—squarely in the globalization process, we may accommodate continuity with the past as well as give an account of new characteristics. Let me return to the Limu case to consider what we may expect from the state when dealing with local crises of the sort experienced in Liangshan. It goes without saying that structural constraints emanating from China's past and present governing practices are unlikely to be completely revamped in the short to medium term. Nevertheless, it is reasonable to hang some hope on the capacity of the Chinese state to realize practice-based improvements. After all, social processes as part of globalization are localized in national and subnational settings (Sassen 2007). The role of the state remains crucial.

Research has identified at least four levels of social factors involved in AIDS interventions: the superstructural (e.g., at the state and global economic levels), the structural (e.g., law and policy internal to the state), the environmental (e.g., immediate living conditions and resources), and the individual (e.g., personal socioeconomic characteristics such as age, sex, education) (Sumartojo 2000). Research and intervention at each level are critical to the successful orchestration of comprehensive intervention efforts. In light of this fourfold requirement, any successful intervention must take into account at least the individual and environmental factors and adopt relevant and appropriate practices on the ground.

A solid local footing is essential for successful intervention; this involves issues of adequate cultural competence and sound social relationships. Indigenous culture and practices are local people's only remaining recourse when the state provides little concrete support. As we have seen in the Limu case, where local lives and activities have continually been hindered by external forces, people's tolerance of suffering and their resilience in the face of daunting challenges can be more than amazing. I have often wondered where such resourcefulness comes from. Local Nuosu seem to be equipped with an inner power that allows them to endure miseries and continue living in a humble yet steadfast manner. Limu's particularities, long suppressed under socialist modernization, have been resuscitated and have acquired new meanings in the course of China's transition toward market capitalism. If the state were to change its problematic practices during local crises and provide proper inducements, I believe that Nuosu social activism—their voluntary participation in the state's or other outside agencies' interventions—could be rekindled.

In this scenario, the first step to successful local crisis intervention is not to change the local people but to change state agents' attitudes and provide them with proper training in regard to local culture and social conditions. Genuine state-society collaboration for the public good requires the "developers" to respect local knowledge and practices and be willing to work with communities previously labeled as "backward" and "superstitious." Local knowledge and practices, held not only by traditional authorities but also by young people with a variety of experiences and skills, are the best channels through which intervention workers can carry out local projects. As I see it, only through this type of bilateral cooperation, which divorces itself from externally imposed guidance and decontextualized, one-size-fits-all models, can the state and local society both benefit from effective interventions.

No sane or reasonable person wants to see the damaging, if unintended, consequences brought about by a reckless leap into global modernity and by the chaotic patchwork of intervention efforts that have taken place in Limu. If the Chinese state does not command the political will to change the current situation and strengthen its legitimacy at the local level, marginalized populations in Limu and elsewhere across the country are likely to remain in limbo. If the state's positive role in development remains dubious, the result may fulfill Marx's prophecy describing the experience of modernity, as echoed by Marshall Berman (1982): "All that is solid melts into air."

Notes

Introduction

1. Scholars have different opinions as to whether the current China is "post-socialist" or not. In consideration of the transitional political economy, I am in agreement with Latham (2002), who argues for the usefulness of thinking of China as post-socialist but not in a chronological sense. Although China remains nominally a state with "actually existing" socialism, it shares many characteristics in common with some of its antecedents, for example, the former Soviet bloc countries.

2. The reoriented worldview of pre-state minorities in the socialist era as based on the imposed nation-state administrative hierarchy receives a thorough treatment in Erik Mueggler's (2001) vivid portrayal of a Yi (Lòlop'ò) community in Yunnan Province.

Chapter 1

1. Among the fifty-five minority nationalities the Chinese government identified, the "Mountain People" (*gaoshan zu*) actually live in Taiwan, where they are officially called "indigenous peoples" (*yuanzhumin*) and were divided into fourteen ethnic groups as of 2008.

2. In the last years of the Qing Dynasty (1644–1911), around 1909, the court established a fortress in Zhaojue and tried to pacify the region—without success. The Republican government (1911–49) withdrew the troops stationed there in 1912, and the local Nuosu rebelled soon afterward. Later, in 1919, the locals successfully captured the town of Zhaojue. Zhaojue remained in the hands of the Nuosu until the early 1950s (Lin 1961, 10–11).

3. Before the 1950s, a small group of the Nuosu who resided close to Han areas became assimilated into certain Han ways of life and thus were called "cooked Yi" (i.e., Han-cultured barbarians), in contrast to the great majority of "raw Yi," who were in Nuosu-dominant areas and never under Han control (Lin 1961).

4. Some researchers classified slaves into two strata: gaxy was even lower than mgajie. In this book, I use only the term "slave" to represent all the people with low status in Limu. My usage here stems from the fact that local people do not make clear distinctions in daily life between these two.

5. *Cyvi* is generally translated as patrilineal clans or lineages. Some scholars use "clan" (e.g., Harrell 2001a; Ma Erzi 2001) and others use "lineage" (e.g., Hill 2001). I distinguish between these two terms circumstantially. Usually the term "lineage" applies to frequent interactions among kin members within close genealogical and geographic distance. For example, lineage members who reside in close proximity usually have an annual meeting at the end of the year. Once in a while, however, these year-end meetings can be expanded—especially when distant kin members encounter major social problems and request assistance from several dispersed lineages that belong to the same clan. In addition, all lineages that belong to the same clan in Liangshan as a whole may also meet once every few years. Therefore, I define "clan" as a translocal kin group, which is different from "lineage" as a localized kin group. The distinction often depends on the context of the social activities involved.

6. Lili nzymo were at one time the rulers in certain Nuosu-dominant areas. Their power was superseded by an array of nuo lineages. In the Ming Dynasty (1368–1644), the Lili nzymo, similar to other nzymo lineages, were driven away from the Nuosu-dominant areas by nuo who later became the de facto rulers there (Ma 1989, 117).

7. It is possible that the Nuosu captured and enslaved all kinds of intrusive outsiders, mostly Han people but sometimes other groups, including even foreigners. For instance, in 1909 the Nuosu killed a British man named Donald Burk and enslaved his followers, who had been on an expedition to Nuosu areas. This incident almost caused a Sino-British dispute (Lin 1961, 10).

8. Nuosu people in Limu referred to the monetary token as *tuotuo yin* (silver ingots). Archival documents may use the term *bai yin* (silver dollars); for example, see Lin (1961).

9. For details on the shift from old weapons to new weapons and its effect on feuds and related customs in old Liangshan, see Lin (1961), especially chapter 8, "Clan Feuds."

10. Whether Nuosu society is a "slave society" is a matter for debate, especially between Chinese ethnologists and Western anthropologists (Harrell 2001a, 2001b; Hill 2001). Hill, in particular, argues that slave labor was not essential to the structures of production in Nuosu society and that, therefore, the Nuosu society was a society with slaves but not a slave society.

11. The incorporation of minority elites into state apparatuses has had controversial effects (Harrell 2007). The Han-dominant state bureaucracy often places low-level minority cadres in a dilemma, since they are caught between the state policies, which may not be popular, and their community relationships. These cadres represent the

state's modernization programs and, in this regard, often ignore or even look down on their own culture. As Harrell suggests, however, the situation is not simply a dichotomy. The assumption of dichotomies between state cadres and ordinary peasants is too simplistic and fails to account for the real dynamic interaction between basic-level cadres and peasants in the everyday life of rural villages.

12. This ethnic identification project identified only forty-one ethnic groups in 1953 (Gladney 1998, 14). The project continued identifying more nationalities until the late 1950s and then added one in 1962 and another in 1979. In the early 1990s, the identification of new nationalities was declared to be closed.

13. The controversy over China's ethnic identification project is extensively debated in many scholarly publications (e.g., Gladney 1998; Li 2004; Litzinger 2000; Mueggler 2001; Mullaney 2006). Harrell (2001a), for instance, distinguished the Nuosu from other Yi groups on the basis of the Nuosu's sui generis kinship and religious systems.

14. Verdery (1996) calls for further studies of the revival of Communist parties in postsocialist states: "The Soviet Union may be irretrievably gone, but the electoral victories of renamed Communist Parties in Poland, Hungary, Bulgaria, and elsewhere have shown that the Party is far from over" (10).

15. The population of Zhaojue County was 201,292 in 1990 (Sichuan sheng 1999).

16. Bimo and many of their family members know the Nuosu written language, yet this is not counted in the literacy category.

17. Personal interview with an official at the Anti-Poverty Office in Zhaojue County, August 17, 2004. The state's criterion for the poverty line was raised to 1,000 yuan in 2001. The previous criterion was 625 yuan. In Limu, the local government still used 625 yuan as the cutoff point, probably because the living standards in rural Liangshan were lower than the living standards in most other locales in China.

18. One *mu* is equivalent to approximately 0.067 hectare. In recent years, 1.0 mu of rice paddies has been able to produce about 300 to 400 kilograms of unhusked rice in Limu. Local peasants told me that the harvest level in the 1980s was about half the current level. In the 1980s, animal waste and sometimes night soil were the only fertilizers used. Since the 1990s, chemical fertilizer has become more affordable and peasants have become more accustomed to its use. With the improvement of certain common agricultural techniques, Limu has begun to produce more grain than in the recent past.

19. In recent years, environmental protection policy has prohibited local people from cutting down trees for construction. The local people can collect only twigs and fallen deadwood for firewood.

20. In some parts of Liangshan, the local government began restricting rural Nuosu families to two children in the 1990s.

21. For example, in the high mountains and in designated leprosy villages, which county and township birth-control officials are reluctant to visit, people often give

birth to as many children as they like. It is common to have from four to seven children in each family there. Even in lower mountain areas such as Limu (elevation 1,900 meters), it is not uncommon to see more than three children per fertile woman. People have different ways of eluding this birth-control policy.

Chapter 2

1. The Nuosu believe that odd numbers are auspicious and even numbers ominous.

2. In Limu, *hlyx pu*, the practice of sharing expenses or costs among lineage members or neighboring families for public matters, does not count married-but-childless couples as independent household units.

3. This is the same as in Mexico, where fatherhood defines what it means to be a good man in the eyes of both men and women (Gutmann 1996, 248).

4. Even by 1997, 97 percent of the villages in Liangshan had no public roads (Heberer 2001).

5. In rural Liangshan, where people are very traditional, they can eat and stay in a lineage member's house as long as they can recite the lineage genealogy correctly. This custom is a testament to the strong kinship ties in Nuosu society. Peasants who cannot recite their lineage genealogy are not seen as genuine Nuosu and may be considered descendants of slaves whose Han ancestors were captured by Nuosu in the past. This practice of reciting lineage genealogy is generally a requirement that falls only on men, although some women may be able to recite genealogies of their natal or their husband's family.

6. In recent years, people from Meigu County have increased their presence in Chengdu. Zhaojue, Meigu, and Butuo are the three major Nuosu-dominant counties in Liangshan.

7. In addition to *yeyi*, two terms later surfaced to denote heroin: *aqu* (which means whiteness, indicating the white powder of heroin) and *ddu* (the Han Chinese word for illicit drugs or poison). In the early 1990s, some heroin users added *bbucy* (medicine) to the suffix *aqu* to create the term *bbucy aqu*.

8. Medical anthropologist Merrill Singer explains how heroin interacts with human brain chemistry: "In the brain, heroin is converted into morphine and binds with natural opiate receptors. . . . Heroin depresses the transmission of nerve impulses that signal pain. . . . Moreover, the drug relieves anxiety, calms muscles, causes drowsiness, and produces a sense of well-being and contentment" (Singer 2006, 45).

9. Interview with Bamo Erha, former chairperson of the People's Consultation Council in Liangshan Prefecture. He conducted a social survey in Liangshan in 1992 and 1993 when an old Nuosu in Butuo County told him about the prevalent use of heroin among the young.

10. There are at least four seasonal rituals in a year: the spring blossom in March,

the summer month of July or August, the autumn harvest, and the Nuosu New Year around November or December. Families will usually wait for their migrating family members to return home to hold these rituals.

11. See the relevant articles in the criminal law at http://www.people.com.cn/item/faguiku/xingf/R1010.html.

12. In socialist China, the government prohibits sales of agricultural land. In Limu, however, peasants sold land behind the back of the township government. During most sales a witness, often a ndeggu or headman, would be present for the transaction. In the 1990s, some drug users sold land to others secretly, that is, without a witness. I was told that disputes occasionally took place afterward because the sellers (drug users) reneged on the sale.

13. Traditionally, only lepers and infants received interment after death. The former are highly stigmatized in Nuosu society (Sichuan sheng 1999).

14. Nuosu who speak Han Chinese languages refer to themselves as Yizu (Yi nationality), which is the state-designated category. But they identify themselves as Nuosu while speaking in their own language.

15. The China-UK Project held similar blood-test programs in other townships of Zhaojue County, Butuo County, and Xichang City. According to Zhaojue County health-campaign information, until mid-2005 this county remained the worst hit by HIV in Liangshan, with 867 HIV/AIDS cases. This number constituted nearly half of the total HIV/AIDS cases in the entire prefecture.

Chapter 3

1. Such firsthand data may be gleaned occasionally and sporadically in local archives, *wenshi ziliao*, edited by local government offices. For example, Alan Baumler provides a narrative excerpted from a local archive magazine of Hubei Province that describes daily life in an opium den (Baumler 2001, 99–107). But Baumler also reminds historians to approach these sorts of valuable local archives with care inasmuch as the Communist government was involved in their collection and compilation.

2. There is another possible explanation for translating *cyvi* as *jiazhi*. Literally, *cy* means kindred within seven generations, and those who are related after seven generations are called *vi* (Ma Erzi 2001, 88). Thus *jiazhi* can also distinguish between the close (*jia*, family) and distant (*zhi*, branch) kin.

Chapter 4

1. In contradistinction to this line of research, Hill (2004) emphasizes the significance of individual agency in her historical analysis of Nuosu conflict resolutions in the pre-state era.

2. Levirate is a traditional practice among the Nuosu.

Chapter 5

1. The DFID's assistance to Sichuan and Yunnan provinces lasted for five years, with a total budget of £15,305,850 (China-UK 2000, 5). This project in Limu was extended until early 2006.

2. Scott (1998) uses the Greek word *mētis* to designate the situated local practical knowledge. He does not simply use the terms "local knowledge" or "local practice" because he wants to emphasize the meticulous situated characteristics of practical knowledge that are embedded in local and individual experiences.

3. Following Mao's nationalistic and pragmatic rationality in regard to primary health care in vast rural areas, the state has also trained health workers to practice Chinese medicine and to use herbs along with biomedicine in hygiene schools.

4. The term "barefoot doctor" was not used until 1968. Before then, the socialist government called them "peasant doctors" (Lucas 1982, 136).

5. Interview with Wu Peiwei, a retired Han doctor. She retired as the director of the former Institute of Dermatology and Venereology (now the Center for STD and Leprosy Control) in Xichang City in 1993.

6. See http://www.photius.com/rankings/world_health_systems.html (accessed January 20, 2005) or Kaufman (2006, 57).

7. In 2003, China launched a new Rural Cooperative Medical Scheme (RCMS) in a few selected areas, which was expanded nationwide in 2007. The new RCMS aims at reducing the high cost of health care that has severely constrained people's lives, particularly in impoverished rural areas, since the collapse of the old RCMS in the 1980s. This new initiative, however, mainly focuses on reducing patients' out-of-pocket expenses for health care while neglecting public health initiatives such as sanitation and health education. Some research even suggests that the new RCMS has not reduced out-of-pocket expenses after all, because it has required township clinics to own more expensive equipment and thus forced patients to pay more for health care (Wagstaff et al. 2009).

8. Some state agencies did try to facilitate official work by turning to indigenous authorities. The incorporation of ndeggu into the courts in Limu and other localities in Zhaojue County is a successful example. One ndeggu who was recruited as a jury member in the Limu court told me that this practice stems from a decision made by the former head of the Zhaojue County court in 1999. The decision resulted from the large number of cases under dispute in the county. This ndeggu went to work at the court every day; his attendance there was more regular than that of any other official jury member. Thus local people might come to the court for an official judiciary settlement or for his ndeggu services. This ndeggu argued that resolutions "in society" are more reliable than resolutions in court: "After the ndeggu mediation, both sides may kill a chicken as settlement and there would no longer be any dispute. But the state law is more complicated and involves more offices, such as the police. People often have lingering problems after a court settlement."

Chapter 6

Part of this chapter was published previously in *Human Organization* 68, no. 4 (2009): 395–405.

1. The Chinese Communist Party considers propaganda to be of great political importance in conveying messages from the top to the masses, and considers slogans (*kouhao*) a key vehicle by means of which to attain its social-engineering goals. For a detailed discussion about the rhetoric and the effect of political slogans on transforming Chinese official ideology, see, for example, Lu's (1999) analysis of political slogans between the 1960s and late 1980s.

2. For example, Waxler's (1981) research on lepers demonstrates that the social construction of stigma is not only imposed by society but often internalized by the lepers themselves.

3. For example, see the Ford Foundation HIV/AIDS Anti-Stigma Initiative: http://www.hivaidsstigma.org/documents/antistigmafactsheet.pdf?CFID=1060268&CFTOKEN=79292170 (accessed January 20, 2007); and the 2002 World AIDS Day Observance message by the president of the Fifty-seventh Session of the United Nations General Assembly (Kavan 2002).

4. Some people still consider death from a drug overdose or an improperly handled injection to be death from illness and hence categorize such deaths as normal. But most of the people with whom I spoke, especially young people, considered such deaths to be accidental and therefore abnormal.

5. Beginning in the late 1950s, people with leprosy were confined in remote leprosy villages in Liangshan, a practice in accordance with the segregation policy for leprosy control in China at large (Leung 2009). Beginning around the mid-1980s, when the segregation policy came to an end with the introduction of multidrug therapy, many cured Nuosu lepers returned to their original rural communities only to encounter crushing stigmatization from the locals. As a result, some chose to return to the leprosy villages to live with peer lepers (Liu 2009a).

Conclusion

1. See http://www.who.int/GlobalAtlas/predefinedReports/EFS2006/EFS_PDFs/EFS2006_VN.pdf; accessed March 20, 2008.

2. See http://data.unaids.org/pub/PressRelease/2006/20060515-PR-GF_en.pdf; and http://www.dfid.gov.uk/pubs/files/central-asia/land_arbitration.pdf; accessed January 22, 2007.

Bibliography

Agar, Michael. 1986. *Speaking of Ethnography*. Beverly Hills, CA: Sage.

AHRN (Asian Harm Reduction Network). 1997. *The Hidden Epidemic: A Situation Assessment of Drug Use in Southeast and East Asia in the Context of HIV Vulnerability*. Bangkok: UNAIDS-APICT.

Alonzo, Angelo A., and Nancy R. Reynolds. 1995. "Stigma, HIV and AIDS: An Exploration and Elaboration of a Stigma Trajectory." *Social Science and Medicine* 41, no. 3: 303–15.

Altman, Dennis. 1998. "Globalization and the 'AIDS Industry.'" *Contemporary Politics* 4, no. 3: 233–45.

Amit-Talai, Vered, and Helena Wulff, eds. 1995. *Youth Cultures: A Cross-Cultural Perspective*. New York: Routledge.

Appadurai, Arjun. 1996. *Modernity at Large: Cultural Dimensions of Globalization*. Minneapolis: University of Minnesota Press.

Arnason, Johann P. 2002. "Communism and Modernity." In Shmuel N. Eisenstadt, ed., *Multiple Modernities*, pp. 61–90. New Brunswick, NJ: Transaction.

Azi Ayue. 1993. *Yizu yiyao* [Yi medicine]. Beijing: Zhongguo yiyao keji chubanshe.

Baer, Hans A., Merrill Singer, and Ida Susser. 1997. *Medical Anthropology and the World System: A Critical Perspective*. Westport, CT: Bergin & Garvey.

Bamo Ayi. 1994. *Yizu zuling xinyang yanjiu* [The study of the Yi's worship of ancestors]. Chengdu: Sichuan minzu chubanshe.

———. 2003. "Zhongguo Liangshan Yizu shehui zhong de bimo" [Bimo in the Liangshan Nuosu society of China]. In Zhongguo Meigu Yizu bimo wenhua yanjiu zhongxin bangongshi, ed., *Meigu Yizu bimo wenhua diaocha yanjiu: lunwen zhuanji* [Research on Meigu Yizu bimo culture: Collected essays], pp. 68–82. Sichuan, Meigu: Zhongguo Meigu Yizu bimo wenhua yanjiu zhongxin bangongshi.

Barnett, A. Doak. 1993. *China's Far West: Four Decades of Change.* Boulder, CO: West-view Press.

Baumler, Alan. 2001. "Reading 10: The Chen Family Opium Den." In Alan Baumler, ed., *Modern China and Opium: A Reader,* pp. 99–107. Ann Arbor: University of Michigan Press.

Beck, Ulrich, and Elisabeth Beck-Gernsheim. 2002. *Individualization: Institutionalized Individualism and Its Social and Political Consequences.* London: Sage.

Bello, David Anthony. 2005. *Opium and the Limits of Empire: Drug Prohibition in the Chinese Interior, 1729–1850.* Cambridge, MA: Harvard University Asia Center.

Berman, Marshall. 1982. *All That Is Solid Melts into Air: The Experience of Modernity.* New York: Simon and Schuster.

Bernard, H. Russell. 2002. *Research Methods in Anthropology: Qualitative and Quantitative Approaches.* Walnut Creek, CA: AltaMira Press.

Beyrer, Chris, et al. 2000. "Overland Heroin Trafficking Routes and HIV-1 Spread in South and South-East Asia." *AIDS* 14, no. 1: 75–83.

Biehl, João. 2005. "Technologies of Invisibility: Politics of Life and Social Inequality." In Jonathan Xavier Inda, ed., *Anthropologies of Modernity: Foucault, Governmentality, and Life Politics,* pp. 248–71. Malden, MA: Blackwell.

Bloom, Gerald. 2001. "China's Rural Health System in Transition: Towards Coherent Institutional Arrangements." Paper presented at the Conference on Financial Sector Reform in China, Beijing, China, September 11–13.

Bloom, Gerald, and Xingyuan Gu. 1997. "Health Sector Reform: Lessons from China." *Social Science and Medicine* 45, no. 3: 351–60.

Bloom, Gerald, Leiya Han, and Xiang Li. 2001. "How Health Workers Earn a Living in China." *Human Resources for Health Development Journal* 5, nos. 1–3: 25–38.

Blumenthal, David, and William Hsiao. 2005. "Privatization and Its Discontents—The Evolving Chinese Health Care System." *New England Journal of Medicine* 353, no. 11: 1165–70.

Bourgois, Philippe. 1999. "Theory, Method, and Power in Drug and HIV-Prevention Research: A Participant-Observer's Critique." *Substance Use & Misuse* 34, no. 14: 2155–72.

———. 2003. *In Search of Respect: Selling Crack in El Barrio.* Cambridge: Cambridge University Press.

Bourgois, Philippe, and Jeff Schonberg. 2009. *Righteous Dopefiend.* Berkeley: University of California Press.

Boyle, Paul, Keith Halfacree, and Vaughan Robinson. 1998. *Exploring Contemporary Migration.* Harlow, UK: Longman.

Burawoy, Michael. 2000. "Introduction: Rethinking for the Global." In Michael Burawoy et al., eds., *Global Ethnography: Forces, Connections, and Imaginations in a Postmodern World,* pp. 1–40. Berkeley: University of California Press.

Burawoy, Michael, and Katherine Verdery, eds. 1999. *Uncertain Transition: Ethnographies of Change in the Postsocialist World*. Lanham, MD: Rowman & Littlefield.

Cai, Yongshun. 2000. "Between State and Peasant: Local Cadres and Statistical Reporting in Rural China." *China Quarterly* 163:783–805.

Callaway, Helen. 1992. "Ethnography and Experience: Gender Implications in Fieldwork and Texts." In Judith Okely and Helen Callaway, eds., *Anthropology and Autobiography*, pp. 29–49. London: Routledge.

Carleheden, Mikael, and Michael Hviid Jacobsen. 2001. "Introduction." In Mikael Carleheden and Michael Hviid Jacobsen, eds., *The Transformation of Modernity: Aspects of the Past, Present and Future of an Era*, pp. ix–xxiii. Aldershot, UK: Ashgate.

Castro, Arachu, and Paul Farmer. 2005. "Understanding and Addressing AIDS-Related Stigma: From Anthropological Theory to Clinical Practice in Haiti." *American Journal of Public Health* 95, no. 1: 53–59.

Chen, C. C. 1989. *Medicine in Rural China: A Personal Account*. Berkeley: University of California Press.

Chen, Nancy N. 2001. "Health, Wealth, and the Good Life." In Nancy N. Chen, Constance D. Clark, Suzanne Z. Gottschang, and Lyn Jeffery, eds., *China Urban: Ethnographies of Contemporary Culture*, pp. 165–82. Durham, NC: Duke University Press.

China Center for Disease Control & Prevention. 2004. HIV/AIDS Surveillance Report. Beijing.

China-UK HIV/AIDS Prevention and Care Project. 2000. Zhong ying xingbing aizibing fangzhi hezuo xiangmu xiangmu beiwanglu [China-UK STD and AIDS prevention cooperation project memorandum]. Beijing: China-UK HIV/AIDS Prevention and Care Project.

———. 2001. *Situational Analysis of STI/HIV/AIDS in Sichuan and Yunnan Provinces*. Beijing: China-UK HIV/AIDS Prevention and Care Project.

China-UK HIV/AIDS Prevention and Care Project in Sichuan Province. 2002. Report of Capacity Assessment of Organizations Related to Prevention and Control of STI/AIDS in Sichuan: Technical Report.

China-UK HIV/AIDS Prevention and Care Project Liangshan Office. 2004. Update of China-UK HIV/AIDS Prevention and Care Project in Liangshan (2001–September 2004). Xichang, Sichuan: China-UK HIV/AIDS Prevention and Care Project Liangshan Office.

Cohen, Cathy J. 1999. *The Boundaries of Blackness: AIDS and the Breakdown of Black Politics*. Chicago: University of Chicago Press.

Cohen, Myron L. 1990. "Lineage Organization in North China." *Journal of Asian Studies* 49, no. 3: 509–34.

———. 1993. "Cultural and Political Inventions in Modern China: The Case of the Chinese 'Peasant.'" *Daedalus* 122, no. 2: 151–70.

Connell, R. W. 1995. *Masculinities*. St. Leonards, New South Wales: Allen & Unwin.

Cornwall, Andrea, and Nancy Lindisfarne, eds. 1994. *Dislocating Masculinity: Comparative Ethnographies*. London: Routledge.

Courtwright, David T. 2001. *Forces of Habit: Drugs and the Making of the Modern World*. Cambridge, MA: Harvard University Press.

Crandon-Malamud, Libbet. 1991. *From the Fat of Our Souls: Social Change, Political Process, and Medical Pluralism in Bolivia*. Berkeley: University of California Press.

Crewe, Emma, and Elizabeth Harrison. 1998. *Whose Development? An Ethnography of Aid*. New York: Zed Books.

Croll, Elisabeth. 2006. *China's New Consumers: Social Development and Domestic Demand*. New York: Routledge.

Davis, Meg. 2003. *Locked Doors: The Human Rights of People Living with HIV/AIDS in China*. Human Rights Watch.

Delaporte, François. 1986. *Disease and Civilization: The Cholera in Paris, 1832*. Cambridge, MA: MIT Press.

Diamond, Norma. 1983. "Model Villages and Village Realities." *Modern China* 9, no. 2: 163–81.

Dikötter, Frank, Lars Peter Laamann, and Zhou Xun. 2004. *Narcotic Culture: A History of Drugs in China*. Chicago: University of Chicago Press.

Dirlik, Arif. 2007. *Global Modernity: Modernity in the Age of Global Capitalism*. Boulder, CO: Paradigm.

Douglas, Mary. 1992. *Risk and Blame: Essays in Cultural Theory*. London: Routledge.

Durkin-Longley, Maureen. 1984. "Multiple Therapeutic Use in Urban Nepal." *Social Science and Medicine* 19, no. 8: 867–72.

Edelman, Marc, and Angelique Haugerud. 2005. "Introduction: The Anthropology of Development and Globalization." In Marc Edelman and Angelique Haugerud, eds., *The Anthropology of Development and Globalization: From Classical Political Economy to Contemporary Neoliberalism*, pp. 1–74. Malden, MA: Blackwell.

Ellis, Mark, Dennis Conway, and Adrian J. Bailey. 2000. "The Circular Migration of Puerto Rican Women: Towards a Gendered Explanation." In Katie Willis and Brenda Yeoh, eds., *Gender and Migration*, pp. 119–50. Cheltenham, UK: Edward Elgar.

Escobar, Arturo. 1995. *Encountering Development: The Making and Unmaking of the Third World*. Princeton, NJ: Princeton University Press.

Evans-Pritchard, E. E. 1940. *The Nuer: A Description of the Modes of Livelihood and Political Institutions of a Nilotic People*. Oxford: Clarendon Press.

Eves, Richard, and Leslie Butt. 2008. "Introduction." In Leslie Butt and Richard Eves, eds., *Making Sense of AIDS: Culture, Sexuality, and Power in Melanesia*, pp. 1–23. Honolulu: University of Hawaii Press.

Farmer, Paul. 1992. *AIDS and Accusation: Haiti and the Geography of Blame*. Berkeley: University of California Press.

Farmer, Paul, Margaret Connors, and Janie Simmons, eds. 1996. *Women, Poverty, and AIDS: Sex, Drugs, and Structural Violence.* Monroe, ME: Common Courage Press.

Farrer, James. 2002. *Opening Up: Youth Sex Culture and Market Reform in Shanghai.* Chicago: University of Chicago Press.

Feng, Xueshan, et al. 1995. "Cooperative Medical Schemes in Contemporary Rural China." *Social Science and Medicine* 41, no. 8: 1111–18.

Fischer, Michael M. J. 2003. *Emergent Forms of Life and the Anthropological Voice.* Durham, NC: Duke University Press.

Frankenberg, Ronald J. 1993. "Risk: Anthropological and Epidemiological Narratives of Prevention." In Shirley Lindenbaum and Margaret Lock, eds., *Knowledge, Power and Practice: The Anthropology of Medicine and Everyday Life,* pp. 219–42. Berkeley: University of California Press.

Friedman, Edward, Paul Pickowicz, and Mark Selden. 2005. *Revolution, Resistance, and Reform in Village China.* New Haven, CT: Yale University Press.

Gao Zhijian. 2002. "Weisheng zhanxian shang de jianbing: Jiefang chuqi sheng weisheng fangyidui zai Xichang Liangshan diqu gongzuo jishi" [In the hygienic front line: Chronology of the provincial anti-epidemic team's work in Xichang of Liangshan during the early days of liberation]. In Zhengxie Liangshanzhou weiyuanhui wenshi ziliao weiyuanhui, ed., *Liangshan wenshi ziliao xuanji* [Anthology of Liangshan cultural and historical documents], vol. 21, pp. 286–92. Xichang: Zhengxie wenshi ziliao weiyuanhui (Internal circulation).

Gaonkar, Dilip Parameshwar. 2001. "On Alternative Modernities." In Dilip Parameshwar Gaonkar, ed., *Alternative Modernities,* pp. 1–23. Durham, NC: Duke University Press.

Gates, Hill. 1996. *China's Motor: A Thousand Years of Petty Capitalism.* Ithaca, NY: Cornell University Press.

Geertz, Clifford. 1973. *The Interpretation of Cultures: Selected Essays.* New York: Basic Books.

———. 1983. *Local Knowledge: Further Essays in Interpretive Anthropology.* New York: Basic Books.

———. 1998. "The World in Pieces: Culture and Politics at the End of the Century." *Focaal: Tijdschrift voor Antropologie* 32:91–117.

Giddens, Anthony. 1990. *The Consequences of Modernity.* Stanford, CA: Stanford University Press.

———. 1991. *Modernity and Self-Identity: Self and Society in the Late Modern Age.* Cambridge: Polity Press.

Giddens, Anthony, and Christopher Pierson. 1998. *Conversations with Anthony Giddens: Making Sense of Modernity.* Cambridge: Polity Press.

Gilmore, David D. 1990. *Manhood in the Making: Cultural Concepts of Masculinity.* New Haven, CT: Yale University Press.

Gladney, Dru C. 1998. *Ethnic Identity in China: The Making of a Muslim Minority Nationality.* Fort Worth, TX: Harcourt Brace College.

Glick Schiller, Nina. 1992. "What's Wrong with This Picture? The Hegemonic Construction of Culture in AIDS Research in the United States." *Medical Anthropology Quarterly* 6, no. 3: 237–54.

Glick Schiller, Nina, Stephen Crystal, and Denver Lewellen. 1994. "Risky Business: The Cultural Construction of AIDS Risk Groups." *Social Science and Medicine* 38, no. 10: 1337–46.

Goffman, Erving. 1963. *Stigma: Notes on the Management of Spoiled Identity.* Englewood Cliffs, NJ: Prentice-Hall.

Golde, Peggy, ed. 1986. *Women in the Field: Anthropological Experiences.* Berkeley: University of California Press.

Goullart, Peter. 1959. *Princes of the Black Bone: Life in the Tibetan Borderland.* London: J. Murray.

Green, Gill, and Elisa Janine Sobo. 2000. *The Endangered Self: Managing the Social Risk of HIV.* London: Routledge.

Greenhalgh, Susan. 1986. "Shifts in China's Population Policy, 1984–86: Views from the Central, Provincial, and Local Levels." *Population and Development Review* 12, no. 3: 491–515.

Guldin, Gregory Eliyu. 1994. *The Saga of Anthropology in China: From Malinowski to Moscow to Mao.* Armonk, NY: M. E. Sharpe.

Gutmann, Matthew C. 1996. *The Meanings of Macho: Being a Man in Mexico City.* Berkeley: University of California Press.

Hahn, Robert A. 1999. "Expectations of Sickness: Concept and Evidence of the Nocebo Phenomenon." In Irving Kirsch, ed., *How Expectancies Shape Experience,* pp. 333–56. Washington, DC: American Psychological Association.

Hall, Stuart. 1992. "The Question of Cultural Identity." In Stuart Hall, David Held, and Tony McGrew, eds., *Modernity and Its Futures,* pp. 273–316. Cambridge: Polity Press.

———. 1996. "Introduction." In Stuart Hall, David Held, Don Hubert, and Kenneth Thompson, eds., *Modernity: An Introduction to Modern Societies,* pp. 3–18. Cambridge, MA: Blackwell.

Haller, Dieter, and Cris Shore, eds. 2005. *Corruption: Anthropological Perspectives.* Ann Arbor, MI: Pluto.

Hammett, Theodore M., et al. 2006. "A Delicate Balance: Law Enforcement Agencies and Harm Reduction Interventions for Injection Drug Users in China and Vietnam." In Joan Kaufman, Arthur Kleinman, and Tony Saich, eds., *AIDS and Social Policy in China,* pp. 214–31. Cambridge, MA: Harvard University Asia Center.

Hann, C. M., ed. 2002. *Postsocialism: Ideals, Ideologies and Practices in Eurasia.* London: Routledge.

Harper, Janice. 2002. *Endangered Species: Health, Illness and Death Among Madagascar's People of the Forest.* Durham, NC: Carolina Academic Press.

Harrell, Stevan. 1995. "Introduction: Civilizing Projects and the Reactions to Them." In Stevan Harrell, ed., *Cultural Encounters on China's Ethnic Frontiers*, pp. 3–36. Seattle: University of Washington Press.

———. 1996. "Introduction." In Melissa J. Brown, ed., *Negotiating Ethnicities in China and Taiwan*, pp. 1–18. Berkeley: Center for Chinese Studies, Institute of East Asian Studies, University of California, Berkeley.

———. 1999. "The Role of the Periphery in Chinese Nationalism." In Shu-min Huang and Cheng-kuang Hsu, eds., *Imagining China: Regional Division and National Unity*, pp. 133–60. Taipei: Institute of Ethnology, Academia Sinica.

———. 2001a. *Ways of Being Ethnic in Southwest China*. Seattle: University of Washington Press.

———. 2001b. "Introduction." In Stevan Harrell, ed., *Perspectives on the Yi of Southwest China*, pp. 1–17. Berkeley: University of California Press.

———. 2007. "L'état, c'est nous, or We Have Met the Oppressor and He Is Us: The Predicament of Minority Cadres in the PRC." In Diana Lary, ed., *The Chinese State at the Borders*, pp. 221–39. Vancouver: University of British Columbia Press.

Harvey, David. 1989. *The Condition of Postmodernity: An Enquiry into the Origins of Cultural Change*. Cambridge, MA: Blackwell.

He, Jing Lin, and Joel Rehnstrom. 2005. "United Nations System Efforts to Support the Response to AIDS in China." *Cell Research* 15, nos. 11–12: 908–13.

He, Na, and Roger Detels. 2005. "The HIV Epidemic in China: History, Response, and Challenge." *Cell Research* 15, nos. 11–12: 825–32.

Heberer, Thomas. 2001. "Nationalities Conflict and Ethnicity in the People's Republic of China, with Special Reference to the Yi in the Liangshan Yi Autonomous Prefecture." In Stevan Harrell, ed., *Perspectives on the Yi of Southwest China*, pp. 214–37. Berkeley: University of California Press.

———. 2005. "Ethnic Entrepreneurship and Ethnic Identity: A Case Study Among the Liangshan Yi (Nuosu) in China." *China Quarterly* 182:407–27.

Herdt, Gilbert H., and Stephen C. Leavitt, eds. 1998. *Adolescence in Pacific Island Societies*. Pittsburgh: University of Pittsburgh Press.

Herek, Gregory M. 1999. "AIDS and Stigma." *American Behavioral Scientist* 42, no. 7: 1106–16.

Herek, Gregory M., and Eric K. Glunt. 1988. "An Epidemic of Stigma: Public Reactions to AIDS." *American Psychologist* 43, no. 11: 886–91.

Herzfeld, Michael. 1985. *The Poetics of Manhood: Contest and Identity in a Cretan Mountain Village*. Princeton, NJ: Princeton University Press.

Hesketh, Therese, and Wei Xing Zhu. 1997. "Health in China: From Mao to Market Reform." *British Medical Journal* 314, no. 7093: 1543–45.

Hibbins, Raymond, and Bob Pease. 2009. "Men and Masculinities on the Move." In Mike Donaldson, Raymond Hibbins, Richard Howson, and Bob Pease, eds., *Migrant Men:*

Critical Studies of Masculinities and the Migration Experience, pp. 1–19. New York: Routledge.

Hill, Ann Maxwell. 2001. "Captives, Kin, and Slaves in Xiao Liangshan." *Journal of Asian Studies* 60, no. 4: 1033–49.

———. 2004. "Provocative Behavior: Agency and Feuds in Southwest China." *American Anthropologist* 106, no. 4: 675–86.

Hill, Ann Maxwell, and Eric Diehl. 2001. "A Comparative Approach to Lineages Among the Xiao Liangshan Nuosu and Han." In Stevan Harrell, ed., *Perspectives on the Yi of Southwest China*, pp. 51–67. Berkeley: University of California Press.

Honig, Emily, and Gail Hershatter. 1988. *Personal Voices: Chinese Women in the 1980's*. Stanford, CA: Stanford University Press.

Hopkins, MaryCarol. 1993. "Is Anonymity Possible? Writing About Refugees in the United States." In Caroline B. Brettell, ed., *When They Read What We Write: The Politics of Ethnography*, pp. 121–29. Westport, CT: Bergin & Garvey.

Hopper, Kim. 2003. *Reckoning with Homelessness*. Ithaca, NY: Cornell University Press.

Hopper, Kim, and Jim Baumohl. 2004. "Liminality." In David Levinson, ed., *Encyclopedia of Homelessness*, vol. 1, pp. 354–56. Thousand Oaks, CA: Sage.

Hou Yuangao et al. 2003. Liangshan aizibing wenti de shehui wenhua fenxi yu bentu fangzhi moshi [The sociocultural analysis of AIDS in Liangshan and a local preventive model]. Report to China-UK STD/AIDS Prevention and Care Project, March.

Hsiao, William. 1995. "The Chinese Health Care System: Lessons for Other Nations." *Social Science and Medicine* 41, no. 8: 1047–55.

Huang, Shu-min. 1988. "Transforming China's Collective Health Care System: A Village Study." *Social Science and Medicine* 27, no. 9: 879–88.

———. 1998. *The Spiral Road: Change in a Chinese Village Through the Eyes of a Communist Party Leader*. Boulder, CO: Westview Press.

Humphrey, Caroline. 1998. *Marx Went Away—But Karl Stayed Behind*. Ann Arbor: University of Michigan Press.

———. 2002. "Does the Category 'Postsocialist' Still Make Sense?" In C. M. Hann, ed., *Postsocialism: Ideals, Ideologies and Practices in Eurasia*, pp. 12–15. London: Routledge.

Hyde, Sandra Teresa. 2007. *Eating Spring Rice: The Cultural Politics of AIDS in Southwest China*. Berkeley: University of California Press.

James, Paul. 2006. *Globalism, Nationalism, Tribalism: Bringing Theory Back In*. London: Sage.

Jay, Mike. 1999. "Why Do People Take Drugs?" *International Journal of Drug Policy* 10, no. 1: 5–7.

Jing, Jun. 2006. "The Social Origin of AIDS Panics in China." In Joan Kaufman, Arthur Kleinman, and Tony Saich, eds., *AIDS and Social Policy in China*, pp. 152–69. Cambridge, MA: Harvard University Asia Center.

Jones, Edward E., et al. 1984. *Social Stigma: The Psychology of Marked Relationships*. New York: W. H. Freeman.

Kalb, Don. 2000. "Localizing Flows: Power, Paths, Institutions, and Networks." In Don Kalb, Marco van der Land, Richard Staring, Bart van Steenbergen, and Nico Wilterdink, eds., *The Ends of Globalization: Bringing Society Back In*, pp. 1–29. Lanham, MD: Rowman & Littlefield.

————. 2002. "Afterword: Globalism and Postsocialist Prospects." In C. M. Hann, ed., *Postsocialism: Ideals, Ideologies and Practices in Eurasia*, pp. 317–34. London: Routledge.

Katz, Irwin. 1981. *Stigma: A Social Psychological Analysis*. Hillsdale, NJ: Lawrence Erlbaum Associates.

Kaufman, Joan. 2006. "SARS and China's Health-Care Response: Better to Be Both Red and Expert!" In Arthur Kleinman and James L. Watson, eds., *SARS in China: Prelude to Pandemic?* pp. 53–68. Stanford, CA: Stanford University Press.

Kaufman, Joan, and Jun Jing. 2002. "China and AIDS—the Time to Act Is Now." *Science* 296, no. 5577: 2339–40.

Kaufman, Joan, Arthur Kleinman, and Tony Saich, eds. 2006a. *AIDS and Social Policy in China*. Cambridge, MA: Harvard University Asia Center.

————. 2006b. "Introduction: Social Policy and HIV/AIDS in China." In Joan Kaufman, Arthur Kleinman, and Tony Saich, eds., *AIDS and Social Policy in China*, pp. 3–14. Cambridge, MA: Harvard University Asia Center.

Kaufman, Joan, and Kathrine Meyers. 2006. "AIDS Surveillance in China: Data Gaps and Research for AIDS Policy." In Joan Kaufman, Arthur Kleinman, and Tony Saich, eds., *AIDS and Social Policy in China*, pp. 47–71. Cambridge, MA: Harvard University Asia Center.

Kavan, Jan. 2002. "Fighting Stigma and Discrimination." World AIDS Day Observance Statements and Messages from the President of the Fifty-seventh Session of the United Nations General Assembly, December 1.

Keyes, Charles F., Helen Hardacre, and Laurel Kendall, eds. 1994. *Asian Visions of Authority: Religion and the Modern States of East and Southeast Asia*. Honolulu: University of Hawaii Press.

Kleinman, Arthur. 1980. *Patients and Healers in the Context of Culture: An Exploration of the Borderland Between Anthropology, Medicine, and Psychiatry*. Berkeley: University of California Press.

————. 1995. *Writing at the Margin: Discourse Between Anthropology and Medicine*. Berkeley: University of California Press.

————. 1999. "Experience and Its Moral Modes: Culture, Human Conditions, and Disorder." In Grethe B. Peterson, ed., *The Tanner Lectures on Human Values*, vol. 20, pp. 355–420. Salt Lake City: University of Utah Press.

Kleinman, Arthur, and Joan Kleinman. 1997. "The Appeal of Experience; the Dismay of Images: Cultural Appropriations of Suffering in Our Times." In Arthur Kleinman,

Veena Das, and Margaret Lock, eds., *Social Suffering*, pp. 1–23. Berkeley: University of California Press.

Koch, Klaus-Friedrich. 1974. *War and Peace in Jalémó: The Management of Conflict in Highland New Guinea*. Cambridge, MA: Harvard University Press.

Kohrman, Matthew. 2005. *Bodies of Difference: Experiences of Disability and Institutional Advocacy in the Making of Modern China*. Berkeley: University of California Press.

———. 2007. "Depoliticizing Tobacco's Exceptionality: Male Sociality, Death and Memory-Making Among Chinese Cigarette Smokers." *China Journal* 58:85–109.

Kwong, Peter. 2001. "Poverty Despite Family Ties." In Judith Goode and Jeff Maskovsky, eds., *The New Poverty Studies: The Ethnography of Power, Politics, and Impoverished People in the United States*, pp. 57–78. New York: New York University Press.

Lan Yajia et al. 2005. *Sichuan sheng aizibing fangzhi gongzuo: Jiandu pinggu de xianzhuang pingjia* [AIDS prevention in Sichuan Province: Evaluating the supervisory system]. Chengdu: China-UK Project.

Langness, L. L., and Gelya Frank. 1981. *Lives: An Anthropological Approach to Biography*. Novato, CA: Chandler and Sharp.

Lash, Scott. 2002. "Foreword: Individualization in a Non-Linear Mode." In Ulrich Beck and Elizabeth Beck-Gernsheim, eds., *Individualization: Institutionalized Individualism and Its Social and Political Consequences*, pp. vii–xiii. London: Sage.

Latham, Kevin. 2002. "Rethinking Chinese Consumption: Social Palliatives and the Rhetorics of Transition in Postsocialist China." In C. M. Hann, ed., *Postsocialism: Ideals, Ideologies and Practices in Eurasia*, pp. 217–37. London: Routledge.

Leavitt, Stephen C. 1998. "The Bikhet Mystique: Masculine Identity and Patterns of Rebellion Among Bumbita Adolescent Males." In Gilbert Herdt and Stephen C. Leavitt, eds., *Adolescence in Pacific Island Societies*, pp. 173–94. Pittsburgh: University of Pittsburgh Press.

Lee, Kelly, and Anthony B. Zwi. 1996. "A Global Political Economy Approach to AIDS: Ideology, Interests and Implications." *New Political Economy* 1, no. 3: 355–73.

Lee, Liming. 2004. "The Current State of Public Health in China." *Annual Review of Public Health* 25:327–39.

Lefebvre, Henri. 1991. *The Production of Space*. Cambridge, MA: Blackwell.

Leng Fuying and Ma Tongyu. 1992. "Jiefang qian Ganluo de jishi maoyi yu nuli maimai" [Periodic markets and slave trades in Ganluo before liberation]. In Zhengxie Liangshanzhou weiyuanhui wenshi ziliao weiyuanhui, ed., *Liangshan wenshi ziliao xuanji* [Anthology of Liangshan cultural and historical documents], vol. 10, pp. 185–90. Xichang: Zhengxie wenshi ziliau weiyuanhui (Internal circulation).

Leung, Angela Ki Che. 2009. *Leprosy in China: A History*. New York: Columbia University Press.

Lewellen, Ted C. 2002. *The Anthropology of Globalization: Cultural Anthropology Enters the 21st Century*. Westport, CT: Bergin & Garvey.

Lewin, Ellen. 2006. "Introduction." In Ellen Lewin, ed., *Feminist Anthropology: A Reader*, pp. 1–46. Malden, MA: Blackwell.

Leys, Colin. 1996. *The Rise and Fall of Development Theory*. Bloomington: Indiana University Press.

Li Shaoming. 2004. "Cong Zhongguo Yizu de rentong tan zuti lilun: Yu Hao Rui (Stevan Harrell) jiaoshou Shangque" [Discussing theorization about the ethnic identity of the Yi with Professor Stevan Harrell]. In Anduo Wei, ed., *Liangshan Yizu wenhua yishu yanjiu* [Research on the culture and art of Yi nationality in Liangshan]. Chengdu: Sichuan minzu chubanshe.

Liangshan zhou duiwai youhao xiehui. 2005. Di san jie Liangshan guoji NGO jiaoliuhui [The third meeting for international NGOs in Liangshan]. September 27–29. Unpublished document.

Lin, Man-Hung. 2004. "Late Qing Perceptions of Native Opium." *Harvard Journal of Asiatic Studies* 64, no. 1: 117–44.

Lin, Yueh-hua. 1961. *The Lolo of Liang Shan*. New Haven, CT: HRAF Press.

Link, Bruce G., and Jo C. Phelan. 1999. "Labeling and Stigma." In Carol S. Aneshensel and Jo C. Phelan, eds., *Handbook of the Sociology of Mental Health*, pp. 481–94. New York: Kluwer Academic/Plenum.

———. 2001. "Conceptualizing Stigma." *Annual Review of Sociology* 27:363–85.

Litzinger, Ralph. 2000. *Other Chinas: The Yao and the Politics of National Belonging*. Durham, NC: Duke University Press.

———. 2002. "Theorizing Postsocialism: Reflections on the Politics of Marginality in Contemporary China." *South Atlantic Quarterly* 101, no. 1: 33–55.

Liu, Shao-hua. 2007. "Emerging Modernity in a Periodic Marketplace of Southwest China." *Taiwan Journal of Anthropology* 5, no. 2: 1–30.

———. 2009a. "Learning to Be Leprosy Doctors in China." Paper presented at the International Conference of the Society for Medical Anthropology of the American Anthropological Association, Yale University, September 27.

———. 2009b. "Contested AIDS Stigmatization in Southwest China." *Human Organization* 68, no. 4: 395–405.

Liu, Xiaoxing. 2001. "The Yi Health Care System in Liangshan and Chuxiong." In Stevan Harrell, ed., *Perspectives on the Yi of Southwest China*, pp. 267–82. Berkeley: University of California Press.

Liu, Xingzhu, and Anne Mills. 2002. "Financing Reforms of Public Health Services in China: Lessons for Other Nations." *Social Science and Medicine* 54, no. 11: 1691–98.

Liu, Yu. 2001. "Searching for the Heroic Age of the Yi People of Liangshan." In Stevan Harrell, ed., *Perspectives on the Yi of Southwest China*, pp. 104–17. Berkeley: University of California Press.

Liu, Yuanli, Keqin Rao, and William C. Hsiao. 2003. "Medical Expenditure and Rural Impoverishment in China." *Journal of Health, Population, and Nutrition* 21, no. 3: 216–22.

Lock, Margaret M., and Mark Nichter. 2002. "Introduction: From Documenting Medical Pluralism to Critical Interpretations of Globalized Health Knowledge, Policies, and Practices." In Mark Nichter and Margaret Lock, eds., *New Horizons in Medical Anthropology: Essays in Honour of Charles Leslie*, pp. 1–34. New York: Routledge.

Lu, Xing. 1999. "An Ideological/Cultural Analysis of Political Slogans in Communist China." *Discourse & Society* 10, no. 4: 487–508.

Lucas, AnElissa. 1982. *Chinese Medical Modernization: Comparative Policy Continuities, 1930s–1980s*. New York: Praeger.

Luo Zhengyou. 1999. "Mingai qian de Zhaojue: Tuanjie shangceng, qingjiao canfei shishi huigu" [Zhaojue before the Democratic Reform: A historical review of uniting the higher classes and eliminating bandits]. In Zhengxie Liangshanzhou weiyuanhui wenshi ziliao weiyuanhui, ed., *Liangshan wenshi ziliao xuanji* [Anthology of Liangshan cultural and historical documents], vol. 18, pp. 150–54. Xichang: Zhengxie wenshi ziliao weiyuanhui (Internal circulation).

Lyttleton, Chris. 2004. "Relative Pleasures: Drugs, Development and Modern Dependencies in Asia's Golden Triangle." *Development and Change* 35, no. 5: 909–35.

Ma Changshou. 2006. *Liangshan Luoyi kaocha baogao (shang yu xia)* [Investigations on the Yi in Liangshan, vols. 1 and 2]. Chengdu: Sichuan chuban jituan.

Ma Erzi. 1999. "Liangshan Yizu jiazhi shenghuo de bianqian" [Changes in clan life of the Liangshan Yi]. *Liangshan minzu yanjiu* [Liangshan ethnic studies] 9:51–63.

———. 2001. "Names and Genealogies Among the Nuosu of Liangshan." In Stevan Harrell, ed., *Perspectives on the Yi of Southwest China*, pp. 81–93. Berkeley: University of California Press.

———. 2003. "Nuosu and Neighbouring Ethnic Groups: Ethnic Groups and Ethnic Relations in the Eyes and Ears of Three Generations of the Mgebbu Clan." *Asian Ethnicity* 4, no. 1: 129–45.

Ma Linying. 2001. "Liangshan dupin wenti de xianzhuang qushi ji qi duice yanjiu" [The current situation, trend, and policy of the drug problem in Liangshan]. Paper presented at Social Science for STI and HIV/AIDS Prevention and Care in China Symposium, Tsinghua University, Beijing, January 8–11.

Ma Linying and Eric Diehl. 2001. "Yingguo chuanjiaoshi Haihengbo dui Liangshan Zhaojue Yiqu yiyao weisheng de yingxiang" [British missionary Anthony Broomhall's influence on medicine and hygiene in Zhaojue County of Liangshan]. *Liangshan minzu yanjiu* [Liangshan ethnic studies] 11:258–63.

Ma Xueliang. 1989. *Yizu wenhua shi* [The cultural history of the Yi]. Shanghai: Shanghai renmin chubanshe.

MacDonald, Robert, and Jane Marsh. 2002. "Crossing the Rubicon: Youth Transitions, Poverty, Drugs and Social Exclusion." *International Journal of Drug Policy* 13, no. 1: 27–38.

Mandel, Ruth Ellen, and Caroline Humphrey, eds. 2002. *Markets and Moralities: Ethnographies of Postsocialism*. Oxford, UK: Berg.

Marcus, George E. 1998. *Ethnography Through Thick and Thin*. Princeton, NJ: Princeton University Press.

Marshall, Mac. 1979. *Weekend Warriors: Alcohol in a Micronesian Culture*. Palo Alto, CA: Mayfield.

Marshall, Patricia A., and Linda A. Bennett. 1990. "Anthropological Contributions to AIDS Research." *Medical Anthropology Quarterly* 4, no. 1: 3–5.

Meigu xian weishengju. 1992. *Meigu xian weisheng zhi* [Megui County health gazette].

Midgley, James. 1986. "Community Participation: History, Concepts, and Controversies." In James Midgley, ed., *Community Participation, Social Development, and the State*, pp. 13–44. London: Methuen.

Modell, John. 1989. *Into One's Own: From Youth to Adulthood in the United States, 1920–1975*. Berkeley: University of California Press.

Morgan, Lynn Marie. 1993. *Community Participation in Health: The Politics of Primary Care in Costa Rica*. New York: Cambridge University Press.

Mose Daer et al. 2008. "Liangshanzhou HIV/AIDS liuxing tedian yu duice fenxi" [Analysis of epidemiological characteristics and countermeasures of AIDS in Liangshan state]. *Xiandai yufang yixue* [Modern preventive medicine] 35, no. 4: 630–35.

Mueggler, Erik. 2001. *The Age of Wild Ghosts: Memory, Violence, and Place in Southwest China*. Berkeley: University of California Press.

Mullaney, Thomas. 2006. "Coming to Terms with the Nation: Ethnic Classification and Scientific Statecraft in Modern China, 1928–1954." PhD dissertation, Columbia University.

Nader, Laura. 1986. "From Anguish to Exultation." In Peggy Golde, ed., *Women in the Field: Anthropological Experiences*, pp. 97–116. Berkeley: University of California Press.

Newman, R. K. 1995. "Opium Smoking in Late Imperial China: A Reconsideration." *Modern Asian Studies* 29, no. 4: 765–94.

Nguyen, Vinh-Kim. 2005. "Uses and Pleasures: Sexual Modernity, HIV/AIDS, and Confessional Technologies in a West African Metropolis." In Vincanne Adams and Stacy Leigh Pigg, eds., *Sex in Development: Science, Sexuality, and Morality in Global Perspective*, pp. 245–67. Durham, NC: Duke University Press.

Nichter, Mark. 1989. *Anthropology and International Health: South Asian Case Studies*. Boston: Kluwer Academic.

Page, J. Bryan. 1997. "Needle Exchange and Reduction of Harm: An Anthropological View." *Medical Anthropology* 18, no. 1: 13–33.

Parker, Richard. 2001. "Sexuality, Culture, and Power in HIV/AIDS Research." *Annual Review of Anthropology* 30: 163–79.

Parker, Richard, and Peter Aggleton. 2003. "HIV and AIDS-Related Stigma and Discrimination: A Conceptual Framework and Implications for Action." *Social Science and Medicine* 57, no. 1: 13–24.

Pearson, Geoffrey. 1987. *The New Heroin Users*. Oxford: Blackwell.

Perry, Elizabeth. 1994. "Trends in the Study of Chinese Politics: State-Society Relations." *China Quarterly* 139:704–13.

Pieke, Frank. 2004. "Contours of an Anthropology of the Chinese State: Political Structure, Agency and Economic Development in Rural China." *Journal of the Royal Anthropological Institute* 10, no. 3: 517–38.

Pigg, Stacy Leigh. 1996. "The Credible and the Credulous: The Question of 'Villagers' Beliefs' in Nepal." *Cultural Anthropology* 11, no. 2: 160–201.

———. 2002. "Too Bold, Too Hot: Crossing 'Culture' in AIDS Prevention in Nepal." In Mark Nichter and Margaret Lock, eds., *New Horizons in Medical Anthropology: Essays in Honour of Charles Leslie*, pp. 58–80. New York: Routledge.

Pilkington, Hilary. 2006. "'For Us It Is Normal': Exploring the 'Recreational' Use of Heroin in Russian Youth Cultural Practice." *Journal of Communist Studies and Transition Politics* 22, no. 1: 24–53.

Pinel, Elizabeth C. 1999. "Stigma Consciousness: The Psychological Legacy of Social Stereotypes." *Journal of Personality and Social Psychology* 76, no. 1: 114–28.

Pun, Ngai. 2005. *Made in China: Women Factory Workers in a Global Workplace*. Durham, NC: Duke University Press.

Qin Heping. 2001. *Sichuan yapian wenti yu jinyan yundong* [The opium problem and antidrug campaigns in Sichuan]. Chengdu: Sichuan minzu chubanshe.

Qubi Shimei and Ma Erzi. 2001. "Homicide and Homicide Cases in Old Liangshan." In Stevan Harrell, ed., *Perspectives on the Yi of Southwest China*, pp. 94–103. Berkeley: University of California Press.

Reid, Gary, and Genevieve Costigan. 2002. *Revisiting the Hidden Epidemic: A Situation Assessment of Drug Use in Asia in the Context of HIV/AIDS*. Fairfield, Victoria: Center for Harm Reduction, Burnet Institute, Australia.

Rofel, Lisa. 1999. *Other Modernities: Gendered Yearnings in China After Socialism*. Berkeley: University of California Press.

———. 2007. *Desiring China: Experiments in Neoliberalism, Sexuality, and Public Culture*. Durham, NC: Duke University Press.

Rosenbaum, Arthur Lewis, ed. 1992. *State and Society in China: The Consequences of Reform*. Boulder, CO: Westview Press.

Rosenbaum, Marsha. 1981. *Women on Heroin*. New Brunswick, NJ: Rutgers University Press.

Rosenthal, Elisabeth. 2000. "In Rural China, a Steep Price of Poverty: Dying of AIDS." *New York Times*, October 28.

Sassen, Saskia. 2007. "Introduction: Deciphering the Global." In Saskia Sassen, ed., *Deciphering the Global: Its Scales, Spaces and Subjects*, pp. 1–18. New York: Routledge.

Schoepf, Brooke G. 2001. "International AIDS Research in Anthropology: Taking a Critical Perspective on the Crisis." *Annual Review of Anthropology* 30:335–61.

Scott, James C. 1998. *Seeing Like a State: How Certain Schemes to Improve the Human Condition Have Failed.* New Haven, CT: Yale University Press.

Segall, Malcolm. 2000. "From Cooperation to Competition in National Health Systems—and Back? Impact on Professional Ethics and Quality of Care." *International Journal of Health Planning and Management* 15, no. 1: 61–79.

Setel, Philip. 1999. *A Plague of Paradoxes: AIDS, Culture, and Demography in Northern Tanzania.* Chicago: University of Chicago Press.

Sewell, William Hamilton. 2005. *Logics of History: Social Theory and Social Transformation.* Chicago: University of Chicago Press.

Sharp, Lesley Alexandra. 2002. *The Sacrificed Generation: Youth, History, and the Colonized Mind in Madagascar.* Berkeley: University of California Press.

Sherman, Susan G., et al. 2002. "Social Influences on the Transition to Injection Drug Use Among Young Heroin Sniffers: A Qualitative Analysis." *International Journal of Drug Policy* 13, no. 2: 113–20.

Sherraden, Margaret Sherrard. 1991. "Policy Impacts of Community Participation: Health Services in Rural Mexico." *Human Organization* 50, no. 3: 256–63.

Shi Jinbo et al. 1999. *Zhaojue xian Yizu juan* [On the Yi in Zhaojue County]. Zhongguo shaoshu minzu xianzhuang yu fazhan diaocha yanjiu congshu [A series of research investigations on the current situation and developments among Chinese minority nationalities]. Beijing: Minzu chubanshe.

Sichuan sheng renkou pucha bangongshi. 2002. *Sichuan sheng 2000 nian renkou pucha ziliao* [Sichuan Province 2000 population census]. Beijing: Zhongguo tongji chubanshe.

Sichuan sheng Zhaojue xianzhi bianzuan weiyuanhui. 1999. *Zhaojue xianzhi* [The gazette of Zhaojue County]. Chengdu: Sichuan cishu chubanshe.

Sidel, Ruth, and Victor W. Sidel. 1982. *The Health of China.* Boston: Beacon Press.

Singer, Merrill. 1997. "Needle Exchange and AIDS Prevention: Controversies, Policies and Research." *Medical Anthropology* 18, no. 1: 1–12.

———, ed. 1998. *The Political Economy of AIDS.* Amityville, NY: Baywood.

———. 2006. *The Face of Social Suffering: The Life History of a Street Drug Addict.* Long Grove, IL: Waveland Press.

Siu, Helen F. 1989. *Agents and Victims in South China: Accomplices in Rural Revolution.* New Haven, CT: Yale University Press.

Skinner, G. William. 1964–65. "Marketing and Social Structure in Rural China," parts 1, 2, and 3. *Journal of Asian Studies* 24, nos. 1–3: 3–43, 195–228, 363–99.

———. 1985. "Rural Marketing in China: Repression and Revival." *China Quarterly* 103:393–413.

Smith, Daniel Jordan. 2004. "Burials and Belonging in Nigeria: Rural-Urban Relations and Social Inequality in a Contemporary African Ritual." *American Anthropologist* 106, no. 3: 569–79.

Solinger, Dorothy J. 1999. *Contesting Citizenship in Urban China: Peasant Migrants, the State, and the Logic of the Market.* Berkeley: University of California Press.

Song Jiayu and Tian Weikuan. 1995. "Liangshan yiyao weisheng shiliao buyi" [A supplementary historical document about medicine and hygiene in Liangshan]. In Zhengxie Liangshanzhou weiyuanhui wenshi ziliao weiyuanhui, ed., *Liangshan wenshi ziliao xuanji* [Anthology of Liangshan cultural and historical documents], vol. 13, pp. 287–96. Xichang: Zhengxie wenshi ziliao weiyuanhui (Internal circulation).

Spence, Jonathan. 1975. "Opium Smoking in Ch'ing China." In Frederic Wakeman, Jr., and Carolyn Grant, eds., *Conflict and Control in Late Imperial China,* pp. 143–73. Berkeley: University of California Press.

State Council AIDS Working Committee Office and UN Theme Group on AIDS in China. 2007. *A Joint Assessment of HIV/AIDS Prevention, Treatment and Care in China.* Beijing: State Council AIDS Working Committee Office & UNAIDS China Office.

Sumartojo, Esther. 2000. "Structural Factors in HIV Prevention: Concepts, Examples, and Implications for Research." *AIDS* 14, suppl. 1: S3–S10.

Sun Xingshen, Shi Tangxi, and Zhu Changhe. 1993. "Jinyan jindu zai Liangshan" [Anti-opium campaign in Liangshan]. In Ma Weigang, ed., *Jinchang jindu* [Abolish prostitution and eradicate narcotics], pp. 197–217. Beijing: Jingguan jiaoyu chubanshe.

Tang, Shenglan, and Gerald Bloom. 2000. "Decentralizing Rural Health Services: A Case Study in China." *International Journal of Health Planning and Management* 15, no. 3: 189–200.

Tang, Shenglan, et al. 1994. *Financing Health Services in China: Adapting to Economic Reform.* Brighton, UK: Institute of Development Studies.

Taylor, Avril. 1993. *Women Drug Users: An Ethnography of a Female Injecting Community.* New York: Oxford University Press.

Tedlock, Barbara. 2003. "Ethnography and Ethnographic Representation." In Norman K. Denzin and Yvonna S. Lincoln, eds., *Strategies of Qualitative Inquiry,* pp. 165–213. London: Sage.

Treichler, Paula A. 1988. "AIDS, Gender, and Biomedical Discourse: Current Contests for Meaning." In Elizabeth Fee and Daniel M. Fox, eds., *AIDS: The Burdens of History,* pp. 190–266. Berkeley: University of California Press.

———. 1999. *How to Have Theory in an Epidemic: Cultural Chronicles of AIDS.* Durham, NC: Duke University Press.

Trocki, Carl A. 1999. *Opium, Empire and the Global Political Economy: A Study of the Asian Opium Trade, 1750–1950.* London: Routledge.

Turner, Victor. 1967. *The Forest of Symbols: Aspects of Ndembu Ritual.* Ithaca, NY: Cornell University Press.

———. 1969. *The Ritual Process: Structure and Anti-Structure.* Chicago: Aldine.

UNAIDS. 2000. *HIV and AIDS-Related Stigmatization, Discrimination and Denial: Forms, Contexts and Determinants.* Research Studies from Uganda and India. Geneva: UNAIDS.

———. 2001. *HIV/AIDS: China's Titanic Peril. 2001 Update of the AIDS Situation and Needs Assessment Report.* Beijing: UN Theme Group on HIV/AIDS in China.

———. 2002. *Report on the Global HIV/AIDS Epidemic, July 2002.* Geneva: The Joint United Nations Programme on HIV/AIDS.

———. 2008. *Epidemiological Fact Sheet on HIV and AIDS: China, 2008 Update.* Geneva: UNAIDS/WHO Working Group on Global HIV/AIDS and STI.

Van Gennep, Arnold. 1960. *The Rites of Passage.* Chicago: University of Chicago Press.

Verdery, Katherine. 1996. *What Was Socialism, and What Comes Next?* Princeton, NJ: Princeton University Press.

Vlahov, David, et al. 2001. "Needle Exchange Programs for the Prevention of Human Immunodeficiency Virus Infection: Epidemiology and Policy." *American Journal of Epidemiology* 154, suppl. 12: S70–S77.

Wagstaff, Adam, et al. 2009. "Extending Health Insurance to the Rural Population: An Impact Evaluation of China's New Cooperative Medical Scheme." *Journal of Health Economics* 28, no. 1: 1–19.

Wallace, Claire, and Malcolm Cross, eds. 1990. *Youth in Transition: The Sociology of Youth and Youth Policy.* London: Falmer Press.

Waxler, Nancy. 1981. "Learning to Be a Leper: A Case Study in the Social Construction of Illness." In Elliot G. Mishler et al., eds., *Social Contexts of Health, Illness, and Patient Care,* pp. 169–94. Cambridge: Cambridge University Press.

Wei, Bu. 2006. "Looking for 'the Insider's Perspective': Human Trafficking in Sichuan." In Maria Heimer and Stig Thøgersen, eds., *Doing Fieldwork in China,* pp. 209–24. Honolulu: University of Hawaii Press.

Weiss, Linda. 1998. *The Myth of the Powerless State: Governing the Economy in a Global Era.* Cambridge: Polity Press.

Weng Naiqun. 2002. "Zaoyu aizibing de Zhongguo shaoshu minzu" [Chinese ethnic minorities in the face of HIV/AIDS]. Paper presented at Harvard-Tsinghua Universities Medical Anthropology Workshop, Beijing, China, June 5–7.

West, C., and D. H. Zimmerman. 1987. "Doing Gender." *Gender and Society* 1, no. 2: 125–51.

White, Sydney D. 1998. "From 'Barefoot Doctor' to 'Village Doctor' in Tiger Springs Village: A Case Study of Rural Health Care Transformations in Socialist China." *Human Organization* 57, no. 4: 480–90.

Whyte, Martin King, and S. Z. Gu. 1987. "Popular Response to China's Fertility Transition." *Population and Development Review* 13, no. 3: 471–93.

Willis, Katie, and Brenda Yeoh, eds. 2000. *Gender and Migration.* Cheltenham, UK: Edward Elgar.

Winnington, Alan. 1959. *The Slaves of the Cool Mountains: The Ancient Social Conditions and Changes Now in Progress on the Remote South-Western Borders of China.* London: Lawrence & Wishart.

Wolf, Eric R. 1982. *Europe and the People Without History.* Berkeley: University of California Press.

World Bank. 1997. *Financing Health Care: Issues and Options for China.* Washington, DC: World Bank.

Wright, Caroline. 2000. "Gender Awareness in Migration Theory: Synthesizing Actor and Structure in Southern Africa." In Katie Willis and Brenda Yeoh, eds., *Gender and Migration*, pp. 3–23. Cheltenham, UK: Edward Elgar.

Wu, Zunyou, Keming Rou, and Haixia Cui. 2004. "The HIV/AIDS Epidemic in China: History, Current Strategies and Future Challenges." *AIDS Education and Prevention* 16:7–17.

Yan, Yunxiang. 2003. *Private Life Under Socialism: Love, Intimacy, and Family Change in a Chinese Village, 1949–1999.* Stanford, CA: Stanford University Press.

Yang, Lawrence Hsin, et al. 2007. "Culture and Stigma: Adding Moral Experience to Stigma Theory." *Social Science and Medicine* 64, no. 7: 1524–35.

Yang, Y., et al. 2005. "Institutional and Structural Forms of HIV-Related Discrimination in Health Care: A Study Set in Beijing." *AIDS Care* 17, suppl. 2: S129–S140.

Yeoh, Brenda S. A., Michael W. Charney, and Chee Kiong Tong, eds. 2003. *Approaching Transnationalisms: Studies on Transnational Societies, Multicultural Contacts, and Imaginings of Home.* Boston: Kluwer Academic.

Zhang Haiyang et al. 2002. Liangshan Yizu diqu xingbing aizibing chuanbo ji fangzhi gongzuo xianzhuang diaocha baogao [Report of investigations on the spread of STI/HIV and its current prevention among the Yi in Liangshan]. Unpublished report to the China-UK HIV/AIDS Prevention and Care Project.

Zhang, Li. 2001. *Strangers in the City: Reconfigurations of Space, Power, and Social Networks Within China's Floating Population.* Stanford, CA: Stanford University Press.

Zhang Rongde. 2002. "Wenquan yijia: Yige bianyuanhua qushi xia de shaoshu minzu cunluo" [A hot-spring Yi community: A marginalized village of the ethnic minority]. Unpublished summer fieldwork report, Department of Ethnology, Central University of Nationalities, Beijing.

Zheng, Yangwen. 2005. *The Social Life of Opium in China.* New York: Cambridge University Press.

Zhou, Yongming. 1999. *Anti-Drug Crusades in Twentieth-Century China: Nationalism, History, and State Building.* Lanham, MD: Rowman & Littlefield.

Zhuang Kongshao, Yang Honglin, and Fu Xiaoxing. 2005. "Xiao Liangshan Yizu 'Huri' minjian jiedu xingdong de yingyong shijian" [Revelation of the 'Tiger's Day' initiative in the Yi ethnic region of Xiaoliangshan]. *Journal of Guangxi University for Nationalities* 27, no. 2: 38–47.

Index